A Ready-to-Use
Activities Program for Students
with Spelling Difficulties

CYNTHIA M. STOWE

THE CENTER FOR APPLIED
RESEARCH IN EDUCATION
Paramus, NJ 07652

Library of Congress Cataloging-in-Publication Data

Stowe, Cynthia M.
    Spelling smart : a ready-to-use activities program for students
with spelling difficulties / Cynthia Stowe.
        p.   cm.
    Includes bibliographical references (p. 415).
    ISBN 0-87628-880-8 (spiral wire) — ISBN 0-13-044978-4 (paper)
    1. English language—Orthography and spelling—Study and
teaching—Activity programs. 2. Language experience approach
in education.
    I. Title.
    LB1574.S69   1995   95-22920
    372.6'32—dc20   CIP

Printed in the United States of America

10   9   8   (spiral/wire)   10 9 8 7 6 5 4 3 2 1 (paper)

ISBN 0-87628-880-8 (spiral/wire)   ISBN 0-13-044978-4 (paper)

**THE CENTER FOR APPLIED RESEARCH
IN EDUCATION**
Paramus, NJ 07652

www.phdirect.com/education

DEDICATION

To Robert who helps me with everything.

ACKNOWLEDGMENTS

My deepest gratitude goes to Cynthia Conway Waring, wonderful teacher and friend, who made this book possible.

Thanks to my many colleagues who have sought excellence in their teaching.

Thanks to my students who have taught and inspired me, especially Bill Klaus, Jr. and Danyel Addes.

Thanks to Susan Kolwicz for all her editorial help and support.

Thanks to Nancy Hope Wilson who helped greatly with the proposal.

Thanks to Kathleen Bridgewater for sharing ideas, and to Winifred Luhrmann for the loan of many valuable books. Thanks, also, to Michael Daley, Jessie Haas, Lorraine Ryan and Jean Shaw, critiquers and supporters all.

ABOUT THE AUTHOR

Cynthia Stowe has worked with students for many years. She is a certified classroom teacher, special education teacher, and school psychologist. She's worked with students of all ages, including adults, in diverse settings.

A main area of interest has always been working with students who have difficulties with traditional curriculum. Her focus on spelling was inspired by some teenage boys with whom she was asked to work. These boys had experienced years of frustration with spelling and did not have high motivation levels regarding the subject. The challenge of helping these boys to succeed initiated her interest in teaching spelling. *Spelling Smart!* was thus developed over a ten-year period.

In addition to her teaching, Ms. Stowe also writes novels for children. Her books include *Home Sweet Home, Good-Bye* (middle grades), *Dear Mom, in Ohio for a Year* (middle grades), and *Not-So-Normal Norman* (grades 3–6).

ABOUT THIS BOOK

Spelling Smart! is a program designed for students, grade 4 through adult, who have difficulty learning to spell through memorization. They recall the spelling of words for a short time only, even when the words are taken from their own writing or from thematic units. Some of these students are labeled as having special needs. Others are not. The latter often perform well in other academic areas, and have a weakness particular to spelling.

This program approaches spelling as a cognitive task. It integrates concepts from the whole language philosophy and strategies from the phonics approach. Instead of asking students to memorize hundreds of individual words, it helps them discover patterns and consistencies. Therefore, it helps students who have weak visual memories learn to apply their good logical thinking skills to the task of spelling.

This program focuses on the structural regularity of English. According to research, approximately 85 percent of the language follows consistent patterns and rules. There are, of course, exceptions. These are presented as interesting variances that reflect the rich historical background of English.

This program presents an overview of the structure of the English language. Six basic concepts are taught:

- SOUNDS—In most words, sounds are associated with letters.
- SYLLABLES—Words are made up of syllables. Multisyllabic words which may appear complicated can be divided into individual syllables, and these can be spelled easily. There are six types of syllables in the English language.
- WORD BUILDING—Words can be built up. In other words, prefixes and/or suffixes can be added to root words to form new words.
- RULES—There are rules which govern how to add endings to root words.
- GENERALIZATIONS—There are generalizations which govern how to choose between different spellings when a given sound is spelled more than one way.
- COMPENSATORY STRATEGIES—It is important to learn compensatory strategies in dealing with words that are not spelled in a regular way.

Spelling Smart! can be used for individual or small group instruction. Special education teachers can present lessons. Other teachers can either take fifteen minutes of their instructional time each day, or they can ask an aide to implement the program. Each lesson is completed over a series of several days.

Spelling Smart! is a complete program. No prior knowledge of how to teach spelling is needed. It is important, however, to start at the beginning of the program even if students already have some spelling skills. In this way, students will learn how to approach the task of spelling.

Organization

Spelling Smart! is organized in the following way. It has two sections: ISSUES AND CONCERNS and THE LESSONS.

The first section of the book, ISSUES AND CONCERNS subsections in which the following are presented:

- Students' feelings about spelling. It discusses typical feelings and presents ways to help students deal with them.

- A short test for checking students' knowledge of the consonant sounds and procedures for teaching these sound/symbol correspondences.

- A short test for checking students' knowledge of the short vowel sounds. and procedures for teaching these sound/symbol correspondences.

- A short test for checking students' knowledge of the consonant blends and consonant digraphs, and procedures for teaching these sound/symbol correspondences.

- Guidelines for assessing the needs of students. Types of spelling problems are discussed. Suggestions on what to do if students have extreme difficulty with basic sound/symbol correspondences are offered.

- Ways of teaching irregular words. It discusses different types of compensatory strategies.

- How and when to teach homonyms. A list of forty common pairs are presented.

- Strategies for teaching dictionary skills.

- Computer spell checks and a discussion of how students can use them effectively.

In the second section of the book, THE LESSONS, 40 lessons are presented. Each lesson consists of the following parts:

- Getting Started
- Introducing New Information
- Practicing with Individual Words
- Practicing Spelling in Context
- Reinforcing Activities
- Extra Interesting Facts

Everything that is needed to present each lesson is given, including a comprehensive word list of the spelling pattern being presented. In addition, worksheets are offered which students can work on during independent learning times.

Some Special Features of This Unique Program

- The teacher creates situations and provides data from which students discover spelling patterns and rules for themselves. You don't just tell them what you want them to know.

- You follow your student's pace as you present lessons.

- Students learn a process. They learn *how* to learn to spell.

- Students do very little writing of isolated words. They write most words in context in sentences.

- Students are held accountable only for the knowledge they possess. If they encounter words that follow unfamiliar patterns or rules, you provide the spelling for them.

- Students edit their own work. You do not correct spelling, rather you provide the information your students need to edit successfully. If they miss an error, you question them in a way that helps them discover it themselves. Helping students focus on their spelling is a major goal of this program.

- Review and practice is carefully built into the program.

- Students make a spelling notebook to record in their own words what they have learned.

- Students decide when they have mastered some information and are ready to be tested if testing is required.

- Spelling is an integrated part of the total learning experience. It is not an isolated skill.

- *Spelling Smart!* is age appropriate for older students. Since emphasis is placed on teaching syllable types early in the program, it is possible to present multisyllabic words that are well within students' abilities to spell. There is no issue with students having "baby" spelling words.

All these factors help you create an environment in which students feel they can become successful spellers. Most poor spellers started out *wanting* to learn but became discouraged by failure. Talk with them about their feelings. Acknowledge that learning to spell appears to be an overwhelming task. Discuss their past difficulties with memorization, explaining that rote learning may not be one of their strengths. Explain that *Spelling Smart!* helps them to learn in a different way. They will learn about the logic of spelling. They will learn to focus on their work, and they will begin to feel better about their progress.

As you guide students through the first lessons, they will gain confidence. Once they begin to succeed, they will demand more challenge.

Cynthia Stowe

THE STRUCTURE AND PHILOSOPHY OF THE LESSON PLAN

This section gives information on the philosophy and methodology of each part of the lesson. Please refer to an actual lesson (preferably not Lesson One) as you read this section.

Getting Started

This is an extremely important part of the lesson, for here your students review previous information and come to own it. *Spelling Smart!* depends upon your students using new information many times and in various ways. They tell you and others about it. They write about it in their notebooks. They use the information so often that it becomes internalized.

The most helpful notebook is a looseleaf binder. Students record each new pattern or rule or generalization on a separate sheet of paper. For example, students will have a separate page for closed syllables, open syllables, the Doubling Rule, and so on throughout the sequence. This format allows your students to find or add information easily.

Introducing New Information

In this section of the lesson, you create situations in which students figure out the new information for themselves. For example, you don't just say, "An open syllable is a syllable that ends in a single vowel." You present some open syllables and ask your students to figure out what is similar about all of them. Thus, you give them an interesting problem to solve, rather than a definition to memorize.

Gaining information in this way develops self esteem. You know that your students are smart enough to figure out these patterns. Soon, they will know it, too.

They are also more likely to remember the information because they were actively engaged in learning it. Passive learning can easily be forgotten.

Practicing with Individual Words

Now you show your students a list of words that demonstrates the new pattern. Usually, the list the students see will be eight to fifteen words long. This list contains words that you have selected and copied from the Word List provided. Give your students as much time as they want to look at the list and notice the pattern.

Then, read the list, asking students to write each word. Individual words are used only at this initial stage, just to provide practice with the new pattern.

Once they have completed their writing, tell your students to ask about any of their spellings of which they are unsure. This procedure is important because it helps them notice their work. Also, it helps them begin to take responsibility for their spelling.

Answer all questions with guiding, careful questions that refer back to the information being presented. Your main goal here is to help your students think about their spelling.

Self-editing is crucial to the *Spelling Smart!* program. Poor spellers have often experienced years of having other people correct their spelling. Even if this has been done in a nurturing way, it has reinforced the idea that someone else is responsible for finding and correcting errors.

Once your students have asked as many questions as they wish, either ask to see their lists, or ask them to tell you how they've spelled the words. Decide between these two options depending upon the needs of your students.

If there are errors that one of your students hasn't noticed, ask him leading questions so that he will notice the problem. For example, suppose you have studied the pattern "k" and "ck," and your student has already discovered that a word ends with a "ck" if the /k/ sound is preceded by one short vowel. Your student, however, has spelled the word "track" as "t-r-a-k."

Show him the list of "k" and "ck" words you originally presented to help him rediscover this generalization. Ask him to tell you about this information. Then say, *"Look at how you've spelled 'track.' Do you feel that's correct?"*

In this way, guide your student to correcting his work. Your goal is never to correct any spelling for him. If the information has been presented, he can figure it out in time.

When working with a group, some students will have errors that others do not. Do not worry about some students hearing information they already know. The repetition will serve as reinforcement.

Practicing Spelling in Context

In this part of the lesson, your students begin to feel mastery of spelling. The number of sentences you present will vary, but the average number is four.

Show your students the sentences you have copied on a separate sheet of paper and that you are going to read. Ask them about any vocabulary words you feel they may not know. See if they have any questions about any of the sentences. In this way, the students become comfortable with the sentences they will write. They also practice noticing spellings.

These sentences have been carefully developed. The words they contain include only those patterns already presented in the learning sequence. Your students will have been given all the information they need to be able to spell these words independently. This gives them a sense of mastery and provides essential review.

In the initial lessons, there are some words in the sentences whose phonetic patterns are unfamiliar to your students. These words are included to make the sentences more interesting and natural.

These words with unfamiliar patterns are underlined in the text. When you write out the sentences for your students, underline these words and also write them on a separate sheet of paper. Say, *"Here are some words that you will need. Just copy them when you come to them."* You write the words out rather than telling your students the spellings to encourage them to notice and relate to written language.

The words "the" and "a" are underlined for the first five lessons. After that, it is assumed that students know these spellings from repeated use. If your students continue to have difficulty with these words, however, continue to provide written models for them.

The words "said," "of," and "to" are underlined through Lesson 11. Again, if your students demonstrate confusion with the spellings after this lesson, provide models for them. Eventually, they will be able to remember these spellings, or they will develop compensatory strategies for them.

Once your students are ready to write, read each sentence through completely. If your students ask you to repeat a sentence, read it through completely again rather than reading just a fragment. You want your students to develop the sense that words are in context. Also, this technique encourages the development of auditory memory.

When your students are finished, ask them if they have any questions about their work. Because people who have difficulty with spelling are often overwhelmed by writing whole sentences, you will answer all questions readily. This procedure is different from the work with individual words, where you only respond with questions and help them recall prior knowledge.

If your students know they can ask about any word, they will feel less intimidated. This process also encourages careful editing.

As your students progress through the program, you may begin to choose to answer with questions again. This is a judgment call. If you are really undecided about what is best, talk with your students and get their opinions.

When the students have asked all their questions, say, *"Are you ready for me to look at your work?"* When they are ready, check the sentences. If there is an error in any sentence, put a small pencil check in the margin. Say, *"Can you find the word that needs to be changed?"*

Once the students have done so, help them correct their errors by questioning. As soon as the error is corrected, erase the pencil mark.

You will notice that many of the sentences provided in *Spelling Smart!* are dialogue and, thus, have quotation marks. Assist your students with the proper use of quotation marks. Talk about them as an interesting punctuation mark. Provide as much help as your students need.

Dialogue is included for three reasons. First, it makes the sentences seem natural and "alive." Second, students often have a natural feel for dialogue and enjoy writing sentences which include it. Third, practicing with dialogue in this formal part of the lesson will help students develop dialogue in their creative writing.

Reinforcing Activities

In this section of the lesson, your students choose from a list of supplementary activities. Allow your students a great deal of choice here. They will naturally gravitate to their areas of strength, and this is an excellent way for them to compensate for their relative weakness with memorization.

Supplementary activities are important. This is often where the knowledge is fully internalized.

These activities can also assist with the pacing of knowledge acquisition. For example, a student who has been learning well and quickly for two months may start acting listless, tired, or confused. This is usually a sign that she needs to practice what she's learned rather than be exposed to new information. Although for some students periods of fatigue are unavoidable, ample time for supplementary activities usually keeps the pace manageable.

In *Spelling Smart!*, only a few activities are repeated in the "Reinforcing Activities" sections of the lessons. This was done so that a wide variety of possibilities could be offered. If students wish to repeat an activity that was introduced in an earlier lesson, however, this is a fine option for them. Once again, the belief is that students will self-select activities that involve their strengths and that will, therefore, be beneficial to them.

Extra Interesting Facts

A short essay called "The Origins of English" is presented immediately before the lessons. This essay gives a very brief account of the history of English. It is most helpful to share this information with your students, either by reading the essay to them or sharing the data more informally. Use your discretion as to how much data to present in one sitting.

Then, as the formal part of each lesson finishes, share the information about the history of individual words and phrases that is provided in "Extra Interesting Facts."

In this section, you will also find discussions of any important exceptions to the pattern, rule, or generalization being presented. These exceptions are not meant to be memorized; rather, they are meant to be seen as interesting variations.

It is extremely important for students of spelling to learn about the history of English. This knowledge helps them to stop seeing the vagaries of English spelling as the enemy. This knowledge helps them become interested and curious about the language.

INDEPENDENT WORK

Finish It!

This activity offers students the opportunity to notice and practice spelling in a protected way. Because they can refer to the word list, they need not be worried about making a mistake with spelling. Instead, they can focus on finding just the right word to complete a meaningful sentence, and they can feel satisfaction in spelling this word correctly.

A Game of Categories

This activity again offers a nonthreatening way to practice spelling. In addition, it gives students a chance to develop logical thinking skills. Some students really enjoy this activity once they begin to gain confidence with it. A few even like to develop their own categories when given word lists.

Look It Up!

This activity is primarily designed to give students practice with a dictionary. Often, people who have difficulty with spelling have developed resistance to using the dictionary. Teachers often hear comments like, *"How can I look up a word if I don't know how to spell it?"*

It's very important to refer to the section on dictionary skills at the beginning of *Spelling Smart!* This section provides information and guidelines on how to help students overcome their resistance to using dictionaries. It also gives techniques that help students become successful with using this critically important tool.

LOOK IT UP! allows students to practice at their own speed. Since some of the words presented are not very common words, you will need to provide your students with a good, comprehensive dictionary.

List It!

Students who experience difficulty with spelling sometimes develop a corresponding resistance to writing. They're afraid that what they write won't be "correct." They think so much about the spelling of words that they don't develop a good expressive flow. They avoid using words they don't know how to spell, and this disrupts their thought processes.

Writing lists is a powerful tool in helping students develop their expository and creative writing, as well as their spelling skills. It is fun and easy. It helps students relax around writing. It also develops their logical thinking and organizational skills.

It is recommended that no attention be paid to errors students make with spelling during the initial lessons. Once students are expressing enthusiasm about writing lists, however, begin to hold them accountable for the spelling patterns, rules, and generalizations they know.

Often, students enjoy sharing their lists with others. If possible, it is very helpful for you to also write a list and share your work. This provides excellent modeling.

Write On!

These activities are offered to help students integrate their development of spelling skills with creative and expository writing. Again, as with the lists, no attention should be paid to spelling errors until students are very comfortable with the activities. Then they should be held accountable only for the spelling information they have already discovered. A good way to help students edit their work is to ask them to check through their work and to look for a specific spelling pattern; for example, words with closed syllables. Guiding editing in this way helps students become more relaxed with it.

As with the lists, students usually enjoy sharing their writing. If they do not wish to do so, however, this needs to be respected. Usually, once they gain confidence with their work, students will be eager to share.

CONTENTS

About This Book . . . . *v*

The Structure and Philosophy of the Lesson Plan . . . . *viii*

Section

ONE

ISSUES AND CONCERNS / 1

Feelings About Spelling 3

The Consonants 5

The Short Vowel Sounds 9

Consonant Blends and Digraphs 11

Assessing the Needs of Students 15

Irregular Words 18

Homonyms 20

Dictionary Skills 23

A Note on Computer Spell Checks 25

The Origins of English 25

Section

TWO

THE LESSONS / 27

Please note: All lessons follow the same familiar format—Getting Started, Introducing New Information, Practicing with Individual Words, Practicing Spelling in Context, Reinforcing Activities, and Extra Interesting Facts—plus reproducibles that include a "Word List," "Finish It!", "A Game of Categories," "Look It Up!", "List It!", and "Write On!"

Lesson One—Closed Syllable: Short "a" 29

Lesson Two—Closed Syllable: Short "i" 38

Lesson Three—Closed Syllable: Short "o" 47

Lesson Four—Closed Syllable: Short "u" 56

Lesson Five—Closed Syllable: Short "e" 65

Lesson Six—Spelling Generalization: "ff, ll, ss" 74

Lesson Seven—Spelling Generalization: "ck" 83

Lesson Eight—Vowel-consonant-e Syllable: "a - e" 93

Lesson Nine—Vowel-consonant-e Syllable: "i - e" 102

Lesson Ten—Vowel-consonant-e Syllable: "o - e" 111

Lesson Eleven—Vowel-consonant-e Syllables: "u - e" and "e - e" 120

Lesson Twelve—Eight Common Suffixes 129

Lesson Thirteen—Suffix "-ed" 139

Lesson Fourteen—The E Rule 148

Lesson Fifteen—Open Syllable: "a" 157

Lesson Sixteen—Open Syllable: "i" 167

Lesson Seventeen—Open Syllable: "o" 177

Lesson Eighteen—Open Syllable: "u" and Open Syllable: "e" 186

Lesson Nineteen—Open Syllable at the end of words: "y" 195

Lesson Twenty—The Doubling Rule 205

Lesson Twenty-One—Six Common Prefixes 215

Lesson Twenty-Two—Vowel Combination Syllable: "ai" 225

Lesson Twenty-Three—Spelling Generalization: "ai" and "ay" 234

Lesson Twenty-Four—Vowel Combination Syllable: "ee" 243

Lesson Twenty-Five—Vowel Combination Syllable: "oa" 252

Lesson Twenty-Six—Vowel Combination Syllable: "ea" 261

Lesson Twenty-Seven—Vowel Combination Syllables: "ie" and "ei" 270

Lesson Twenty-Eight—Vowel Combination Syllable: "oo" 280

Lesson Twenty-Nine—Vowel Combination Syllable: "ow" 289

Lesson Thirty—The Y Rule 298

Lesson Thirty-One—Consonant-le Syllables: "ble" and "dle" 308

Lesson Thirty-Two—Consonant-le Syllables: "ple" and "gle" 317

Lesson Thirty-Three—Consonant-le Syllables: "tle, fle, cle, kle" 326

Lesson Thirty-Four—Spelling Generalization: "ch, tch" 335

Lesson Thirty-Five—Spelling Generalization: "ge, dge" 344

Lesson Thirty-Six—R-Controlled Syllable: "ar" 353

Lesson Thirty-Seven—R-Controlled Syllable: "or" 362

Lesson Thirty-Eight—R-Controlled Syllables: "er, ir, ur" 371

Lesson Thirty-Nine—Final Vowel Combination Syllables: "tion" and "sion" 380

Lesson Forty—The Doubling Rule with Multisyllabic Words 389

ANSWER KEYS / 401

BIBLIOGRAPHY / 415

Section

ISSUES
AND
CONCERNS

FEELINGS ABOUT SPELLING

The first question is: Why do teachers need to deal with students' feelings about spelling? How important are these feelings?

The answer: Students' feelings about spelling are critically important.

Think for a moment about a task that is extremely difficult for you, a task where you have faced failure, even embarrassment. Perhaps that task is parallel parking, hitting a baseball, or cooking. Now, ask yourself these questions:

1. Do you seek out opportunities to work on that task?

2. Do you work hard to improve your skills on that task?

If your answer is "Yes" to these questions, you are an amazingly mature person. Most people tend to avoid tasks that are difficult for them. When faced with such a task, most people tend to spend a great deal of their available energy protecting themselves from feelings of inadequacy and defeat. Then they feel overwhelmed and confused, sometimes angry. Very little energy is left over to actually do any work on improving their skills.

Students who have difficulty with spelling are confronted by their "failure" continually in academic settings. Even if teachers are sensitive and nurturing, the students know they have not spelled the words the same way the other students have. In addition, they sometimes have to face weekly spelling tests. As students get older and proceed through the grades, the pressure to spell words in the standard way increases, and students feel more and more pressure.

Is it surprising that these students have little energy left over to focus on spelling? Sometimes, students will make a valiant effort and decide that they will "learn how to spell, right now, right here."

One student reports that when he was in elementary school, he decided he would memorize every single one of his spelling words for his test. And he did. He memorized the series of letters for the first word, then the second and so on throughout the entire list of words. He memorized the letters in one unbroken string. For example, if the first word was "car," the second, "tree" and the third, "lamp," he memorized, "c . . . a . . . r . . . t . . . r . . e . . . e . . . l . . . a . . . m . . . p." The system worked fine until, one week, the teacher dictated the spelling words in a different order.

Look at the energy, dedication, and hard work it took to memorize that list of letters. After the system failed, do you think the student was likely to keep trying at that same level, or do you think he gave up just a little and put more of his energies into protecting himself?

Many, if not most, students who have difficulty with spelling have made such amazing efforts in the past. When we see them now after years of failure, many look like they just don't care. "Spelling isn't important," they say. Or, "It doesn't matter how I spell. I can use a spell check."

How can teachers help these students begin to feel comfortable with spelling? How can students put aside old habits of not focusing on spelling? How can students get the courage to try just one more time?

The first thing for the teacher to do is to acknowledge the students' feelings. It is important to talk about how difficult it has been to not succeed with such an ever-present task.

If students have difficulty expressing their feelings, the teacher can encourage this discussion. It's best not to say, "I know that you're feeling . . ." upset, angry or another emotion. It's better to say, "Many people feel . . ." or "I think you could have been discouraged by . . . " or "One way people respond to this is by . . . ."

It's important to respect students' privacy around their feelings. If they don't want to talk about how they feel, they should not feel pressure to do so. Opening the subject up for students is only an **invitation** for them to talk.

Mostly, give your students time to talk about their feelings if they wish to do so. This is not a waste of time. It is an important part of their instruction.

The second thing for the teacher to do is to explain that most spelling instruction expects students to memorize the letters in a word and to retain that memory over a long period of time. Tell your students that the ability to memorize relatively meaningless letters is not related to intelligence at all. Many extremely bright, even brilliant people, have great difficulty memorizing the spelling of words.

HAVING TROUBLE MEMORIZING SERIES OF LETTERS MEANS THAT A PERSON HAS TROUBLE MEMORIZING SERIES OF LETTERS. IT MEANS NOTHING ELSE.

At this point, it is often helpful to talk about people's strengths and weaknesses. If you feel comfortable, share with your students an area in which you do not feel particularly strong. If you wish, you can keep this discussion less personal and more general.

Next, tell your students that *Spelling Smart!* is not based on memorization. Tell them that it is based on patterns found in words, and that they will primarily use their good common sense and logical thinking in learning to spell.

A third important area for the teacher to discuss is the difficulty of spelling English. This is often a place where you can share some of the information in the section "The Origins of English" on pages 25 to 26. Providing time to talk about the many languages from which English has "borrowed" words is extremely important. It helps students realize that they are learning to spell one of the most challenging languages in the world.

Talk is important, but *Spelling Smart!* also offers specific help for students regarding their negative feelings about spelling. *Spelling Smart!* stresses the following:

1. The pacing of knowledge acquisition can be slow and easy. There is no need to rush. There is no list of words that needs to be learned each week. It is far more important for students to feel relaxed and comfortable with the material than it is for them to move along quickly. In this way, they will retain what they learn, and they will begin to feel better about their competence with spelling.

2. The "Reinforcing Activities" provide practice, rest, and the ability to use a strength in an area of weakness. These are not frill activities that can be offered "if there's

time." These are an important part of the lesson, where students can work at their own pace and begin to relax around spelling.

Likewise, the "Independent Work" provides opportunities for students to practice their spelling skills in a nonthreatening way. The "List It!" and "Write On!" activities also encourage them to integrate their new spelling knowledge into their writing. This often helps students feel better about both skills.

3. The "Extra Interesting Facts" section provides information on word and phrase derivations. In some cases, it tells about words that have "died" in English. It is most helpful to present this information in a relaxed way. English is, after all, a fascinating language with a diverse history. If students can become interested in how English reflects other cultures and historical events, it often helps them feel less resentful about the many irregular spellings. They can also become intellectually curious about the origins of specific words, and this can help them begin to develop the habit of focusing on spelling.

THE CONSONANTS

Even with older students, it is essential to do some diagnostic work before you begin the lessons. In Lesson One, it is assumed that students know the consonant sounds, short vowel sounds, consonant blends, and digraphs. Students may appear to know these sounds and, in fact, they **may** know all of them. On the other hand, they may only know some of them. The few they don't know can keep them from succeeding.

This section focuses on the consonant sounds. Before giving the following test, explain to your students that you are checking to see if they have any gaps in their knowledge. Tell them that people can sometimes go through many years of school and still not know certain letter sounds. Explain that, if you discover any such gaps, you will work together to fill them.

Diagnostic Assessment of Consonant Sounds

Provide your students with pencils and lined paper. Ask them to number their papers from 1 to 24.

Say, *"I am going to say some sounds. When you hear the sound, please write down the letter that represents that sound. Most of the time, I will not give you a word associated with the sound. I will do that only when more than one letter represents a given sound."*

(Be careful to produce a pure sound for each consonant; for example, for /b/, say /b/ as in "bat," as opposed to /bl/ as in "blue." Also, you may repeat sounds if students ask you to do so. Make note of these requests, however, as they may indicate a pattern of difficulty hearing or discriminating sounds.)

Say, *"It is now time to begin. Please write the letter that represents the sound."*

Sounds	Correct Answers
1. /d/	d
2. /m/	m
3. /k/ as in "cat"	c
4. /t/	t
5. /s/ as in "sit"	s
6. /l/	l
7. /g/ as in "game"	g
8. /w/	w
9. /h/	h
10. /j/ as in "jam"	j
11. /b/	b
12. /kw/	q
13. /f/	f
14. /z/ as in "zipper"	z
15. /r/	r
16. /j/ as in "giant"	g
17. /ks/	x
18. /n/	n
19. /s/ as in "city"	c
20. /y/	y
21. /k/ as in "kite"	k
22. /v/	v
23. /z/ as in "is"	s
24. /p/	p

If your students know all the consonant sounds, proceed to the Diagnostic Assessment of short vowel sounds on page 9. If they need to learn the sound/symbol correspondence of "b," "d," "f," "h," "j," "k," "l," "m," "n," "p," "r," "t," "v," "w," "x," "y," or "z," teach them in the same way that "b" is taught in the following sample lesson.

A SAMPLE LESSON FOR TEACHING THE SOUND/SYMBOL CORRESPONDENCE OF "B"

Gather together some objects or pictures of objects that begin with the /b/ sound; for example: ball, bat, bell, bow, button. Be careful that all the objects begin with a pure /b/ sound and not a consonant blend such as /br/ as in "brick." Share these objects with your students and talk about each one. Ask your students to find other objects that begin with /b/. They can also find pictures of such objects.

Then say the following words: ball, bat, bell, bow, button.
"What do you hear at the beginning of these words?"
"That's right. You hear a /b/ sound."
Record the following words: ball, bat, bell, bow, button.
"What do you see at the beginning of these words?"
"Yes, you see the letter 'b.'"
Ask your students to write the letter "b," and also to copy a few words that begin with this letter. If your students need more practice with this sound/symbol correspondence, repeat this activity with new objects.

Some students find it helpful to have a key word they associate with a given letter; for example, their key word for /b/ might be "bat." Some students like to write this key word on a piece of paper and to have this to refer to whenever they wish.

TEACHING THE SOUND/SYMBOL CORRESPONDENCES OF "Q," "C," "G," AND "S"

Present the letter "q" in the same way you did for the letter "b." You will need to add the information that "q" never appears alone in English, but that it is always followed by a "u."

The last three letters are unusual because they each represent two different sounds. The letter "c" represents the sound /k/ and the sound /s/ (usually before "e," "i" and "y"). The letter "g" represents the sound /g/ and the sound /j/ (usually before "e," "i," and "y"). The letter "s" can represent the sounds /s/ and /z/.

It is best to present these letters after all the other consonants have been presented. The following illustrates how to teach them.

A SAMPLE LESSON FOR TEACHING THE SOUND/SYMBOL CORRESPONDENCES OF "C"

You will begin with the /k/ sound that "c" can represent. First, gather together objects or pictures of objects that begin with the letter "c" representing the /k/ sound. Share these objects and pictures with your students and talk about each one.

Then say the following words: cap, cat, coat, cup, cut.

"What sound do you hear in the beginning of these words?"

"I agree that you hear the /k/ sound. This is the same sound that the letter 'k' can represent."

Record the following words: cap, cat, coat, cup, cut.

"What do you see at the beginning of all these words?"

"That's correct. You see the letter 'c.' This letter can represent the /k/ sound."

As with the lesson for /b/, ask your students to write the letter "c" and to copy some words that begin with this letter. Some students may wish to make a key word card.

Then say, *"The letter 'c' is unusual because it can represent a second sound."*

Gather objects or pictures of objects that begin with the letter "c" representing the /s/ sound. Share these objects with your students and talk about each one.

Say the following words: celery, cent, cereal, cider, cyclone.

"What do you hear at the beginning of these words?"

"Good, you hear the /s/ sound."

Record the following words: celery, cent, cereal, cider, cyclone.

"What do you see at the beginning of these words?"

"Yes, you see the letter 'c.' Therefore, we know that the letter 'c' can represent both the /k/ sound and the /s/ sound."

Ask your students to write the letter "c" and to copy some words that begin with "c" representing the /s/ sound. Some students may wish to make a key word card.

Further Discussion on Teaching Sound/Symbol Correspondences for Consonants

Allow your students to proceed at their own pace. Especially in these early stages, it is best that students not feel overwhelmed and confused. Introduce games, at times, to provide reinforcement of the learning. One good game is Sound Bingo.

Make up Bingo cards and put a letter in each square. Then, the caller says selected sounds and the players can cover up the letter or letters that represent that sound. The first player to cover a line, or the whole card if you prefer, wins the game. Even better, students have valuable practice and reinforcement.

Another way to help students become comfortable with the consonants is to talk with them about their origins. The history of the alphabet is a fascinating subject. Tell your students that English letters started out as pictures of people, animals, or things. As time went on, these pictures became stylized, partly because people did not want to take the time to draw the careful pictures.

The letter "m" has an interesting history. The Phoenicians, an ancient people, were sea explorers. Their word for water was "mem." Their letter "m," which is very similar to our "m," started out as a picture of ocean waves.

Do you know why "z" is the last letter of the alphabet? Apparently, "z" was the sixth letter in the Greek alphabet. When the Romans borrowed from the Greeks, they felt they didn't need the "z," so they dropped it. They changed their minds later, however, and added "z" to the end of their alphabet.

THE SHORT VOWEL SOUNDS

In this section, you will continue with diagnostic work. You will assess your students' knowledge of the short vowel sounds /a/, /i/, /o/, /u/ and /e/. The use of "y" as a vowel will not be discussed until much later in the program.

Tell your students that you want to see how familiar they are with short vowel sounds. Explain that these sounds are found in many words, and it is important to discover if everyone knows them. If someone needs to learn one or more short vowel sounds, you will work on it together.

Diagnostic Assessment of Short Vowel Sounds

Provide your students with pencils and lined paper. Ask them to number their papers from 1 to 25.

Say, *"I first want to see if you know what the vowels are. Please write the five vowels on your paper from 1 to 5. Sometimes, the letter "y" is used as a vowel, but don't put that one down. List the other five vowels."*

When your students are finished, say, *"I am going to say some words that begin with a short vowel sound. After I say the word, write down the vowel you feel it begins with. If you're not sure, take a guess.*

Words	Correct Answers
6. odd	o
7. act	a
8. end	e
9. it	i
10. us	u
11. enter	e
12. opposite	o
13. imperfect	i
14. adolescent	a
15. uncover	u

Say, *"I am now going to say some words that have vowel sounds in the middle of the word. Listen carefully, and then write down the vowel you feel is in each word."*

Words	Correct Answers
16. cup	u
17. tap	a
18. pit	i
19. bell	e
20. sod	o
21. list	i
22. pond	o
23. rust	u
24. bent	e
25. camp	a

If your students know all the short vowel sounds, proceed to the diagnostic assessment of consonant blends and digraphs on pages 12 and 13. Sometimes, this is a judgment call as to when to proceed, because some students demonstrate occasional confusion, especially with the vowels in the middle of words.

The general rule is to provide some instruction on the sound/symbol correspondence if confusion is seen. Do not wait until full mastery is achieved, however, to proceed through the program. Since the vowel sounds are among the hardest sounds to discriminate, some students may need the practice provided in the actual lessons of *Spelling Smart!* to attain full mastery.

SAMPLE LESSON TEACHING THE SOUND/SYMBOL CORRESPONDENCE OF THE SHORT VOWEL "A"

"Today, we are going to work with a short vowel sound."
Say the following words: act, after, ant, apple, at.
"What vowel sound do you hear at the beginning of all these words?"
"Good, you hear the /a/ sound as in 'ant.'"
Record the following words: act, after, ant, apple, at.

"What vowel do you see in the beginning of these words?"

"Yes, you see the letter 'a.' As you have heard, its short vowel sound is /a/ as in 'ant.' Let's use the word 'ant' as the key word to help us remember that sound."

Ask your students to write the letter "a," and to copy a few words that contain this short vowel. Make a card with the word "ant" written on it as a key word card.

Further Discussion on Teaching the Short Vowel Sounds

These sounds are among the hardest for students to discriminate between. For that reason, the procedure for teaching them is different from that with consonants. Instead of presenting objects or pictures of objects, you begin presenting words. Then, a main focus becomes establishing a key word for each short vowel sound.

You can establish your own key words. One suggestion is: "ant" for /a/, "in" for /i/, "on" for /o/, "under" for /u/, and "edge" for /e/. One interesting thing you can do is make a small ant figure out of clay. Get a box like a shoe box and label "in" inside the box, "on" on the cover of the box, etc. The ant can sit in the box, on the cover of the box, under the box, and at the edge (attached with tape perhaps?). This is just one manner of providing a tangible prop to help students remember the key words and, thus, the short vowel sounds.

It is important to provide reinforcement once all the short vowels are presented. Sound Bingo, as described in "The Consonants" on page 8, is a good game for this. Another possibility is Sound Scatter. This game can be played individually or in a group. Make up a deck of cards, each card having one short vowel written on it. For a group game, every player gets five cards to start.

Scatter the rest of the cards on the table. Say a short vowel sound (or a word with that sound if your students are ready for this). The first player tries to find a card with the correct vowel sound from the table. If she selects the correct vowel, she gets to keep the card. if she selects a different one, she has to give up one of her cards. Players stop playing if their cards run out. The player with the most cards at the end wins the game.

If only one student is playing this game with a teacher, he "wins" if he gets all the cards. He "loses" if he has to give up all his cards.

As with the teaching of consonants, it is interesting to learn about the origins of vowels. It is believed that our letter "A" comes from the Phoenicians. These people called "A" aleph, which stood for "ox." The letter was originally a V (to represent the horns of oxen?) with a line across it. The Greeks turned it around.

Oxen were very important to the Phoenicians because they helped with planting. The letter "A" may begin our alphabet because its original derivation referred to animals who helped provide life-giving food.

CONSONANT BLENDS AND DIGRAPHS

It is important to assess students' knowledge of consonant blends and digraphs because these letter combinations occur in so many English words. Sometimes, students have difficulty hearing them and/or deciding which letters to put in combination. Many of these difficulties can be corrected by a small amount of instruction.

Consonant blends are combinations of two or three consonants in which the individual sounds can all be heard. Consonant digraphs are combinations of two consonants that together make one unique sound.

Tell your students that this is the last formal diagnostic work you will do. If it is discovered that they are not familiar with some of these consonant combinations, you will work on them together.

Diagnostic Assessment of Consonant Blends and Digraphs

Provide your students with pencils and lined paper. Ask them to number their papers from 1 to 26.

Say, *"I am going to say some consonant combinations, or blends, that occur frequently in the English language. After I say the blend and give an example of a word that begins with it, please write the consonant combination down. You will be writing down two or three letters. For example, if I say /sc/ as in 'scare,' you will write down 'sc.' Now, let's begin."*

Sounds	Correct Answers
1. /dr/ as in "drive"	dr
2. /sl/ as in "sled"	sl
3. /cl/ as in "cloud"	cl
4. /tr/ as in "truck"	tr
5. /gr/ as in "great"	gr
6. /tw/ as in "twine"	tw
7. /bl/ as in "blue"	bl
8. /sp/ as in "spoon"	sp
9. /pl/ as in "plead"	pl
10. /str/ as in "street"	str
11. /fl/ as in "flag"	fl
12. /cr/ as in "cry"	cr
13. /sw/ as in "sweet"	sw
14. /br/ as in "brick"	br
15. /pr/ as in "prove"	pr
16. /gl/ as in "glad"	gl

Say, *"Sometimes, consonant blends occur at the end of words. After I say the combination and give an example of a word that ends with it, please write down the two consonants that make the sound."*

Sounds	Correct Answers
17. /nd/ as in "and"	nd
18. /lt/ as in "melt"	lt
19. /ct/ as in "fact"	ct
20. /nt/ as in "punt"	nt
21. /pt/ as in "accept"	pt

Say, *"In these next five sounds, two consonants combine to make one unique sound. Write down the two consonants which, together, make this one unique sound."*

Sounds	Correct Answers
22. /sh/ as in "ship"	sh
23. /ch/ as in "church"	ch
24. /th/ as in "thumb"	th
25. /ph/ as in "phone"	ph
26. /wh/ as in "what"	wh

If your students know these consonant blends and digraphs, proceed to Lesson 1 of *Spelling Smart!* If they need instruction, refer to the following sample lessons.

As with short vowels, it is a judgment call as to how much instruction to provide on these patterns. Students do need to have a good grasp of the consonant digraphs. Fortunately, these are often easier for students to master than the blends. Concerning the latter, it is important for students to have a good awareness of them.

It's not necessary to wait for full mastery, however. Often, students need the practice provided in the lessons of *Spelling Smart!* for them to achieve this level.

SAMPLE LESSON FOR TEACHING THE SOUND/SYMBOL CORRESPONDENCE OF THE CONSONANT DIGRAPH "CH"

"Today, we are going to work with two consonants that, together, make one unique sound."
     Say the following words: chase, chill, chip, chum, church.
     "What sound do you hear at the beginning of all these words?"
     "Yes, you hear the /ch/ sound as in 'chin.'"
     Record the following words: chase, chill, chip, chum, church.
     "What letter combination do you see at the beginning of these words?"
     "Good, you see 'ch' together. This combination of two consonants that makes one unique sound is called a consonant digraph. You don't have to remember this name, just know that this is a special kind of pattern which occurs in English."
     Ask your students to write the 'ch' combination. Then ask them to copy some words that begin with 'ch.' (At this point, focus is placed on digraphs in the initial position in words. As you proceed through the lessons of *Spelling Smart!*, you will point them out in other places in words.)
     Ask your students to make a key word card for "ch," which they can refer to whenever they wish to do so. A good key word is "chin."

SAMPLE LESSON FOR TEACHING THE SOUND/SYMBOL CORRESPONDENCE OF THE CONSONANT BLEND "BL"

"Today, we are going to work with a consonant blend. This is a combination of two consonants that occur together. If you listen carefully, you can hear both their sounds."
     Say the following words: black, blast, bloom, blow, blue.
     "If you listen carefully, which two consonant sounds do you hear at the beginning of these words?"
     "I agree that you hear /b/ and then the /l/ sound."
     Record the following words: black, blast, bloom, blow, blue.
     "What two consonants do you see at the beginning of these words?"
     "That's right, you see the consonants 'b' and 'l.' These consonants occur together quite frequently in English."
     Ask your students to write the "bl" combination, and then to copy several words that begin with this blend. Practice with this blend until students demonstrate a comfortable familiarity with it.

Further Discussion on Teaching Consonant Blends

Hearing and spelling consonant blends in the final position in words is quite difficult for some students. It's important to present these final consonant blends, but expect that some students will have difficulty with them. Just be aware of each student's needs in this area, and provide extra support as you proceed through the program.

It is critically important not to continue too long, making sure every student completely knows every consonant blend. As long as students have some abilities to spell these letters, it is time to move on. Staying too long at this level can cause students to become discouraged and bored.

Some students find it very helpful to work with a tangible prop when they are learning consonant blends. For example, you can give your students some small beads. Ask them, *"How many sounds do you hear when you hear /br/ or /pl/ or /str/ . . . ? Count out the beads that represent these sounds."* It appears strange, but for some students, this is a very helpful technique.

ASSESSING THE NEEDS OF STUDENTS

In this section, typical needs of students will be discussed. These needs fall into four major categories: cognitive, emotional, behavioral, and learning style. In the following subsections, these general areas will be presented, along with associated spelling difficulties. Specific ways to meet these needs will be included. Finally ways to assess the needs of students will be discussed.

Cognitive

This area includes logical thinking skills, organizational skills, and the ability to think abstractly. If students have significant difficulty with all of these areas, it may be that *Spelling Smart!* is not the spelling program of choice for them. These students might do better with a program based on drill, repetition, and visual memory.

If, however, students just have some weakness in these areas, the following modifications can support them:

1. Provide additional time for all aspects of the program, especially the reinforcing activities.

2. Talk with students a great deal about the structure of English. Make charts and posters to visually represent this structure.

3. If students have difficulty with certain abstract concepts such as consonants and vowels, explain what these things are. For example, with vowels, our mouths can stay open. With consonants, a part of our mouth (lips, tongue, or teeth) close quickly. Have your students feel this with their own mouths. You can also use a mirror to show them how this looks.

4. Whenever possible, use tangible props to support learning. You might continue to use objects to represent patterns being studied throughout the program instead of ending with this technique after the presentation of consonants.

Some students may be gifted in the cognitive area. These students will profit from the intellectual stimulation of additional work on the history of English, and the etymology of specific words. See the Bibliography for the names of good books to refer to in this area.

Emotional

For some students, emotional needs are so significant that they must be addressed before learning can occur. Some students are so afraid they will fail that they are reluctant to try. Others will begin a task, but will abandon it as soon as it becomes a little difficult. Still others will approach academic tasks with feelings of being overwhelmed and confused. Some students feel angry. The following are recommended to deal with these feelings:

1. Offer reassurance that you will only ask students to do what you know they can do. If students feel that something is too difficult, you will ask them to tell you this, and you will discuss the issue.

2. At the beginning of each learning session, tell your students exactly what you will be doing that day. For example, you can tell them you will be asking them to discuss some information presented yesterday, you will be offering some new information, and you will be asking them to spell ten words.

Some students need to feel they are progressing quickly. These students often need challenge. For these students, select multisyllabic words from the word list for them to spell. Encourage them to select challenging reinforcing activities.

Behavioral

As all teachers know, the area of behavior is a significant area of need for some students. These students can exhibit hyperactivity, with the resultant difficulty of staying with any academic task. Or they may have trouble paying attention to a topic that does not immediately capture their interest. Still others approach any new learning situation with hostility.

The following often help with these issues:

1. Keep learning sessions relatively short. Within the learning session, vary the types of modalities utilized.

2. For active students, provide legitimate outlets for their energy during the lesson.

3. If necessary, contract with students as to what they will accomplish each day. By accomplishing their agreed-upon goals, students can earn free time.

4. Try to make the activities personally meaningful to the students. This is where the reinforcing activities can be critically important.

Learning Style

This area is a place where careful assessment of learning strengths and weaknesses is required. Is your student a conceptual learner? Does he need to see an overall picture of what he will learn before the details begin to make sense? Does he remember best what he sees? Or hears? Does he need to interact with the material: talk about it, work with it, play with it before he can remember the information?

Spelling Smart! utilizes so many modalities within the program that many learning styles are accommodated. There is one skill area, however, that is very important to discuss. This is auditory discrimination.

Spelling Smart! assumes that students can learn the consonants, short vowel sounds, consonant blends, and digraphs relatively easily given proper instruction. If a student has serious difficulty with these sound/symbol correspondences, it is possible that he has a problem with auditory discrimination.

People who have significant difficulty with auditory discrimination have trouble hearing the differences between sounds. Often, they can't discriminate between short vowel sounds, or between consonant sounds such as /f/ and /v/ and /th/. They often have trouble recognizing the different sounds in consonant blends. Now, if they can't hear them, how can they possibly spell them?

These students need to be taught specifically about the sounds. Often, speech and language clinicians or educational therapists will help them to recognize how the sound feels in their mouths and vocal cords. A program like *Auditory Discrimination in Depth* by Charles H. Lindamood and Patricia C. Lindamood (DLM Teaching Resources, 1969 and 1975) can help students with significant needs in this area.

The following are recommendations to accommodate learning styles:

1. If one of your students needs to know "the whole picture" before learning the particulars, give a quick overview of the structure of English. For example, present the six syllable types as being the major syllables in the English language.

2. The general rule is: Utilize a student's strength to compensate for a weakness. Thus, if a student has poor visual skills but strong auditory ones, utilize a lot of auditory cues in your instruction.

3. If you suspect that a student has significant difficulty with auditory discrimination, bring your concerns to a school psychologist or speech and language clinician. Your student's needs may require formal evaluation so that he can receive the proper help.

How to Assess a Student's Needs

Many teachers ask, *"But how can I tell what my students need? I'm not a trained evaluator."*

Teachers have many skills that can go a long way toward assessing what their students need. At times, it's important for school psychologists and other educational diagnosticians to administer standardized tests. Often, however, teachers can figure out how to best help their students by pursuing the following steps:

First, it's important to get to know your student as a person. Try to spend some time with her during informal moments; for example, during recess or at a choice time in class. Does your student's behavior change when she is not being asked to complete some academic task? Does she have a sense of humor? Does she prefer to listen or to talk?

Next, look at her records. If she is receiving special education services, there will be a lot of information about learning style in her file. If she is not receiving these services, check her regular school records. What has her attendance been like? What subjects has she excelled at? Where has she experienced difficulty? Is she successful in art? Are there behavioral notes that indicate any needs?

Continue your investigation by carefully observing your student during instruction times. Is she more engaged when she is talking about a topic, or when she is listening to another student or teacher? Does she seem to relate to visual cues provided during instruction? Does she stay on task during independent work times? Give yourself enough time for observation so that any important clues can emerge.

A next critical step is to talk to people. If possible, ask teachers who have taught your student in the past. Have they discovered anything special about her learning needs? When was your student most successful and least successful with academics? If they could now change some instructional method they used with your student, what would that be?

Next, talk with your student about her learning style. Ask her to tell you when she feels she is most successful. When does schoolwork seem easiest, or hardest? Are there any special pitfalls that keep her from concentrating on schoolwork? Does she need quiet? Or does she like a comfortable social environment with a little background chatter in which to work?

Last, when you actually begin to work, notice how your student responds. Ask her to tell you how she feels she is learning. Regularly ask her for feedback concerning how she feels the lessons are going. Ask her to tell you which techniques and approaches are most successful and least successful in assisting her learning.

Students are often surprised to be asked these questions, and they tend to be reticent in the beginning. Once they realize, however, that you believe they have valuable information about their own learning, students will be extremely helpful in providing this information.

IRREGULAR WORDS

This section discusses the difficult topic of teaching irregular words. English has borrowed a great deal from other languages. When this occurred, the spelling of the original language was usually maintained.

This borrowing has created a wide variety of diverse spellings that appear to follow no patterns. Also, the pronunciations of some words have changed drastically over the years, but the spellings have stayed the same. This has added to the confusion. It is estimated that these "irregular" spellings comprise approximately 15 percent of the English language.

The traditional way for students to learn these words is to memorize them. Usually, students write them over and over. Verbal drill sometimes occurs.

Teachers are left, therefore, with the dilemma of how to teach these words to students who have weak memorization skills. *Spelling Smart!* advocates this position: The main goal is to help students become comfortable with the 85 percent of English that follows regular patterns. If too much attention is placed on irregular words, this can detract from this goal. There are some irregular words that are practical for students to have access to early in their learning. There are only a few of these, however.

Introduce irregular words that are extremely common. Students may wish to use words like "you" and "for" in their writing. As discussed before, the words "the," "a," "said," "of," and "to" are presented in the sentences that students write for practice with spelling in context. The way these words are introduced in the lessons is one good way to teach irregular words. A written model is provided. It is not expected that students will memorize these words. With continued use, it is hoped that they will come to learn them, but this memorization task is not stressed. The written model is provided for as long as is necessary.

There are different ways of giving models. Some teachers write each irregular word on an index card for the students to see. Others ask students to copy the spellings in their notebooks. Some people write the irregular words on the inside cover of the notebook. You can also help your students create their own personal dictionaries. A small wire-bound notebook works well for this. It is cautioned, however, to limit the number of words in this dictionary. Some students want to include many words. Whenever they come upon an irregular word they don't know, they wish to record it. If too many words are included, however, it makes the personal dictionary cumbersome and less usable.

Encourage your students not to worry about the spellings of a lot of irregular words. Especially in the early stages of the program, explain to them that they will be learning many patterns and that, in time, they will be able to spell many words by themselves. Then the words that have irregular patterns will not seem to be so overwhelming.

By the time students begin to have a basic understanding of the structure of the language, they often begin to remember the irregular words more easily. It may be that their anxiety around spelling has decreased and, therefore, they can more efficiently access the memory skills they do possess. Even though their memorization skills may be weak, they do exist.

As students progress through *Spelling Smart!*, you may wish to do some formal work with irregular words. This can serve as a break between formal lessons. This is recommended in two areas:

1. where there in a group of words that are irregular but follow consistent patterns
2. high visibility words your students may wish to know

An example of the first type of irregular words are words in which there are silent letters. Common silent letters are:

"k" with "n" as is "knot"
"g" with "n" as in "gnome" and "sign"
"w" with "r" as in "write"

It is believed that, in the past, these letters were pronounced. It is fun for students to now add the sounds and to "talk" in the ancient way.

Present the information about silent letters and talk about it. Ask your students if they wish to have a page for silent letters in their notebooks. They can try to find as many words as they can with these silent letters. They can also try to find examples of other silent letters, such as "b" with "m" as in "numb."

You may also wish to present some high visibility irregular words. Examples of these are the numbers, the days of the week, and the months of the year.

For example, if you wish to present the numbers from one to twelve, write them all down in a list for your students. Look at each word, and discuss all words that follow known patterns. For example, if your students have already discovered closed syllables and vowel-consonant-e syllables, talk about how "six," "seven," and "ten" are all closed syllables, and how "five" and "nine" are vowel-consonant-e syllables.

Discuss with your students what type of written model they would like for the others. Since this is a group of words, would it be helpful to include the words they already know in the model? Talk about any irregularities they notice in the spellings of these words.

To complete the lesson, do a little work with etymology. You can, for example, discuss where the number "eleven" comes from. Tell your students that many ancient societies based their number systems on people's ten fingers. The Anglo-Saxons did this.

If Anglo-Saxons had to count one more than ten, they said the count was "endle-ofen," or "one left over." Thus, our "eleven" evolved from this ancient source.

HOMONYMS

Homonyms are words that sound the same but have different spellings and meanings. They pose great challenges for people who have difficulty with spelling.

Spelling Smart! recommends that homonyms be introduced as an interesting aspect of the English language. This should be done only when students are well into the program and have at least worked with closed, vowel-consonant-e, and open syllables. By this time, students often begin to notice homonyms in their reading. They are often expressing either curiosity about them or frustration with them, or both.

Homonyms can be presented as supplements to regular lessons, or they can be introduced instead of a regular lesson. However this is done, it is very important that only a few homonyms are presented at one time. Teachers sometimes make the mistake of doing a homonym unit and introducing several pairs. This tends to create confusion for people who have difficulty with memorization.

The following is a list of forty common homonym teams:

1. aloud, allowed
2. ate, eight
3. be, bee
4. berry, bury
5. blew, blue
6. board, bored

(continued on next page)

forty common homonym teams (continued)

7. brake, break
8. buy, by, bye
9. coarse, course
10. dear, deer
11. dew, do, due
12. eye, I
13. flour, flower
14. for, fore, four
15. groan, grown
16. guessed, guest
17. hear, here
18. hole, whole
19. hour, our
20. knew, new
21. knight, night
22. know, no
23. knows, nose
24. made, maid
25. mail, male
26. meat, meet
27. one, won
28. passed, past
29. read, red
30. right, rite, write
31. road, rode, rowed
32. sail, sale
33. sew, so, sow
34. shone, shown
35. some, sum
36. son, sun
37. their, there, they're
38. to, too, two
39. waist, waste
40. weak, week

You can select the teams to be presented according to the interests of your students. It is highly recommended, however, that the first two homonym teams to be introduced are: "to," "too," "two" and "their," "there," "they're." These homonyms are so common that students will feel greatly empowered once they begin to understand them.

The following illustrates a good way to teach homonyms. Since many of these words are irregular, the procedure varies from teaching other regular patterns.

Presenting the Homonyms "To," "Too," and "Two"

1. Introduce the following chart for students to complete:

Word	Sentence to Be Completed
two	a. Pam went _____ the store.
to	b. "It's _____ cold to go swimming," Tom said.
too	c. Henry ate _____ hot dogs.
too	d. Martha wanted to go for a walk, _____.

Challenge your students to figure out which word belongs in each sentence. Enlist other people's help if necessary.

2. Provide as many sentences as are needed from which your students can figure out the meanings of each word.

3. Once the meanings are established, record the three words with their meanings and sample sentences on a card or chart that is highly visible to students.

4. Ask your students to record this information in their notebooks.

5. Allow the model to be used for as long as your students need it. Expect that your students will now be able to edit their own writing for these homonyms.

Further Discussion on Presenting Homonyms

Provide additional reinforcement by using one or all of the following:

1. Play homonym concentration. Once a few homonyms have been presented, get a stack of blank cards such as 3 × 5 inch index cards. Write a homonym on one card, and then write its meaning on a separate card. Repeat this process for all the members of all the homonym teams.

   Place all cards face down on the table. The first player turns two cards around. If a word matches with its meaning, the player keeps the cards and gets another turn. If not, she has to place the cards face down again and the next player gets a chance. The person who has collected the most cards at the end, wins the game.

2. Play the "I'm thinking of" game. Ask your students to write a series of sentences, each one of which follows the following format:

    He went to the _____ and got a great buy on a pair of jeans, and then he went for a _____ on the lake.

    (Choose between *sale* and *sail*.)

    Students write their sentences on a chalkboard or large paper and challenge their peers to complete them correctly. Students gain a point for every word of theirs that is filled in correctly. (This twist encourages them to write meaningful sentences. It also reinforces their writing a lot of sentences.)

3. Another activity that supports the learning of homonyms is to "collect" them. Have a large piece of paper available in the classroom on which homonym teams can be recorded. Students often notice these teams in their reading, and they enjoy making a list of them.

    The teams collected in this way are not meant to be mastered. The goal of this activity is to help students become interested in homonyms. It's fun to see how many of them are present in the English language.

In the few cases where members of homonym teams follow regular patterns that have already been presented, use this as additional information as students study the words. Examples of teams that follow these patterns are: "be" and "bee" (open syllable and vowel combination syllable with "ee"), "made" and "maid" (vowel-consonant-e syllable and vowel combination syllable with "ai"), and "pain" and "pane" (vowel combination syllable with "ai" and vowel-consonant-e syllable).

DICTIONARY SKILLS

A great deal can be gained by spending some time with dictionary skills. People who have difficulty with spelling often dislike using dictionaries. Some are openly resistive to them.

This is very understandable. After all, if a student has poor spelling skills, he probably will have experienced a great deal of failure with dictionaries in the past. How, for example, would a student have approached looking up the word "aristocrat" if he had no idea of its beginning? Once again, we see the old dilemma, "How can I look it up if I don't know how to spell it?"

Also, some teachers, in their efforts to help students with dictionary skills, have given long and complex assignments before students had any confidence or skill with the dictionary. These attempts to have students "practice" and thus improve, often only reinforced feelings of frustration and failure.

How, then, can you help students who perceive dictionaries as being confusing and complex?

A major way to start is to help students become familiar and comfortable with the physical structure of the dictionary. There is, after all, a very standard physical structure upon which all dictionaries are based: the alphabet.

It is a good idea to check that your students have familiarity with the design of the alphabet. Do they know, for example, that there are 26 letters, and that "m" and "n" are approximately in the middle? Could they say if "g" is in the first half of the alphabet? Where is "r"?

With some students, you need to do some activities with the alphabet before you even ask them to open the dictionary. This needs to be done with great care because of the childlike look of the work.

Spelling Smart! recommends that if it is apparent students are not familiar with the structure of the alphabet, you speak openly about this in a private setting. Tell your students that this is one of those gaps in knowledge that can be easily corrected. Just a little work with this will make it much easier for them to use the dictionary. Then, begin work with the following activity.

First, make a set of individual alphabet letters. One way to do this is to photocopy an alphabet out of a book like *Modern Display Alphabets: 100 Complete Fonts, selected and arranged by Paul E. Kennedy* from the *Franklin Photolettering Catalogue,* (Dover Publications Inc., New York, 1974). Glue the alphabet page onto heavy paper, and then cut out squares around each letter.

Create a private working space. Ask each student to place these letters, which are given in random order, into their alphabetic sequence. Repeat this activity with students attempting to become faster and more efficient. Continue this activity until students are clearly aware of the sequence.

It's now time to start work with the actual dictionary. Ask your students to hold the dictionary in their hands and to try to open it to where there are words with the letter "m." They only get one try and they have to use their sense of where this letter may be. Repeat this activity with all the letters until students can get quite close with each try.

Students enjoy this activity. It can be a good "filler" for those few extra minutes left over from other class lessons.

The comment often comes up, "But some letters have more words than others." Some students enjoy actually counting the pages of certain letters and comparing them to others. They like looking for answers to questions like, "What letter has the most words?" "What letter has the least words?"

Another important thing to do that helps students become comfortable with the dictionary is to ask your students to just look through the dictionary to see how it's organized. Look at the front section to see what information it provides. What's at the end? Do dictionaries differ in the information they provide?

Once students have a good sense of the physical structure of the dictionary, it is helpful to check their knowledge of guide words. First, ask your students to explain how they work. If students understand these valuable tools, the following will provide good practice for using them:

1. Ask your students to find certain guide words.

2. Present the two guide words of a particular page on the chalkboard. Ask students to brainstorm about which words will be present on that page. Then, check to see how accurate their list is.

3. Present a guide word. Ask students to list words they feel will occur before and after that guide word. Check the dictionary for accuracy.

You have dealt with the physical structure of the dictionary and the use of guide words. It is now helpful to spend some time looking at the structure of individual word entries. Some people use dictionaries for years and never really know what all those "funny" marks mean. Some knowledge of the way entries are presented can make them seem much more "user friendly."

Dictionaries vary in the exact information they include for each word listed. Select a dictionary your students are likely to use, and look up a common word in it. Write out all of the information presented, including all of the strange marks and abbreviations, if present. Then, discuss the entry. If you are confused about some piece of information, check in the front of the dictionary, because it will list the meanings of its entry system as well as its abbreviations.

To complete your study, which can be ongoing as students proceed through the program, spend a little time reading about the history of dictionaries. Encyclopedias have valuable information about this.

Students like to learn that the Chinese had a dictionary-type book, which they called the *Shuo Wen*, as early as 150 B.C. One of the early dictionaries in the English language was published in 1604 A.D. by Robert Cawdrey. This author only included difficult words in his book. His listing of approximately 2,500 words was meant to help people when they got stumped by a hard word, not a common one.

If approached properly, students can begin to see the dictionary as a friend rather than as a foe. Have as many dictionaries available as you can (many used bookstores sell them), and encourage your students to see them as a valuable resource.

A NOTE ON COMPUTER SPELL CHECKS

Some people say, "Why teach spelling any more? Students can just use spell checks."

As valuable as these tools are, a certain level of expertise is required to use them effectively. In order for a spell check to recognize a word, it has to be presented approximately correctly. Often, spell checks give options of different words that the writer has to choose among. Spell checks cannot discriminate between homonyms. Also, it is very frustrating for a writer if too many words are misspelled on a page. In this case, using the spell check becomes extremely time consuming.

In spite of these limitations, spell checks can be extremely valuable for people who have difficulty with spelling. Once students have some good spelling skills, spell checks can empower them. The tool frees them to risk including harder words in their writing. They gain independence because they can do a first-run edit of their work. A main goal of *Spelling Smart!* is to help students gain enough spelling ability for them to be able to use spell checks efficiently.

THE ORIGINS OF ENGLISH

Do you think the English language began in England? It is a logical assumption, but it is not true. Scholars now believe that as little as 2 percent of the English language originated in the British Islands!

A tribe called the Celts originally migrated to Britain. Since their new home was rich with minerals and good farmland, however, they were often invaded. Julius Caesar brought his Roman soldiers in 55 B.C. and, also, a few Latin words.

When Rome withdrew its armies to defend home territory, Britain was again open to invasion. In 449 A.D., the Anglos, Saxons, and Jutes crossed the sea from Denmark and Germany and conquered the land. They brought a language we now call Old English. Strangely, this language did not mix with the Celtic language but, instead, overpowered it. Only a few Celtic words are now known (some people say less than twelve), all of which deal with special features of the British land. One of these words is "crag" which means a high rock.

The Anglo-Saxon influence on our modern-day English is very powerful. A computer analysis has shown that our 100 most-often-used words—such as "you," "is," and "the"—all come from Anglo-Saxon.

Christianity became a major factor in the development of the language, however, when monks from Rome arrived in the British Isles in the year 597 A.D. With their religion, they also brought many new words from Latin.

And, then, English was affected even more. Between 750 and 1050, the Scandinavian people began to raid and settle on the island. Old Norse, the language these people spoke, was similar to Old English, but also had different words as well. Nine hundred specific words are all documented as coming from the "new" language. These are all one-syllable words like "skin," "hit," and "get."

The Norman Invasion in 1066 brought the French language of Normandy to Britain. The Norman conquerors were originally not interested in speaking English, and they spoke only French. Old English survived as the common spoken language of the people.

Conquerors, however, often intermarry with the conquered, and married people do talk with one another. Thus, by the time the French finally lost their military hold on Britain in 1204, a huge number of French words had worked their way into English.

It would have been complicated enough if English had remained the same since that time. But it has not. We would probably not be able to understand the English of 1204. The language has evolved through the passage of time and, also, from contacts with other peoples who have introduced their words, their phrases, and their perceptions. English contains words from all over the world.

And English has not stopped changing. What person in the early 1900s would know what a microchip was, or even a computer? Would he or she understand the sentence, "Hey, check out that dude"?

Let's turn from the spoken word and look for a moment at written language. Once dictionaries were formed, the spellings of words remained constant. Because English has "borrowed" so much from so many languages, often the ways the words were spelled in their original languages were borrowed as well. Spelling records the vagaries and the rich historical backgrounds of many English words. Through the spellings we see a glimpse of the cultures and peoples who have influenced the language. This is why the spelling of English is so varied and interesting.

Section

THE
LESSONS

CLOSED SYLLABLE
Short "a"

▣ GETTING STARTED

Talk with your students about how they will be learning to spell, but they will not have to memorize the spelling of words. Tell them that they will be discovering the structure of the English language.

◖ INTRODUCING NEW INFORMATION

Ask your students if they know what a syllable is. If they are not sure of this, ask them to say words like "ta-ble" and "tel-e-vi-sion." Help them to understand that a syllable is a separate and unique unit of sound, and that a word can have one or more syllables. It often helps students to tap the desk top in front of them whenever they hear a new syllable.

When the students understand the concept of a syllable, say the following words: am, bat, fan, hand, map, tag.

"How many syllables do you hear in each of these words?"
"That's correct, one."
Record the following words: am, bat, fan, hand, map, tag.
"What do you notice about all these words?"
"Yes, a single, short vowel is followed by at least one consonant. In a syllable where a single, short vowel is followed by at least one consonant, the syllable is called a closed syllable."
Say the following words: am, bat, fan, hand, map, tag.
"What sound do you hear in all of these words?"
"That's correct, /a/ as in 'ant.'"
Record the following words: am, bat, fan, hand, map, tag.
"What letter do you notice in all of these words?"
"That's correct, short 'a'. Today, we will be studying words that have short 'a' in them. All of the syllables we will be spelling will be closed syllables."

❖ PRACTICING WITH INDIVIDUAL WORDS

Select a manageable number of words from the word list provided on page 32 for your students to spell.

❦ PRACTICING SPELLING IN CONTEXT

Select a manageable number of sentences from the following list for your students to write. Dictate these sentences to your students. The words that do not follow regular patterns, or whose patterns have not yet been presented to the students, are underlined. Provide a written model of these words for your students to copy. For more detailed instructions on how to work with these sentences, refer to page x.

The man has a stamp.

Stand up and grab that mask.

Dan had a hat, a fan, and a plan.

The cat will trap the ant in the sand.

At last, Sam sat and was glad.

An ant can travel fast.

Pat ran as fast as Fran.

Ask Nat to get a damp rag.

The man had a tan hat with a hatband.

Pam swam past the raft.

◙ REINFORCING ACTIVITIES

Allow your students to choose from the following list of activities:

1. Make combinations of closed syllable words with short "a"—for example, "a mad ant," "a grand plan," "a tan flag," and "a damp stamp." Write sentences using these phrases or draw illustrations for them.

2. Play concentration with a friend. Take index cards and write the words you are learning, one to a card. Make two cards of each word. When you have made approximately ten pairs of words, place them face down on the table. The first player turns two cards over. If they match, he keeps them and he has another turn. If not, he places them face down again, and the second player gets a turn. The winner is the person who collects the most cards.

3. Play a sentence game with a friend. Write 15 words on index cards, one word per card. Place all 15 words face side down on the table. The first player randomly selects two cards. If she can say a good sentence using both cards, she keeps the cards. The winner is the person who collects the most cards.

4. LITERATURE CONNECTION: See if you can find the classic tale *Millions of Cats,* written and illustrated by Wanda Gag (Coward Publishers, 1928.) As you read and enjoy this tale, notice the word "cat" written over and over in the text. Also, notice the syllable type and spelling of the author's last name.

▣ EXTRA INTERESTING FACTS

The word "samp," which refers to corn meal made into porridge, comes from the Native American Algonquian language (na-saump). The Native Americans who met the English people on the shores of America not only gave them food and knowledge, but also shared their language.

WORD LIST

SHORT "A," ONE-SYLLABLE WORDS

am	gas	plan
ant	gasp	plant
as	glad	raft
ask	grand	rag
bad	grasp	ramp
bag	had	ran
band	hand	rap
bat	has	rat
blast	hat	sand
brag	jam	sat
brand	lab	slam
can	lad	slap
cap	lamp	snap
cat	land	stab
clam	lap	stamp
clap	last	stand
clasp	mad	swam
dam	man	tag
damp	map	tan
drag	nag	tap
fact	nap	tramp
fan	pan	trap
fast	pant	van
fat	past	wag
flag	pat	zap

SHORT "A," TWO-SYLLABLE WORDS

hatband	rattan
madcap	sampan

FINISH IT!

Fill in the blanks with words from the word list.

1. They went down the river in a _____.

2. "I am _____ you got your good news," Ann said.

3. Sam lit the _____ so they could see to read.

4. He traveled across the country in his _____.

5. Tara made _____ from the grapes in her backyard.

6. The man got lost because he did not have a _____.

7. Sonia hailed a _____ to take her to the museum.

8. Jan _____ quickly and won the race.

9. "That letter needs a _____," the postmistress said.

10. It was lovely to rest on the _____ at the beach.

WORD LIST

lamp	ran
cab	sand
jam	raft
stamp	van
glad	map

Name _____   **Date** _____

A GAME OF CATEGORIES

Choose words from your word list that belong in each category.

PEOPLE

_____

_____

_____

_____

_____

THINGS PEOPLE DO

_____

_____

_____

_____

_____

THINGS PEOPLE FEEL

_____

_____

_____

_____

ANIMALS

_____

_____

_____

_____

WORD LIST

cat	man
grasp	Sam
sad	clap
Gram	rat
ask	bad
ant	clam
lad	gasp
brag	tramp
glad	mad

Name _____   **Date** _____

LOOK IT UP!

Look up the listed words in your dictionary. Then match each word with its correct definition.

1. blanch		a.	a fastener made of metal
2. sampan		b.	short of being enough
3. asp		c.	smooth and agreeable
4. scant		d.	a boat
5. apt		e.	a healing crust for a wound
6. hasp		f.	to take away the color
7. rattan		g.	a breakfast food made of ground corn
8. scab		h.	a strip of palm used to make furniture
9. bland		i.	a snake
10. samp		j.	something that is relevant

Now choose five words from the above list and use each one in a sentence.

1. _____

   _____

2. _____

   _____

3. _____

   _____

4. _____

   _____

5. _____

   _____

Name _____ **Date** _____

LIST IT!

Write a list of types of hats. Think of many different kinds of hats, such as cowboy hats, ski masks, and even bicycle helmets. Don't worry if you don't know how to spell some words. Just practice with the closed syllable words that have short "a" and make your best guess for the others.

_____

_____

_____

_____

_____

_____

_____

_____

_____

_____

_____

_____

_____

_____

Name _____   **Date** _____

WRITE ON!

The closed syllable word "map" represents a most useful tool in our daily lives. On a separate sheet of unlined paper, draw a map of your classroom or of another place with which you are familiar. If you wish, draw a map of an imaginary place.

Once you have finished your map, use the following situation to begin a story:

You are in your classroom (or other real or imaginary place). You hear a loud noise, but you cannot locate its source. The noise seems to be very close. What do you do?

_____

_____

_____

_____

_____

_____

_____

_____

_____

_____

_____

_____

Name _____   **Date** _____

CLOSED SYLLABLE
Short "i"

▣ GETTING STARTED

Introduce your students to their spelling notebooks. Tell them they will be recording the information they are discovering about the English language in this notebook. Ask them to tell you what they remember about closed syllables from Lesson One, and then assist them in making a page in their notebooks where they will define closed syllables.

Ask your students to tell you the short vowel they have been studying. Ask them to make a second page in their notebooks that illustrates this short vowel in closed syllables.

When they are finished ask your students to make guesses about how many types of syllables are found in the English language. Discuss their guesses. Tell them there are six types of syllables and that, in time, they will be studying all of them.

◖ INTRODUCING NEW INFORMATION

Say the following words: bit, is, hid, lip, pin, swim.
"What sound do you hear in all these words?"
"That's correct, /i/ as in 'in.'"
Record the following words: bit, is, hid, lip, pin, swim.
"What type of syllable is in all of these words?"

"Yes, they are all closed syllables. What vowel do you notice in all of these words?"
"That's correct. All of these closed syllable words contain the short vowel 'i'."

❖ PRACTICING WITH INDIVIDUAL WORDS

Select a manageable number of words from the word list provided on page 41 for your students to spell.

⑤ PRACTICING SPELLING IN CONTEXT

Select a manageable number of sentences from the following list for your students to write. Dictate these sentences to your students. The words that do not follow regular patterns or whose elements have not yet been presented to the students are underlined. Provide a written model of these words for your students to copy. For more detailed instructions on how to work with these sentences, refer to page ix.

<u>The</u> film is <u>a</u> hit.

Lift that plastic lid <u>off</u> that dish.

<u>Many</u> fish swim in <u>the</u> Atlantic.

That kid, Tim, is fantastic!

Liz hid <u>the gold</u> pin in <u>the</u> attic.

Dan can ask his twin, Sam, <u>to</u> assist him.

At <u>the</u> picnic, <u>the</u> ants bit Jim.

"<u>I</u> admit that <u>I</u> am sad," <u>said</u> Pam.

That rabbit is swift, <u>but</u> that pig is <u>not</u>.

<u>The</u> indignant man did <u>not</u> ask Pam <u>to</u> sit.

◼ REINFORCING ACTIVITIES

Allow your students to choose from the following list of activities:

1. Make combinations of closed syllable words with short "a" and short "i" in them; for example, "the slim man," "a brisk wind," "a fantastic rabbit," and "a frantic kid." Write sentences using these phrases or draw illustrations for them.

2. Make a word design. Take a piece of drawing paper and a felt pen or colored pencil and choose a word that you wish to write; for example, "pin." Write your word using large letters over and over on your paper in a design. It works well to border your paper with your word and then to write it on the diagonals. Write your word as many times as you wish and then color in your design if you choose to do so.

3. Play a pantomime game with a friend. Choose ten closed syllable words with short "i" such as "limp" and "picnic." Write the words where your friend can see them. Pantomime one of your words and let him guess which one you are acting out. Then let him have a turn.

4. LITERATURE CONNECTION: The closed syllable short "i" word "wind" represents a force of nature we are all aware of during our days. Much rich literature has been written about the wind. Two examples are the poem *Ode to the West Wind* by Percy Bysshe Shelley (1792–1822) and the American folk ballad *Hear the Wind Blow.* Try to find these classic works in your library, or search out other literary references to the wind.

▧ EXTRA INTERESTING FACTS

The closed syllable word "ship" has a fascinating history. It is believed to have its origins in an old Germanic word that means "to hollow out." The first ships were hollowed out logs. The old Germanic word "skipam" led to the more modern German word "schiff."

WORD LIST

SHORT "I," ONE-SYLLABLE WORDS

big	him	risk
bit	hip	shin
chin	hit	ship
chip	in	silk
crib	is	sip
crisp	it	sit
did	kid	skip
dig	lid	snip
drip	lift	spin
fig	limp	swim
fin	lip	thin
fish	mist	tip
fist	pig	trip
fit	pin	wig
grin	print	wind
grip	rib	wish
hid	rip	

SHORT "I," TWO- AND THREE-SYLLABLE WORDS

admit	frantic	plastic
Atlantic	inflict	rabbit
attic	impact	tactic
bandit	insist	tidbit
candid	intact	traffic
catnip	kidnap	transit
district	limpid	transmit
drastic	misfit	victim
fabric	napkin	zigzag
fantastic	picnic	

FINISH IT!

Fill in the blanks with words from the word list.

1. The ____________________ got caught before he left the bank.
2. They planned carefully for their ____________________ to New York City.
3. When he was tired, the baby would sleep in his ____________________.
4. The cat played happily with her ____________________.
5. "Please ____________________ your name on the application so I can read it," the woman said.
6. Liz and Pedro went swimming and then had a ____________________ at the beach.
7. She fell and broke her ____________________.
8. He put the ____________________ next to his plate on the table.
9. "I will just sit down and ____________________ my tea," Tanisha told Tim.
10. He ordered ____________________ and chips at the diner.

© 1996 by Cynthia Stowe

WORD LIST

catnip	trip
print	sip
hip	bandit
napkin	crib
fish	picnic

Name ______________________________ **Date** ______________

A GAME OF CATEGORIES

Choose words from your word list that belong in each category.

THINGS PEOPLE DO

_____

_____

_____

_____

_____

PARTS OF THE BODY

_____

_____

_____

_____

_____

FOOD

_____

_____

_____

MATERIALS

_____

_____

_____

_____

WORD LIST

skin	insist
tin	hip
fig	grin
swim	lip
silk	plastic
chin	admit
mint	fish
fabric	skip
shrimp	rib

Name _____   Date _____

LOOK IT UP!

Look up the listed words in your dictionary. Then match each word with its correct definition.

1. brim   a.   a light color
2. wisp   b.   not interesting, dull
3. griffin   c.   to be very upset
4. insipid   d.   the edge
5. candid   e.   to do something easily but not in a convincing way
6. glib   f.   a thin piece, as in a small strand of hair
7. tint   g.   to send off, especially over a long distance
8. tidbit   h.   sincere and honest
9. transmit   i.   an imaginary animal from mythology
10. frantic   j.   a tiny piece of food or a choice piece of gossip

Now choose five words from the above list and use each one in a sentence.

1. _____

_____

2. _____

_____

3. _____

_____

4. _____

_____

5. _____

_____

Name _____   **Date** _____

LIST IT!

Write a list of different kinds of fish. If you aren't an expert on fish and don't know many more than "codfish" and "trout," you can always look up "fish" in the encyclopedia or in another reference book to see what you can find. Try to spell the closed syllable words with short "a" and short "i" correctly, but just make your best guess on the others.

_____

_____

_____

_____

_____

_____

_____

_____

_____

_____

_____

_____

_____

Name _____ **Date** _____

WRITE ON!

The closed syllable word "wish" represents something that is most important to all of us: a desire we have for ourselves or for others. On this page, express a wish that you have. Your wish can be general, as in a hope for the world, or it can be very specific. For example, you can state what you wish to accomplish this year.

_____

_____

_____

_____

_____

_____

_____

_____

_____

_____

_____

_____

_____

_____

Name _____   **Date** _____

CLOSED SYLLABLE
Short "o"

GETTING STARTED

Ask your students to tell you about the type of syllable they have been studying. Which short vowels have they been working with so far?

Ask your students to take out their notebooks and to talk about words with short "a" in them. When they are finished, assist them in making a new page in their notebooks that illustrates short "i" in closed syllable words.

INTRODUCING NEW INFORMATION

Say the following words: cot, drop, hog, pond, rob, shop.
"What sound do you hear in all these words?"
"That's right, /o/ as in 'on.'"
Record the following words: cot, drop, hog, pond, rob, shop.
"What kind of syllables are in all of these words?"
"Yes, they are all closed syllables. What vowel do you notice in all of these words?"
"That's correct. All of these closed syllable words contain the short vowel 'o'."

❖ PRACTICING WITH INDIVIDUAL WORDS

Select a manageable number of words from the word list provided on page 50 for your students to spell.

Ⓢ PRACTICING SPELLING IN CONTEXT

Select a manageable number of sentences from the following list for your students to write. Dictate these sentences to your students. The words that do not follow regular patterns or whose elements have not yet been presented to the students are underlined. Provide a written model of these words for your students to copy. For more detailed instructions on how to work with these sentences, refer to pages ix and x.

"Is that a fossil?" Sam asked.

Ron and Liz had a picnic by the pond.

At last, Pam is better and can jog.

"Stop that hotrod," said the cop.

Dan is not fond of codfish.

Tim cannot contact his twin in Scotland.

"That bobcat is our mascot," Jim said.

At the shop, the man had on a top hat.

Don got a blond wig and a dish with a cat on it at the shop.

On his trip, Tom cannot stop in Wisconsin.

▣ REINFORCING ACTIVITIES

Allow your students to choose from the following list of activities:

1. Make combinations of closed syllable words with short "a," short "i," and short "o"; for example, "sad in Wisconsin," "a gallant frogman," "a blond bandit," and "at that picnic." Write sentences using these phrases or draw illustrations for them.

2. There are goblins throughout folklore. First check your dictionary to see exactly what goblins are. Are they the same as ghosts? Then, draw some goblins of your own.

3. Play a game with a friend or two. Write down ten closed syllable words with short "o" in them where everyone can see them. The first player mentally selects a word. The other players ask questions to which there is a "yes" or "no" answer. For example, "Does your word represent an animal?" A total of ten questions may be asked. The first person to guess the word gains a point and he selects the next

word. If no one guesses the word after ten questions, the first player gains a point and selects another word.

4. LITERATURE CONNECTION: Have you read the classic story *The Hobbit* by J. R. R. Tolkien (published in paperback by Houghton Mifflin, copyright 1937)? This tale then continues on as the *Lord of the Rings Trilogy.* If you enjoy fantasy, be sure to find these books.

⊰ EXTRA INTERESTING FACTS

The word "gossip" illustrates how words can evolve in the English language. "Gossip" is recorded in the A.D. 1300 to 1400 time period as "godsibbe" (god had the same meaning it does now, and sibbe meant a close relative). "Godsibbe" then meant a close relative, often a godmother. A godmother is a person who is appointed by the parents to be a child's special guardian.

The word evolved to include close friends and relatives. Since most people tend to tell secrets to those close to them, the word "godsibbe" evolved to "gossip," as in "the telling of tales."

But other people who study language have a different opinion on how "gossip" evolved from "godsibbe." These people believe that "godsibbe" referred to both the godfather and the godmother of a child. These were important roles in early times, and the "godsibbes" would often have to talk together to discuss the well being of the child. Thus, the word "gossip" evolved from this closeness.

WORD LIST

SHORT "O," ONE-SYLLABLE WORDS

bog	god	pop
bond	got	pot
blond	hog	rob
blot	hop	romp
chop	hot	rot
cob	job	shop
cod	jog	shot
cop	jot	slot
cot	log	smog
crop	lot	snob
dot	mob	sob
drop	mop	spot
flop	nod	stomp
fog	not	stop
fond	on	top
frog	pod	trot
gob	pond	

SHORT "O," TWO- AND THREE-SYLLABLE WORDS

agnostic	cosmic	optic
allotment	fossil	pompom
bobcat	frogman	poplin
cannot	goblin	ramrod
combat	gossip	Scotland
concoct	hobgoblin	stopgap
constant	hobnob	tiptop
contact	hotrod	tomcat
contract	mascot	tonsil
contrast	nostril	Wisconsin

FINISH IT!

Fill in the blanks with words from the word list.

1. He went to the pond to see if he could catch a _____.

2. Be careful not to _____ that box," Hannah told Max.

3. Edinburgh is the capital city of _____.

4. Amir always cuts his _____ hair short in the summer.

5. "If I can't run, then I'll _____ to the finish line," Dana said.

6. They signed the _____ to sell their house.

7. The _____ directed traffic all afternoon in the hot sun.

8. "It's not true, it's just _____," Mr. Santiago said.

9. As soon as she fixed the engine, Sara's _____ was ready to go.

10. Pat and Sam sat by the _____ and fed the ducks.

WORD LIST

Scotland	drop
hop	cop
frog	gossip
contract	hotrod
pond	blond

Name _____   **Date** _____

A GAME OF CATEGORIES

Choose words from your word list that belong in each category.

ANIMALS

_____

_____

_____

_____

_____

PEOPLE

_____

_____

_____

_____

_____

PLACES

_____

_____

_____

_____

WAYS OF MOVING

_____

_____

_____

_____

WORD LIST

cop	pond
cod	trot
Don	frog
Wisconsin	frogman
bobcat	hop
convict	tomcat
jog	Scotland
Tom	hog
bog	plod

Name _____   **Date** _____

LOOK IT UP!

Look up the listed words in your dictionary. Then match each word with its correct definition.

1. noggin   a. a fern's leaf
2. bombastic   b. refers to the sense of sight
3. lop   c. a little cup
4. bodkin   d. wet ground, as in a swamp
5. frond   e. earth that has grass growing in it
6. wombat   f. an animal found in Australia
7. sod   g. a tool that makes holes in cloth
8. concoct   h. refers to speaking or writing that is pompous but has little meaning
9. optic   i. to put together, to scheme
10. bog   j. to cut off or trim

Now choose five words from the above list and use each one in a sentence.

1. _____

_____

2. _____

_____

3. _____

_____

4. _____

_____

5. _____

_____

Name _____   **Date** _____

LIST IT!

Write a list of different uses for a pot. You can list the normal uses, such as "to cook food in" and "to carry water in." However, try to think of unusual ones, such as "to wear as a hat." Enjoy using your imagination.

_____

_____

_____

_____

_____

_____

_____

_____

_____

_____

_____

_____

_____

_____

_____

Name _____   **Date** _____

WRITE ON!

Find a friend to work with and also find a picture of a frog. Do not show your picture to your friend. Tell your friend that you will be giving her written directions on how to draw something, but don't tell her what she will be drawing. Write your directions on how to draw a frog on this page. Then see how closely your friend's drawing duplicates your frog.

_____

_____

_____

_____

_____

_____

_____

_____

_____

_____

_____

_____

_____

_____

_____

Name _____   **Date** _____

CLOSED SYLLABLE
Short "u"

🔳 GETTING STARTED

Ask your students to take out their notebooks and to talk about the syllable type and the short vowels they have been studying. Since they have not yet created a page in their notebook for short "o" in closed syllable words, assist them in doing so.

If your students wish, allow them time to write down more examples of words with short "a" and short "i" on the appropriate pages.

◖ INTRODUCING NEW INFORMATION

Say the following words: bug, cup, gust, mud, rush, sun.
"What sound do you hear in all these words?"
"That is correct, /u/ as in 'under.'"
Record the following words: bug, cup, gust, mud, rush, sun.
"What kind of syllables are in all of these words?"
"Yes, they are all closed syllables. What vowel do you notice in all of these words?"
"That's right. All of these closed syllable words contain the short vowel 'u.'"

❖ PRACTICING WITH INDIVIDUAL WORDS

Select a manageable number of words from the word list provided on page 59 for your students to spell.

Ⓢ PRACTICING SPELLING IN CONTEXT

Select a manageable number of sentences from the following list for your students to write. Dictate these sentences to your students. The words that do not follow regular patterns or whose elements have not yet been presented to the students are underlined. Provide a written model of these words for your students to copy. For more detailed instructions on how to work with these sentences, refer to page ix.

The pig sat in the mud.

Pat had a pumpkin muffin and a cup of coffee.

"Subtract that sum and then stop," Bob said.

At dusk, Pam sat in the rustic cabin.

Tom is as snug as a bug in a rug.

It is fun to run to the sunlit summit.

"If you must hiccup, do not do it in public," Dan said.

Fran had a fit in the shop, but Jim had a tantrum.

"I trust that Liz can swim," Ron said.

The druggist is on a trip to Dublin.

▣ REINFORCING ACTIVITIES

Allow your students to choose from the following list of activities:

1. Make combinations of closed syllable words with short "a," short "i," short "o," and short "u" in them; for example, "the dump at dusk," "trust us," "a plump rabbit," and "a plastic cactus." Write sentences using these phrases or draw illustrations for them.

2. Find two or more friends to play a game. First, make a deck of cards, each card containing one closed syllable word with a vowel you have studied. The caller reads from the deck of cards, while the players sit with their backs to her. If the caller says a word that contains a short "u" sound, the players should stand up. The first person to stand up has the next turn calling. If a player stands up when a word contains a short "a," "i," or "o," she has to sit down for the rest of the game.

3. Clichés are expressions that have become so common that we rarely think about where they came from or what they really mean. The expression "He's as snug as a bug in a rug" is one of these. Two other examples are "She's driving me up the wall" and "Let's hit the road." Make a list of as many clichés as you can think of, and also ask other people for examples.

4. LITERATURE CONNECTION: Puns are words that sound alike but have different meanings. People play with puns; for example, the author Sam Levenson wrote a story he called *In One Era and Out the Other.* The story is about how when the hero was a little boy (in a different ERA), he would go for hikes in Central Park with his friends, but only because he did not listen to the objections raised by his mother (in one EAR and out the other). This story is reprinted in *The Random House Book of Humor,* selected by Pamela Pollack, illustrated by Paul Zelinsky (Random House, 1988).

Watch for other puns in literature, or listen for them as people speak.

⊵ EXTRA INTERESTING FACTS

The English language is always changing. Some words change their form and other new words are sometimes added to reflect the experiences of modern life. There are also words, however, that have become obsolete. Take, for example, the word "crug."

"Crug" was first used in the early 1800s in a school in England. We think it meant the crusts of bread the students were fed. They dipped these crusts into beer to make them more appetizing. At that time, "crug" meant food.

Are you glad we no longer use this word? How would you like to say to a friend, "Let's go over to the caf and get some crug"?

WORD LIST

SHORT "U," ONE-SYLLABLE WORDS

bug	gun	rug
bulb	gust	run
bump	hug	rush
bus	hunt	rust
but	jug	slug
club	jump	slum
crust	just	slump
cup	lump	spun
cut	mud	stunt
drum	must	sum
dug	mug	sun
dump	nut	trust
dust	plump	tub
fun	pub	tug
fund	pump	up
grunt	pup	us
gulp	rub	

SHORT "U," TWO- AND THREE-SYLLABLE WORDS

abduct	hiccup	pumpkin
adjust	humdrum	rustic
album	induct	rumpus
cactus	instruct	submit
campus	insult	subtract
discuss	misconduct	summit
disgust	mistrust	sunlit
druggist	muffin	tantrum
fungus	possum	unfit
gumdrop	public	until

FINISH IT!

Fill in the blanks with words from the word list.

1. He joined the _____ so he could learn about computers.

2. At the parade, the marcher beat his _____.

3. Dona has a beautiful _____ growing in her living room.

4. They bring the trash to the _____ every Saturday.

5. Javon put the photos in the _____.

6. They went sailing in the _____ of Mexico.

7. Jennifer visited the college _____ to see what it was like.

8. The _____ of two plus two is four.

9. "Do not _____ my intelligence by telling me that joke," Lisa said.

10. "We must _____ out the basement," Sam said, "because it is full of water."

© 1996 by Cynthia Stowe

WORD LIST

dump	Gulf
sum	club
cactus	insult
pump	campus
drum	album

Name _____   **Date** _____

A GAME OF CATEGORIES

Choose words from your word list that belong in each category.

FOOD
(Not from the Animal Kingdom)   **ANIMALS**

_____   _____

_____   _____

_____   _____

_____   _____

_____

SOUNDS WE MAKE   **THINGS THAT CAN HOLD WATER**

_____   _____

_____   _____

_____   _____

WORD LIST

jug	mug
gumdrop	muffin
cub	hiccup
hum	pumpkin
possum	thrush
tub	gulp
grunt	pup
plum	cup
mollusk	nut

Name _____   **Date** _____

LOOK IT UP!

Look up the listed words in your dictionary. Then match each word with its correct definition.

1. lug   a. a tube-like structure through which substances like liquid can move

2. hubbub   b. a person who knows a lot; for example, an Indian person who knows about Hinduism

3. induct   c. a type of cloud

4. dud   d. to carry something heavy

5. pundit   e. a hard growth on the skin

6. callus   f. a lot of sounds mixed together

7. pug   g. to take away by force or trickery

8. abduct   h. a small dog

9. duct   i. a person or thing that is not effective

10. nimbus   j. to bring into an organization or a position of honor

Now choose five words from the above list and use each one in a sentence.

1. _____

_____

2. _____

_____

3. _____

_____

4. _____

_____

5. _____

_____

Name _____ **Date** _____

LIST IT!

Write a list of things or living creatures that can jump. Two examples are "a motorcycle" and "a horse." Remember to spell all closed syllable words with the short vowels "a," "i," "o," and "u" in them correctly, but just try your best on other words.

_____

_____

_____

_____

_____

_____

_____

_____

_____

_____

_____

_____

_____

_____

Name _____ **Date** _____

△△△△△△△△△△△△△△△△△

WRITE ON!

Use the following to help you begin to write a story:

It is dusk and you are lost in the woods. A great gust of wind pushes you into a clearing and you come upon a hut. Gratefully, you enter and find a table in the center of the room. On this table are:

1. a gun
2. a bicycle pump
3. a bag of gumdrops
4. a child's toy bus
5. a brush

Whom do these objects belong to? Why are they here in this deserted hut? Can you use them to find your way home?

_____

_____

_____

_____

_____

_____

_____

_____

_____

_____

_____

Name _____   **Date** _____

CLOSED SYLLABLE
Short "e"

◉ GETTING STARTED

Talk with your students about the closed syllables with which they have been working. Ask them to take out their notebooks and to tell you some of the closed syllable words they find most interesting. Then assist your students in making a page in their notebooks for short "u" in closed syllables.

◖◉ INTRODUCING NEW INFORMATION

Say the following words: bet, den, elf, held, leg, yes.
"What sound do you hear in all of these words?"
"That's right, /e/ as in 'edge.'"
Record the following words: bet, den, elf, held, leg, yes.
"What kind of syllables are in all of these words?"
"Yes, they are all closed syllables. What vowel do you notice in all of these words?"
"That's correct. All of these closed syllable words contain the short vowel 'e.'"

❖ **PRACTICING WITH INDIVIDUAL WORDS**

Select a manageable number of words from the word list provided on page 68 for your students to spell.

§ **PRACTICING SPELLING IN CONTEXT**

Select a manageable number of sentences from the following list for your students to write. Dictate these sentences to your students. The words that do not follow regular patterns or whose elements have not yet been presented to the students are underlined. Provide a written model of these words for your students to copy. For more detailed instructions on how to work with these sentences, refer to page ix.

<u>The</u> vet kept pets at his kennel.

"Just rest in bed," Liz <u>said</u>.

Jim got upset and went <u>to the</u> cabin.

Sam has <u>a</u> problem with his kitten.

<u>The</u> bandit has fled and hidden himself.

Ben slept in <u>the</u> tent.

<u>The</u> jet did not stop in Wisconsin.

Pam went <u>to</u> <u>the</u> dentist.

Tom can attempt <u>to</u> win <u>the</u> contest with his hotrod.

Meg has <u>a</u> pet hen that can jump in <u>a</u> basket.

▣ **REINFORCING ACTIVITIES**

Allow your students to choose from the following list of activities:

1. Make combinations of closed syllable words with all five of the short vowels in them; for example, "a hidden object," "the problem with Fred," and "a red sunset." Write sentences using these phrases or draw illustrations for them.

2. The following game involves some preparation. First, make up a game board so that when you roll the dice, players can begin at START, move their pieces a specified number, and then win when they reach FINISH. When the game board is completed, ask some friends to help you make up a pack of cards. On the back of the cards, write down words which contain short vowels in closed syllables, one per card. On the face side, write the definitions. The game is played by rolling the dice, moving your piece the specified number, and then trying to name the word for which you see the definition at the top of the card deck. If a player is correct, he stays where he is. If he is wrong, he moves back to his original position.

3. Select some text, either a newspaper article or a favorite story or poem. Look through the text and see how many closed syllable words with short vowels you can find. If you wish, record some of the more interesting words in your notebook.

4. LITERATURE CONNECTION: We think of sleds as toys with which to have fun or as tools upon which to carry supplies. Sleds took on a new purpose in 1940, however, when, day after day, the children of a small town in Norway hurried past Nazi soldiers who had invaded their land. For on their sleds, these children had hidden nine million dollars' worth of Norwegian gold bullion. *Snow Treasure* by Marie McSwigan, illustrated by Andre LaBlanc (E.P. Dutton and Company, 1942) tells the true story of the remarkable courage of these children who helped save their country's gold.

⊟ EXTRA INTERESTING FACTS

Words in English often come from older words, but they can also originate in other ways as well. For example, the word "denim," which represents a fabric most of us wear, comes from the city where it was made. "Denim" was originally called "serge de Nimes" because it was manufactured in the city of Nimes in the south of France. "Serge de Nimes" was shortened to "de Nimes," and then evolved to "denim."

WORD LIST

SHORT "E," ONE-SYLLABLE WORDS

bed	kept	self
best	led	send
bet	leg	slept
blend	lend	spend
crest	melt	swept
den	men	ten
desk	mend	tent
elf	met	test
end	nest	vest
fed	net	web
felt	peg	wed
get	pen	went
held	pest	west
help	pet	wet
hen	red	yes
jest	rent	yet
jet	rest	

SHORT "E," TWO-SYLLABLE WORDS

absent	helmet	problem
basket	hidden	puppet
bonnet	himself	rotten
cobweb	hundred	sudden
contest	insect	sunset
dentist	invent	tennis
enlist	itself	triplet
expect	kitten	trumpet
goblet	magnet	tunnel
happen	mitten	upset

FINISH IT!

Fill in the blanks with words from the word list.

1. He sat at his _____ and wrote a letter.

2. He went to the _____ to get his tooth pulled.

3. Tim and José _____ well after hiking all day in the mountains.

4. The _____ laid an egg and then sat on it.

5. "Your being late is no _____," said Ieesha.

6. The spider had spun a beautiful _____ in the basement.

7. Jan helped the _____ carry the table.

8. "Kim has been playing the _____ since fifth grade," Gus said.

9. She was so excited she won the tennis match, she jumped over the _____.

10. Sam got a job so that he could pay the _____.

WORD LIST

hen	net
trumpet	dentist
cobweb	problem
slept	rent
men	desk

Name _____   Date _____

A GAME OF CATEGORIES

Choose words from your word list that belong in each category.

HAVING TO DO WITH NUMBERS

_____

_____

_____

_____

_____

FROM THE ANIMAL KINGDOM

_____

_____

_____

_____

_____

CONTAINERS

_____

_____

_____

_____

THINGS TO WEAR

_____

_____

_____

_____

WORD LIST

hen	vessel
bonnet	ferret
keg	mitten
ten	triplet
goblet	basket
seven	belt
insect	octet
helmet	kitten
hundred	mussel

Name _____   Date _____

LOOK IT UP!

Look up the listed words in your dictionary. Then match each word with its correct definition.

1. Zen	a.	a little fish
2. despot	b.	a sect in the Buddhist religion
3. millet	c.	plant that is grown to produce a fiber for rope
4. hemp	d.	a type of seaweed
5. dispel	e.	a musical notation
6. smelt	f.	a grain used for food
7. clef	g.	a ruler who has a great deal of power
8. inflect	h.	a type of fishing net
9. trammel	i.	to turn or change, as in a tone of voice
10. kelp	j.	to drive away, to scatter

Now choose five words from this list and use each one in a sentence.

1. _____

_____

2. _____

_____

3. _____

_____

4. _____

_____

5. _____

_____

Name _____ **Date** _____

LIST IT!

Write a list of things that are red. Two examples are "a stop sign" and "an apple." Be creative and try to think of things from different areas of your life. (How about "a very cold nose"?)

_____

_____

_____

_____

_____

_____

_____

_____

_____

_____

_____

_____

_____

_____

Name _____   **Date** _____

WRITE ON!

This is a cooperative creative writing activity. Find a friend or two who want to write stories. Sit in a circle, either at a table or at desks. Each person needs a piece of writing paper and a pencil.

Every person will write one sentence to begin a story. Examples of good starting sentences are:

a. Fred sped down the hill on his sled.

b. Mary heard a yelp outside her tent.

c. The man rode west into the sunset.

When every person has finished writing his or her first sentence, pass the paper to the person on the right and he or she will write the next sentence. Once that is finished, pass the paper again. Continue working on your cooperative stories until you want to stop.

There are only two rules to this activity:

1. Each person can only write one sentence at a time.

2. No one can kill a character someone else invented.

You can use this space to start your story or to experiment with good first lines.

_____

_____

_____

_____

_____

_____

Name _____ **Date** _____

SPELLING GENERALIZATION "ff, ll, ss"

▣ GETTING STARTED

Ask your students to tell you the type of syllable they have been studying. Give them the choice of looking through their notebooks or of just remembering some closed syllable words, and talk about these words. Then give your students time to make a page in their notebooks for short "e" in closed syllable words.

◖ INTRODUCING NEW INFORMATION

Record the following words: cliff, fluff, off, puff, scuff, sniff.
"What type of syllable are all of these words?"
"That's right, they are all closed syllable words. What do you notice about the way they are spelled?"
"Yes, they all end in a double 'f.'"
"Do they all have one syllable?"
"Yes."
Record the following words: bill, dell, hull, mill, tell, yell.
"Are these all closed syllable words?"
"That's correct. What do you notice about how they are spelled?"

"Yes, they all end in double 'l.'"
Record the following words: bless, class, fuss, kiss, press, toss.
"What type of syllable are all these words?"
"Yes, they are closed syllables, and what do you notice about their spellings?"
"I agree. They all end in double 's.'"
Place all three word lists in front of your students. *"Today, you are going to discover your first spelling generalization, in other words, a general principle about how to spell certain words. Look at these words and tell me what you have discovered."*
"That is right. In a one-syllable word that has a single short vowel and that ends with the letters 'f,' 'l' or 's,' you double the letters 'f,' 'l,' and 's.'"

❖ PRACTICING WITH INDIVIDUAL WORDS

Select a manageable number of words from the word list provided on page 77 for your students to spell.

⑤ PRACTICING SPELLING IN CONTEXT

Select a manageable number of sentences from the following list for your students to write. Since students have now been spelling the words "the" and "a" for the past five lessons, it is assumed they can now spell them. Therefore, these words will no longer be underlined in this text. If, however, your students have difficulty spelling "the" and "a," continue to provide the written model for them.

Jill got a glass of milk.

Ben will miss Liz on his trip.

"If you can, spell 'chill,'" Pam said.

Jess will tell us not to rush.

Jeff is still stiff and cannot run.

"It was a thrill to win the contest," Tom said.

The dress is tan with big red dots.

Tell Sam not to sell his big brass bell.

Russ will travel to the Atlantic with his class.

Jen felt ill, but she did not ask to stop and rest.

Don and Bess sat on the grass and had a picnic.

▣ REINFORCING ACTIVITIES

Allow your students to choose from the following list of activities:

1. Select rhyming pairs of words ending with "ff," "ll," or "ss" in them; for example, "stress" and "chess," "gruff" and "stuff," and "fell" and "smell." Use your word pairs in sentences. If you wish, illustrate some of your sentences.

2. Think about the word "tall." What does it mean? Try to write the word in a way that conveys its meaning; for example, Tall . Do the same thing with the word "small"; for example, small . How about "hiss"? hi_s___s Look through your notebook and find other words that are interesting to write in ways that convey their meanings.

3. Find two dictionaries and a friend. Choose five words with "ff," "ll," or "ss" in them. Then see who can find the five words the quickest.

4. LITERATURE CONNECTION: Tall tales are stories that are not exactly full of lies; they are full of exaggerations. Such a story might begin: My dog is so big, I have to buy leather for his collar by the yard.

   Tall tales often tell of legendary heroes. Such a book is *Pecos Bill* by Steven Kellogg (William Morrow and Co., Inc., 1986). This is a picture book that can be enjoyed by all ages. See if you can find *Pecos Bill* or other tall tales in your library.

☒ EXTRA INTERESTING FACTS

Words like "tall," "fall," and "ball" follow the regular pattern of having "ll" at the end of the word, but the vowel "a" sounds different than in words such as "grass" and "staff." The letter "l" at the end of words like "tall" seem to influence the sound of the vowel.

Some words with the letter "s" at the end of them also have slightly different vowel sounds; for example, "cross" and "toss." The word "off" gives further evidence of vowel sounds being easily changed.

There are also some exceptions to the "ff," "ll," "ss" generalization. Words such as "as," "his," "if," and "is" should be doubled but are not. And then we have words like "add," "fizz," "odd," and "egg," where a different consonant is doubled.

People do not know the reasons for all the irregularities in English. Some are explainable. For example, the word "egg" was brought into English from the Norse language in which it was spelled "egg."

Try not to worry about the exceptions. Most words are regular. It's interesting to notice the exceptions, and a dictionary and computer spell-check will help you spell them.

WORD LIST

FF, LL, SS WORDS

bass	fell	loss	smell
bell	fill	lull	sniff
bill	fluff	mass	snuff
bless	frill	mess	spell
bliss	fuss	mill	spill
bluff	glass	miss	staff
brass	gloss	mull	stiff
dress	grass	pass	still
chess	grill	pill	stress
chill	gruff	press	stuff
class	gull	puff	swell
cliff	hill	sass	tell
cuff	hiss	scruff	thrill
cull	huff	scuff	trill
cuss	ill	sell	twill
dell	jell	shell	well
dill	kill	shrill	whiff
doll	kiss	sill	will
drill	lass	skiff	yell
dull	less	skill	

✠ ✠ ✠ ✠ ✠ ✠ ✠ ✠ ✠ ✠ ✠ ✠ ✠ ✠ ✠ ✠ ✠ ✠

FINISH IT!

Fill in the blanks with words from the word list.

1. Sarah bought a new _____ at the mall.

2. They were tired after they climbed up the _____.

3. He could not cut the _____ because his lawn mower was broken.

4. She had great skill at playing the game of _____.

5. "Hurry up, or you'll _____ the opening of the play," Sam said.

6. The boy _____ off his bike, but he did not get hurt.

7. Janac found a large, perfect _____ on the beach.

8. "If you don't want the paper, _____ it in the recycling bin," Maria said.

9. Lamar had a fever and felt very _____.

10. The dog was behind the house, so Don had to _____ to get his attention.

WORD LIST

miss	toss
dress	fell
shell	ill
chess	grass
yell	hill

Name _____   **Date** _____

A GAME OF CATEGORIES

Choose words from your word list that belong in each category.

PEOPLE

_____

_____

_____

_____

_____

RELATING TO SOUND

_____

_____

_____

_____

_____

RELATING TO OUR NOSES

_____

_____

_____

_____

LAND FORMATIONS

_____

_____

_____

_____

WORD LIST

Jill	dell
cliff	sniff
shrill	Jeff
whiff	bell
snuff	hill
Bill	yell
trill	smell
bluff	hiss
Bess	Russ

Name _____   **Date** _____

LOOK IT UP!

Look up the listed words in your dictionary. Then match each word with its correct definition.

1. joss   a. a little stream

2. miff   b. a plant that belongs to the mustard family

3. skiff   c. a god in China

4. twill   d. a fabric that has diagonal lines in its weave

5. cress   e. a small, isolated valley

6. rill   f. to be in a bad mood

7. snell   g. to select from a group

8. dell   h. a small boat

9. cull   i. a short piece of fiber that holds a fish hook

10. hull   j. the outside cover of a fruit or seed

Now choose five words from the above list and use each one in a sentence.

1. _____

_____

2. _____

_____

3. _____

_____

4. _____

_____

5. _____

_____

Name _____ **Date** _____

LIST IT!

Write a list of things that are made out of glass; for example, a glass bottle and a light bulb. If you get stuck and can't think of any more, look around the room. Or, you can look through a magazine for ideas.

_____

_____

_____

_____

_____

_____

_____

_____

_____

_____

_____

_____

_____

_____

_____

Name _____   **Date** _____

WRITE ON!

It is enjoyable to write a tall tale because you don't have to be overly concerned about telling the truth. You can also make outrageous statements that make people laugh. On this page, write some tall tale statements. Two are started for you here:

1. Russ fell down the hill so fast he . . .

2. The lass was so strong she . . . .

Once you have finished writing some of these sentences, select one and expand it into a true tall tale.

_____

_____

_____

_____

_____

_____

_____

_____

_____

_____

_____

Name _____ **Date** _____

SPELLING GENERALIZATION "ck"

⊡ GETTING STARTED

Talk with your students about the "ff," "ll," "ss" spelling generalization they have discovered. Assist them in making a page about this generalization for their notebooks. Give them the choice about whether they wish to add the exceptions to their notebooks.

◖ INTRODUCING NEW INFORMATION

"Today, you are going to discover a second spelling generalization."
Say the following words: back, check, duck, frock, pick, shack.
"What sound do you hear at the end of each of these words?"
"That's right, you hear the /k/ sound, as in 'kitten.'"
Record the following words: back, check, duck, frock, pick, shack.
"What do you notice about how all these words are spelled?"
"Yes, they all have 'ck' directly after the short vowel. Make up a generalization for this."
"Good, when the /k/ sound comes right after a short vowel, the /k/ sound is spelled with a 'ck.'"

Record the following words: backtrack, bucket, chicken, jacket, pocket, rucksack. *"Is the /k/ sound spelled with a 'ck' at the end of a syllable also?"*
"That's right. The /k/ sound is spelled with 'ck' when it comes directly after a short vowel at the end of a word or at the end of a syllable."

❖ PRACTICING WITH INDIVIDUAL WORDS

Select a manageable number of words from the word list provided on page 87 for your students to spell.

☯ PRACTICING SPELLING IN CONTEXT

Select a manageable number of sentences from the following list for your students to write.

Jack and Jill went up that hill.

Rick has a flat bed truck.

Pam had a chicken leg and ham at the potluck.

At last, the clock struck ten and Tom left.

"It is a shock that Mack is sick," Don <u>said</u>.

Sam put his backpack on and ran up the hill <u>to</u> the cabin.

Jack put the check in his pocket.

Jen had on a black jacket and a tophat.

"Tom can unlock this padlock," Fran <u>said</u>.

The ship hit the dock in the fog.

▣ REINFORCING ACTIVITIES

Allow your students to choose from the following list of activities:

1. Select rhyming pairs of words with "ck" in them; for example, "locket" and "pocket," "trick" and "wick," and "black" and "shack." Use your word pairs in sentences. If you wish, illustrate some of your sentences.

2. Make a crossword puzzle for a friend to solve. First, get some graph paper or make your own. Then write a word, one letter per square. Select a letter from that word and begin a second word, and then continue. Your crossword puzzle will look something like this:

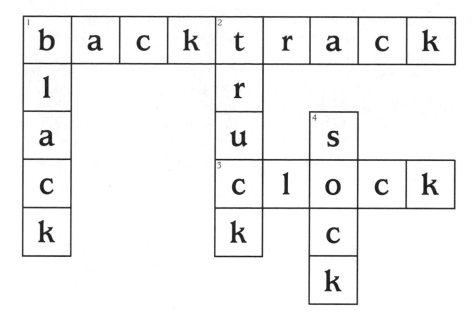

Once you have your puzzle, write out definitions to each word; for example, in the puzzle above, 2. (Down) is "a vehicle that can haul things." Give your friend the list of definitions and an empty puzzle form and see if he or she can solve the puzzle.

3. Tongue twisters are combinations of words that are funny and difficult to say, especially if you try to repeat them. A familiar tongue twister is "How much wood would a woodchuck chuck if a woodchuck could chuck wood?" Another is "Peter Piper picked a peck of pickled peppers."

   Try to invent some tongue twisters of your own. You can start with familiar combinations, such as "Pick a peck of popcorn," if you like.

4. LITERATURE CONNECTION: Folk tales have been important in cultures throughout the world. These are stories meant for all ages, often passed down orally from one generation to the next.

   "Jack" is a frequent main character in folklore in western civilization. *Jack and the Beanstalk* is a popular story. A somewhat less known tale is *Jack the Giant Killer*. Find these folk tales in your library and, as you enjoy reading them, try to figure out why these stories have endured for so many years.

⅀ EXTRA INTERESTING FACTS

Just as words have interesting histories, so do some of our expressions. "To get the sack" now means to be fired from a job. In football, if a quarterback is "sacked," he is not very pleased about the experience.

Where does "to get the sack" come from? There are two theories. The first is based in Roman times, when people who were convicted of terrible crimes were put in a sack and thrown into the river.

The second comes from the early 1600s in France, when craftsmen brought their tools to a job in a sack. While they were working, they gave the sacks to their employer. When they were no longer needed, the employer gave them back their sacks.

We should make note of one exception to the spelling generalization you have discovered in this lesson. When a word of more than one syllable ends with the /ik/ sound, the word usually ends with the letters "ic" rather than "ick". Examples of these words are: Atlantic, clinic, fabric, plastic.

WORD LIST

"CK," ONE-SYLLABLE WORDS

back	jack	shack
black	kick	shock
block	lack	sick
brick	lick	snack
buck	lock	snuck
check	luck	sock
chick	mock	struck
click	neck	stuck
clock	nick	tack
crack	pack	thick
deck	peck	tick
dock	pick	track
duck	pluck	trick
flock	quick	truck
frock	rack	wick
hack	rock	wreck
heck	sack	

"CK," TWO-SYLLABLE WORDS

attack	fullback	rickrack
backpack	haddock	setback
backtrack	handpick	shamrock
bedrock	henpeck	slapstick
blackjack	lipstick	unlock
chicken	locket	unpack
chopstick	padlock	unstuck
cutback	pocket	wedlock
drumstick	potluck	
flashback	ransack	

✤ ✤ ✤ ✤ ✤ ✤ ✤ ✤ ✤ ✤ ✤ ✤ ✤ ✤ ✤ ✤

FINISH IT!

Fill in the blanks with words from the word list.

1. Manuel made a _____ potpie for supper.

2. Pam fell off the dock and hurt her _____.

3. Tom wished Mack good _____ as they began the race.

4. It was a _____ to see how high the river was after the storm.

5. Rick had a _____ to when he was a circus performer.

6. They climbed the big _____ on the shore and sat and watched the ocean.

7. "_____ out the pie and see if it's ready to come out of the oven," Kanisha said.

8. Sam lost the money because he had a hole in his _____.

9. "Let's rest and have a _____ before we get back to work," Anna said.

10. There was barely a _____ of dust in the immaculate living room.

WORD LIST

flashback	shock
speck	pocket
back	chicken
check	snack
luck	rock

Name _____   **Date** _____

A GAME OF CATEGORIES

Choose words from your word list that belong in each category.

BEHAVIORS THAT ARE NOT POSITIVE

to_____

to_____

to_____

to_____

to_____

THINGS PEOPLE WEAR

_____

_____

_____

_____

_____

RELATING TO MONEY

_____

_____

_____

_____

RELATING TO THE OCEAN

_____

_____

_____

_____

WORD LIST

locket	attack
rollback	kickback
henpeck	shipwreck
haddock	trick
check	jacket
mock	pollack
sock	buck
dock	ransack
lipstick	backpack

Name _____   **Date** _____

LOOK IT UP!

Look up the listed words in your dictionary. Then match each word with its correct definition.

1. bannock
2. hack
3. penstock
4. placket
5. wrack
6. gimcrack
7. wicket
8. hummock
9. alpenstock
10. mattock

a. a stick used by mountain climbers
b. a gate that is used to control water flow
c. an inexpensive thing like a knickknack
d. a tool like a pickax
e. a flat cake made on a griddle
f. something that is ruined
g. to cut crudely, as with an ax
h. a small hill
i. an opening at the top of a skirt, or a pocket
j. a small gate or a small door, often near larger ones

Now choose five words from the above list and use each one in a sentence.

1. _____

_____

2. _____

_____

3. _____

_____

4. _____

_____

5. _____

_____

Name _____ **Date** _____

LIST IT!

Write a list of things that are made out of bricks. List as many as you can think of; for example, "a house" and "a chimney." Then·take a short walk either around your school or home to look for other things made out of bricks.

_____

_____

_____

_____

_____

_____

_____

_____

_____

_____

_____

_____

_____

_____

_____

Name _____   **Date** _____

WRITE ON!

Newspapers often have interesting stories. First, get a newspaper and select an article you like. Notice how the article clearly states who the story is about and what has happened.

If you know of something interesting that has occurred recently, write a newspaper article about that. If not, invent a story.

Imagine that a famous rock-and-roll band has come to your community. Think about some mishaps that could befall this band and write about one of them.

A possible headline for one such story is:

ROCK-AND-ROLL BAND GETS STUCK IN TRUCK!

_____

_____

_____

_____

_____

_____

_____

_____

_____

_____

_____

_____

_____

Name _____   **Date** _____

VOWEL-CONSONANT-E SYLLABLE
"a-e"

▣ GETTING STARTED

Ask your students to tell you about the two spelling generalizations they have discovered. Talk with them about the "ck" generalization, and assist them in making a page for their notebook about this generalization. If they wish, they can include the one main exception to this generalization (/ik/ is usually spelled "ic" at the end of a multisyllabic word).

Ask your students to talk with you about the first type of syllable they have learned. Ask them to tell you the important characteristics of closed syllables.

◖ INTRODUCING NEW INFORMATION

"Today, you are going to discover a second type of syllable."
Say the following words: age, chase, gate, lame, rave, vase.
"What sound do you hear in all of these words?"
"That's right, long 'a.'"
Record the following words: age, chase, gate, lame, rave, vase.
"What do you notice about all of these words?"

"Yes, they all have the vowel 'a' followed by a consonant, and then the letter 'e.' Do you hear the 'e'?"

"That's correct, the 'e' is silent. This type of syllable is called a vowel-consonant-e syllable, because a vowel is always followed by a consonant and then by a silent 'e.' Today, we are going to work with words that are spelled with the vowel 'a' in this syllable type. In the words with two or more syllables, you will find both closed and vowel-consonant-e syllables."

❖ PRACTICING WITH INDIVIDUAL WORDS

Select a manageable number of words from the word list provided on page 96 for your students to spell.

⑤ PRACTICING SPELLING IN CONTEXT

Select a manageable number of sentences from the following list for your students to write.

Jane gave the cupcake <u>to</u> Dave.

Pam made a black dress and a red cape.

At his age, he can still skate?

It is a shame that the ship is unsafe.

"That jade is fake," Liz <u>said</u>.

Sam put grape jam on his pancake.

"Dave will blame Tom," Pam <u>said</u>.

The tame ape made a racket in his cage.

Put that tape in that box and save it.

"It is a mistake <u>to</u> call Jake that," Don <u>said</u>. "That nickname will enrage him."

◼ REINFORCING ACTIVITIES

Allow your students to choose from the following list of activities:

1. Find three "a-consonant-e" words that rhyme; for example, "same," "name," and "game," or "take," "rake," and "bake." Try to make a good logical sentence with each set of three words. An example sentence for the last set given is: "Take the rake inside, and then bake a cake." (There is even an extra rhyming word in this sentence.) If you wish, illustrate one or more of your sentences.

2. Play a letter-scatter game. Select five words with "a-consonant-e" syllable types. It is probably best to choose one-syllable words, such as "page," "cake," "date,"

"space," and "name." Cut out little cubes of paper at least one-inch square and then put the letters from your chosen words on the squares (one letter per square). Give the squares to a friend, and see if he can duplicate your words. To be fair, tell him that all five words are "a-consonant-e" words. And, if he gets really stuck, you can give him hints on one or two of the words.

3. "Take Me Out to the Ballgame" is a song that is part of the American national heritage. If you don't know the words of this song, find a song book such as *Rise Up Singing,* edited by Peter Blood-Patterson (A Sing Out Publication, 1988.) As you learn this song for enjoyment, notice the "a-consonant-e" words in the lyrics.

4. LITERATURE CONNECTION: There are many "a-consonant-e" words associated with the sport of baseball. We have already noted a popular song. Look at all the "a-consonant-e" words in the following: baseball, home plate, off base, Hall of Fame, Babe Ruth. Can you think of others?

Go to your library and look at some books on baseball. Even if you are not now interested in the sport, you will find that it will become more appealing once you know something about it.

⊠ EXTRA INTERESTING FACTS

In Lesson Four, you learned of the word "crug" which had been used by people when they were referring to food. Another word that has "died" in our language is the word "flesh-spade." For a moment, try to figure out what it means.

Do you give up? A "flesh-spade" is a fingernail. Perhaps the person who invented this word used her fingernail, the hard part at the tip of her flesh, to dig in the earth and act as a spade.

We now need to discuss a peculiarity in the spelling of English. English words never end with the letter "v." Usually, an "e" is added to the word so that "v" will not be the last letter. What this means is that there are some words, such as "have," where even though the syllable type looks like a vowel-consonant-e syllable, the vowel "a" is not long.

WORD LIST

A-CONSONANT-E, ONE-SYLLABLE WORDS

age	fame	race
ape	flame	rake
ate	gale	rate
bake	game	safe
base	gate	sake
blade	grace	same
blame	grape	shade
brake	hate	shame
brave	lace	shape
cage	lake	space
cake	lame	take
came	made	tame
chase	make	trace
crave	name	wage
drape	pale	wake
face	pave	wave
fade	plate	

A-CONSONANT-E, TWO- AND THREE-SYLLABLE WORDS

backstage	handshake	pancake
confiscate	helpmate	pavement
cupcake	hotcake	shipmate
disgrace	inflame	shipshape
engage	inflate	sunshade
enrage	invade	unmake
escape	landscape	unsafe
fixate	misplace	update
frustrate	mistake	
handmade	nickname	

❅ ❅ ❅ ❅ ❅ ❅ ❅ ❅ ❅ ❅ ❅ ❅ ❅ ❅ ❅ ❅

FINISH IT!

Fill in the blanks with words from the word list.

1. The cat washed her _____ with her paw.

2. It was too hot in the sun, so they sat in the _____.

3. It was fortunate that everyone was able to _____ from the fire.

4. "If you _____ the cake in the oven for too long, it will get dry," Don said.

5. The little girl was in first _____.

6. There were huge cracks in the _____, which made it hard to walk.

7. "Can you please _____ out the trash?" Sam asked.

8. Anthony's family went to the _____ for summer vacation.

9. The _____ was released back into the ocean through the efforts of many people.

10. "I can _____ this book into French," Indira said.

WORD LIST

bake	grade
face	translate
take	escape
whale	lake
pavement	shade

Name _____   **Date** _____

A GAME OF CATEGORIES

Choose words from your word list that belong in each category.

RELATING TO AN ERROR

_____

_____

_____

_____

_____

FOOD

_____

_____

_____

_____

_____

RELATING TO FIRE

_____

_____

_____

_____

ANIMALS

_____

_____

_____

_____

WORD LIST

mistake	kale
ape	blaze
pancake	whale
inflame	misstate
cupcake	flame
drake	hotcake
misplace	grape
crane	bake
misname	mistranslate

Name _____ **Date** _____

LOOK IT UP!

Look up the listed words in your dictionary. Then match each word with its correct definition.

1. efface		a.	a type of rock with many thin layers
2. hake		b.	a type of cabbage
3. cognate		c.	to blur, as in a memory
4. shale		d.	to make a joke
5. jape		e.	to completely satisfy a hunger or desire
6. inculpate		f.	having the same family background
7. kale		g.	to chatter foolishly
8. prate		h.	a fish from the sea
9. wane		i.	to blame or cause to look guilty
10. sate		j.	to become dim

Now choose five words from the above list and use each one in a sentence.

1. _____

_____

2. _____

_____

3. _____

_____

4. _____

_____

5. _____

_____

Name _____ **Date** _____

LIST IT!

Write a list of things you can put either in or on top of a pancake. Of course, you will think of blueberries and maple syrup, but also consider bananas and other fruit. Have you ever thought of a peanut butter sauce for a pancake? You may become the inventor of a famous new recipe!

_____

_____

_____

_____

_____

_____

_____

_____

_____

_____

_____

_____

_____

_____

_____

Name _____   **Date** _____

WRITE ON!

In American folklore, there is a tradition called "GOOD OR BAD?" You begin by making a statement to set the story stage; for example:

"Tom took a plane ride to California."
Then, you alternate between good and bad statements; for example:
"That's good."
"No, that's bad. The pilot got sick."
"That's bad."
"No, that's good. The co-pilot took over."
"That's good."
"No, that's bad, the . . . . "
You can either continue with this GOOD OR BAD? or begin one of your own.

_____

_____

_____

_____

_____

_____

_____

_____

_____

_____

Name _____   **Date** _____

VOWEL-CONSONANT-E SYLLABLE "i–e"

▣ GETTING STARTED

Talk with your students about the two syllable types discovered so far. Mention some of your favorite words with "a-consonant-e" in them, and ask them to tell you some of the words they like. Provide time for your students to make a page in their notebooks for "a-consonant-e" words.

◖● INTRODUCING NEW INFORMATION

"Today, we are going to continue working with vowel-consonant-e syllables, but we will be working with a different vowel."

Say the following words: bite, drive, lime, rice, spike, wide.

"What sound do you hear in all of these words?"

"Yes, long 'i.'"

Record the following words: bite, drive, lime, rice, spike, wide.

"What do you notice about all of these words?"

"That's right. They all end with an 'i,' a consonant, and an 'e.' The 'i' is long, and the 'e' is silent. What kind of syllable do you think this is?"

"I agree, it's a vowel-consonant-e syllable. In the words you will be working with in this lesson, you will find both closed and vowel-consonant-e syllables."

❖ PRACTICING WITH INDIVIDUAL WORDS

Select a manageable number of words from the word list provided on page 105 for your students to spell.

⑤ PRACTICING SPELLING IN CONTEXT

Select a manageable number of sentences from the following list for your students to write.

Jess sat in the sunshine.

"The prize is a trip <u>to</u> Scotland," Mike <u>said</u>.

Rick set the pile <u>of</u> brush on fire.

Did Liz invite Nick?

"The drive is quite nice, and Fred will like it," Pam <u>said</u>.

Fran gave Tim a smile and a handshake, not a kiss.

"The cabin is rustic . . . and full of mice," Sam <u>said</u>.

The umpire did not like the man at bat.

Jen put the white mice in a cage.

Dan put ice and a slice of lime in his glass of Sprite®.

◨ REINFORCING ACTIVITIES

Allow your students to choose from the following list of activities:

1. Find three "i-consonant-e" words that rhyme; for example, "bride," "hide," and "wide," or "slice," "nice," and "ice." Make sentences with these sets of words. An example for the last set given is, "She put a nice slice of smoked salmon on some ice." If you wish, illustrate one or more of your sentences.

2. Play the card game "War." Make a deck of cards by writing a one syllable word on each card. Write words with both closed syllables and vowel-consonant-e syllables. When your deck is finished, find a friend to play with. Each person receives half of the deck. All closed syllable words are worth one point. "A-consonant-e" words are worth two points, and "i-consonant-e" words are worth three. On a signal, each player places one card on the table. The player who places a card with more value gets to take all the cards. If it's a tie, you repeat the procedure. The player with more cards at the end of the game is the winner.

3. Have you ever heard the cliché, "Time will tell"? It means that, in time, the answer to many things will become obvious. Think for a moment, however, about the specific words used in this cliché and about their literal meaning; then,

illustrate this literal meaning. For example, you could draw a picture of a clock talking.

If you wish, also illustrate the cliché, "He can stop on a dime."

4. LITERATURE CONNECTION: Crime is a topic for much literature. Stories on crime range from despairing tales of tragedy to lighter who-dunnits. Popular authors are Arthur Conan Doyle (for his Sherlock Holmes character), Agatha Christie (for her Hercule Poirot and Miss Marple characters), and Dorothy Sayers (for her Lord Peter Wimsey character). Check out mystery books in your library and see if there are some you enjoy.

⅀ EXTRA INTERESTING FACTS

We write almost every day, but do we think about where the word "write" came from? It is related to a very old German word "writan." The main concept behind the word is that of scratching or cutting, as in the German word "reissan," which means "to tear." The earliest type of writing was done by cutting marks on stone or wood. When people progressed to paper, the word origin remained.

In Lesson Eight, you discovered that English words never end with the letter "v." Instead, the letter "e" is placed after the "v." There are some "i-consonant-e" words, therefore, where the "i" is not long, as in "give," "active," and "captive."

WORD LIST

I-CONSONANT-E, ONE-SYLLABLE WORDS

bike	hike	side
bite	hide	size
bribe	ice	slice
bride	kite	smile
chime	life	spite
crime	like	strive
dice	mice	tide
dime	nice	tile
dine	nine	time
dive	pine	tribe
drive	pipe	vine
file	price	while
fine	prize	white
fire	quite	wife
five	rice	wise
glide	ripe	write
gripe	shine	

I-CONSONANT-E, TWO-SYLLABLE WORDS

admire	excite	midline
advise	exile	offside
backfire	grapevine	snakebite
bagpipe	hillside	sunrise
bedside	incite	sunshine
bedtime	inside	textile
campfire	inspire	umpire
clockwise	invite	unlike
dislike	landslide	unwise
empire	lifetime	vampire

FINISH IT!

Fill in the blanks with words from the word list.

1. It was a windy day, so the _____ flew high.

2. The little boy took a huge _____ of carrot cake.

3. On the 4th of July, the firemen made a _____ on the village green.

4. "Do you have the _____ to help me mow the lawn?" Tara asked.

5. The _____ wore a long flowing gown.

6. "Please _____ me a letter from Spain and let me know how you're enjoying your vacation," Tanya said.

7. "The _____ of the car is too high for my budget," Kareem said.

8. The horror movie had a particularly frightening _____ in it.

9. Lien had to walk a _____ to school.

10. It was raining, so they had to go _____.

WORD LIST

time	slice
bride	price
bonfire	kite
mile	write
vampire	inside

Name _____   **Date** _____

A GAME OF CATEGORIES

Choose words from your word list that belong in each category.

RELATING TO NUMBERS

_____

_____

_____

_____

_____

COMPARED TO SOMETHING ELSE

_____

_____

_____

_____

_____

TYPES OF FIRES

_____

_____

_____

_____

SOMETHING TO EAT OR DRINK

_____

_____

_____

_____

WORD LIST

Sprite®	rocklike
grassfire	lime
catlike	twice
prime	campfire
wine	gemlike
five	bonfire
apelike	thrice
nine	rice
brushfire	lifelike

Name _____ **Date** _____

LOOK IT UP!

Look up the listed words in your dictionary. Then match each word with its correct definition.

1. apprise   a. a spike or sharp point

2. rife   b. soggy ground that has a lot of mud

3. expansive   c. similar to a fox

4. mire   d. to tell or notify

5. sublime   e. beautiful or majestic

6. tine   f. a trick

7. vulpine   g. occurring in abundance

8. subside   h. to settle or to become less intense

9. rile   i. to make angry or upset

10. wile   j. that which expands

Now choose five words from the above list and use each one in a sentence.

1. _____

_____

2. _____

_____

3. _____

_____

4. _____

_____

5. _____

_____

Name _____ Date _____

LIST IT!

Write a list of things that can be used for a prize. Think of common prizes, such as a T-shirt or a car. Also, think of less common prizes that are not related to objects; for example, a day off. If you wish, you can list some prizes you would like.

_____

_____

_____

_____

_____

_____

_____

_____

_____

_____

_____

_____

_____

_____

Name _____   **Date** _____

WRITE ON!

Crime has become a great problem in our society. Write a short essay that expresses your opinion about crime. You can discuss what you believe are the causes of crime, how people should be treated by the court system, ways to lower the crime rate, or any other topic about which you feel strongly.

_____

_____

_____

_____

_____

_____

_____

_____

_____

_____

_____

_____

_____

_____

Name _____   **Date** _____

VOWEL-CONSONANT-E SYLLABLE
"o-e"

▣ GETTING STARTED

Ask your students to look through their notebooks and to tell you something they have discovered about the structure of the English language. Then give them time to make a page for "i-consonant-e" syllable words.

◖● INTRODUCING NEW INFORMATION

"Today, we are going to work with a third vowel-consonant-e syllable. We will be working with a different vowel."

Say the following words: bone, code, home, nose, smoke, vote.

"What sound do you hear in all these words?"

"That's right, long 'o.'"

Record the following words: bone, code, home, nose, smoke, vote.

"What do you notice about all of these words?"

"Yes, they all have an 'o,' a consonant, and an 'e.' The 'o' is long, and the 'e' is silent. What kind of syllable is this?"

"Yes, it's a vowel-consonant-e syllable. The words you will be working with in this lesson contain both closed syllables and vowel-consonant-e syllables."

❖ PRACTICING WITH INDIVIDUAL WORDS

Select a manageable number of words from the word list provided on page 114 for your students to spell.

⬣ PRACTICING SPELLING IN CONTEXT

Select a manageable number of sentences from the following list for your students to write.

Jane ran <u>to</u> get the phone.

The sun shone on the grove.

"<u>I</u> hope that Jill will vote," Pat <u>said</u>.

Jess went home and had a Coke®.

"That joke is not a joke <u>I</u> like," Dave <u>said</u>.

That note will expose a crime.

"Mike can <u>practice</u> his backstroke and sidestroke at the lake," Fran <u>said</u>.

Bob drove, and Ben rode with him <u>to</u> Wisconsin.

Sam fell and broke his hipbone . . . and his trombone.

The smoke rose <u>to</u> the top <u>of</u> the cabin.

◼ REINFORCING ACTIVITIES

Allow your students to choose from the following list of activities:

1. Find three "o-consonant-e" words that rhyme; for example, "smoke," "woke," and "broke," or "cone," "stone," and "shone." Make sentences with these sets of words. An example for the last set is, "The sun shone as he sat on the stone and ate his cone." If you wish, illustrate one or more of your sentences.

2. Challenge yourself with a dictionary game. You will need a dictionary and a stopwatch. Choose a favorite "o-consonant-e" word like "nose." Ask a friend to time you as you look up "nose" for the first time. Notice where "nose" is located in the dictionary. Is it in the middle of the book or a little beyond? Notice the guide words on the page where "nose" is located.

   Close your dictionary and then try to find "nose" again. Try to beat your own first time. For this game, you can either continue with the same word for several trials, or you can switch to new words.

3. Make up words from selected letters. For this game, you are given the vowels "o" and "e." You may also select any ten consonants you wish. Challenge a friend or challenge yourself, and see how many words you can find hidden in your twelve

letters. Since you have "o" and "e," you can look for "o-consonant-e" words. You can also try to find closed syllable words. As you play this game, you will discover that some consonants are definitely more useful than others.

4. LITERATURE CONNECTION: Jokes can either make us chuckle or downright guffaw. They can poke fun at human nature or derive their silliness from play with words.

Jokes can be created in the form of poetry, and a master of this sort of poem is Ogden Nash. Check your library for poems by him. Six of his poems can be found in the book *Houseful of Laughter* by Bennett Cerf (Random House, 1963).

⧉ EXTRA INTERESTING FACTS

Our modern word "home" comes from the Old English word "ham," which meant where a person lives, including her village as well as her house. Place names like "Birmingham," with its "ham" ending, remind us of this old word's original meaning. Nowadays, we think mainly of "home" as the particular house or apartment in which we reside.

WORD LIST

O-CONSONANT-E, ONE-SYLLABLE WORDS

bone	globe	prose
broke	grove	quote
choke	hole	robe
chose	home	rode
close	hope	role
code	hose	shone
Coke®	joke	smoke
cone	lone	spoke
cope	mole	stone
cove	nose	stove
dole	owe	those
dome	phone	tone
dope	poke	vote
dose	pole	woke
doze	pose	wrote
drove	probe	zone
froze	prone	

O-CONSONANT-E, MULTISYLLABIC WORDS

backbone	flagstone	milestone
backstroke	foxhole	pothole
compote	gemstone	primrose
disclose	hipbone	sandstone
enclose	impose	sidestroke
explode	indispose	sunstroke
expose	invoke	trombone
flagpole	limestone	wishbone

FINISH IT!

Fill in the blanks with words from the word list.

1. Jane _____ a long letter to her sister in Rome.

2. The reporter would not _____ her source of information.

3. The speaker _____ too softly, and no one could hear him.

4. They _____ strawberries in the freezer for the winter.

5. "Will you please _____ the door behind you when you leave?" Khalil asked.

6. Dan _____ all the invitations to his party.

7. The fireman checked the _____ to make sure it did not have a hole in it.

8. They will _____ the game until it stops raining.

9. "It's so warm in the sun, I'll probably _____ off," Josephine said.

10. The little boy enjoyed his ice cream _____.

WORD LIST

postpone	handwrote
disclose	froze
doze	cone
close	hose
wrote	spoke

Name _____   **Date** _____

A GAME OF CATEGORIES

Choose words from your word list that belong in each category.

BONES

_____

_____

_____

_____

_____

STONES

_____

_____

_____

_____

_____

TO DISTURB SOMETHING

_____

_____

_____

_____

FOOD

_____

_____

_____

_____

WORD LIST

limestone	expose
backbone	millstone
sole	cone
gallstone	chinbone
poke	scone
hipbone	gemstone
wishbone	compote
bulldoze	explode
sandstone	ringbone

Name _____   **Date** _____

LOOK IT UP!

Look up the listed words in your dictionary. Then match each word with its correct definition.

1. cote
2. stoke
3. mangrove
4. rove
5. drone
6. indispose
7. Gladstone
8. milestone
9. palindrome
10. grope

a. to add fuel to a fire
b. to make unwell or unable
c. a small shed for animals
d. an important event in a person's life
e. a type of tree or shrub that grows in swampy ground
f. to search blindly, to feel your way
g. to make a monotonous sound
h. a carriage with enclosed seats for passengers
i. to wander around with no definite destination
j. a sentence or word that reads backwards or forwards the same, like "Hannah"

Now choose five words from the above list and use each one in a sentence.

1. _____

_____

2. _____

_____

3. _____

_____

4. _____

_____

5. _____

_____

Name _____ **Date** _____

LIST IT!

Most of us enjoy a cone on a hot summer day. Make a list of the different kinds of ice cream that can go in a cone. Use common ones, such as vanilla and chocolate, or think of less common flavors, such as pumpkin. If you wish, invent some flavors of your own.

_____

_____

_____

_____

_____

_____

_____

_____

_____

_____

_____

_____

_____

_____

Name _____ Date _____

WRITE ON!

The following will help you write a story:

It is the year 2417, and you are on a one-person mission to explore a far-off section of the galaxy. Two weeks ago, you sent out a probe from your spaceship to try to establish contact with intelligent life.

Your probe has just returned. It has a message for you. The message is:

Home . . . Close . . . Black Hole.

What should you do? What will happen next? Write a story to answer these questions.

_____

_____

_____

_____

_____

_____

_____

_____

_____

_____

_____

Name _____   **Date** _____

VOWEL-CONSONANT-E SYLLABLES
"u-e" and "e-e"

▣ GETTING STARTED

Ask your students to tell you about the three types of vowel-consonant-e syllables they have discovered. Discuss some of the words that contain this syllable type.

Talk about some words that have more than one syllable type; for example, closed and vowel-consonant-e. Then provide time for your students to make a page in their notebook for "o-consonant-e" words.

◖ INTRODUCING NEW INFORMATION

"Today, we are going to continue to work with vowel-consonant-e syllables, but instead of only working with one vowel, we are going to work with two."

Say the following words: cube, dude, flute, June, spruce, Yule.

"What sound do you hear in all these words?"

"Yes, you hear /oo/ as in 'moon.'"

Record the following words: cube, dude, flute, June, spruce, Yule.

"What do you notice about all of these words?"

"That's correct, they all have a 'u,' a consonant, and an 'e.' The 'e' is silent. What kind of syllable is this?"

"I agree, it's a vowel-consonant-e syllable."
Say the following words: eke, eve, gene, Pete, theme, these.
"What sound do you hear in all of these words?"
"Yes, long 'e.'"
Record the following words: eke, eve, gene, Pete, theme, these.
"What do you see in all of these words?"
"That's right, they all have an 'e,' a consonant, and another 'e.' The first 'e' is long, and the last 'e' is silent. What kind of syllable is this?"

"Yes, it's the fifth vowel-consonant-e syllable. Today, we will be working with words that contain all the vowel-consonant-e syllables. Some of our words will also have closed syllables in them."

❖ PRACTICING WITH INDIVIDUAL WORDS

Select a manageable number of words from the word list provided on page 123 for your students to spell.

Ⓢ PRACTICING SPELLING IN CONTEXT

Select a manageable number of sentences from the following list for your students to write.

Jane is a fantastic athlete.

That kitten is cute.

The huge spruce fell on the shed.

Steve put the glass vase on the shelf.

The mule sat and did not get up.

"Luke will assume that it is a trick," Fran <u>said</u>.

Late June is a time <u>of</u> sun and fun.

Beth and Meg went on a trip <u>to</u> Crete.

"Take these mice and put them in that cage," Steve <u>said</u>.

Pete will use his rake and will finish the job.

▣ REINFORCING ACTIVITIES

Allow your students to choose from the following list of activities:

1. Find pairs of words with "e-consonant-e" or "u-consonant-e" syllables that begin with the same letter; for example, "eve" and "eke," or "tube" and "tune." Make sentences with these pairs of words. An example for the last pair is, "The tune

was carried by the long metal tube." If you wish, illustrate one or more of your sentences.

2. Make a magic square letter game. Draw a square like the one below, and then fill it with letters of your choice. Since you have been studying "u-consonant-e" and "e-consonant-e" syllables, you might wish to include at least one "u" and one or two "e"s.

t	b	d
L	u	n
e	k	e

Once your square is completed, try to find as many words as you can. The letters must touch each other sequentially, but you can go up or down or across. Some good words found in the magic square drawn here are: tune, dune, duke, Luke, eke, end, bun, tub.

3. Draw a HUGE picture. Select an object that is very small; for example, a tack or a tiny piece of string. Get a large piece of paper and draw your object as big as you can. This is a real challenge, so don't worry if it takes you one or two tries to be successful with your drawing. Adding color, especially for shading, makes these HUGE pictures very interesting.

4. LITERATURE CONNECTION: When Chinese people first came to America, they brought with them a rich folklore. "The Cure" is one such story. It can be found in the book *Tongues of Jade* by Laurence Yep (Harper Collins Publishers, 1991). In this book, Mr. Yep has translated and retold many Chinese-American tales.

"The Cure" is a story of magic. Another story in *Tongues of Jade*, however, deals more directly with issues of human nature. Read "The Teacher's Underwear" and enjoy a humorous and poignant tale.

⊟ EXTRA INTERESTING FACTS

Have you ever wondered where the names of our months come from? It is believed that June comes from Juno, the Roman goddess who was the protectress of women and, also, the goddess of marriage. The month of June in Roman times was called "Junius mensis," or "Juno's month."

But scholars feel that the month's name did not come directly from Latin. Rather, they think it first was adopted into Old French "juin," and from the Old French found its way into English.

WORD LIST

E-CONSONANT-E, ONE-SYLLABLE WORDS

Crete	eve	theme
eke	gene	these

E-CONSONANT-E, TWO-SYLLABLE WORDS

athlete	concrete	impede
benzene	discrete	stampede
blaspheme	extreme	

U-CONSONANT-E, ONE-SYLLABLE WORDS

brute	fuse	prune
chute	huge	rude
crude	June	rule
cube	jute	ruse
cute	lube	spruce
dude	lute	truce
duke	mule	tube
dune	muse	tune
fluke	mute	use
flute	plume	Yule
fume	prude	

U-CONSONANT-E, TWO-SYLLABLE WORDS

accuse	dispute	infuse
assume	enthuse	intrude
astute	exclude	misrule
attune	excuse	misuse
commune	globule	Neptune
costume	immune	transfuse
Danube	include	transmute
diffuse	induce	volume

FINISH IT!

Fill in the blanks with words from the word list.

1. The _____ is one of the wind instruments.

2. The students picked "Mardi Gras" as the _____ for their dance.

3. The boy was angry because the salesman was _____ to him.

4. The electric _____ needed to be replaced when the lights went out.

5. "Please _____ me," Fred told Pam. "I need to leave early."

6. They went to the island of _____ for their vacation.

7. Anne can swim and run and is, in general, a very fine _____.

8. "I _____ you will eat all of that candy," Mohammad said.

9. They poured the _____ for the foundation.

10. The two sides declared a _____ to discuss their differences.

WORD LIST

fuse	excuse
flute	assume
concrete	theme
athlete	Crete
rude	truce

Name _____   **Date** _____

A GAME OF CATEGORIES

Choose words from your word list that belong in each category.

PEOPLE

_____

_____

_____

_____

_____

THINGS PEOPLE DO

_____

_____

_____

_____

_____

CHARACTERISTICS OF PEOPLE

_____

_____

_____

_____

RELATING TO MUSIC

_____

_____

_____

_____

WORD LIST

rude	cute
intrude	Bruce
lute	postlude
Luke	exclude
Gene	tune
dispute	crude
accuse	flute
Steve	Pete
huge	include

Name _____   **Date** _____

LOOK IT UP!

Look up the listed words in your dictionary. Then match each word with its correct definition.

1. discrete   a   to agree to something, often to accept the duties of a job

2. flume   b. to place obstacles in the way of action or movement

3. impede   c. to stick to something

4. transmute   d. a color

5. accede   e. a member of the Shoshonean tribe

6. Ute   f. made up of separate parts

7. adhere   g. a bird that belongs to the loon family

8. astute   h. smart and cunning

9. puce   i. a narrow chute that carries water

10. grebe   j. to change or convert from one form to another

Now choose five words from the above list and use each one in a sentence.

1. _____

_____

2. _____

_____

3. _____

_____

4. _____

_____

5. _____

_____

Name _____   Date _____

LIST IT!

Many things enthuse us. In other words, they make us enthusiastic. Make a list of things that enthuse you. You can include possessions or things you would like to own, but don't forget to think about other forms of inspiration as well, like a friend's smile.

_____

_____

_____

_____

_____

_____

_____

_____

_____

_____

_____

_____

_____

Name _____ **Date** _____

WRITE ON!

An athlete can be a person who is successful hitting home runs in baseball, or a person who enjoys jumping rope or throwing horse shoes. Find an athlete and ask her/him if he/she is willing to be interviewed. If so, prepare some questions ahead of time, such as:

1. How did you first become involved with your favorite sport?

2. What is difficult for you about your sport?

Once your interview is completed, either write it out in essay form or offer the information you have gained in an oral presentation.

Write your questions here.

_____

_____

_____

_____

_____

_____

_____

_____

_____

_____

_____

_____

Name _____ **Date** _____

EIGHT COMMON SUFFIXES

▣ GETTING STARTED

Discuss closed and vowel-consonant-e syllable types, and then ask your students to tell you about words they see in their everyday lives that represent them; for example, the word "stop" on Stop signs and the word "name" on applications and other papers. Suggest that all of you will look for more representative words during the school day.

Talk with your students about the two vowel-consonant-e syllables they have recently discovered. Provide time for them to make two pages for their notebooks, one page for "u-consonant-e" words and one page for "e-consonant-e" words.

◖ INTRODUCING NEW INFORMATION

"Today, we will be working with suffixes. Suffixes are endings that are added to words to change either their meanings or their word forms. Suffixes are endings like 's,' 'ful,' or 'less.'"

Write out the following on either a large piece of paper or the chalkboard. Then say, *"You already know a lot about suffixes. Match the suffixes with their correct meanings in the chart below."*

Suffixes	Meanings
1. -ful (hopeful)	a. the most
2. -s (cats)	b. state of being (an adjective becomes a noun)
3. -ment (placement)	c. more than one
4. -less (homeless)	d. makes an action happen in the present tense
5. -es (boxes)	e. without
6. -ing (jumping)	f. more than one
7. -ness (sadness)	g. full of (a noun becomes an adjective)
8. -est (fastest)	h. something exists because of an action (a verb becomes a noun)

If your students have difficulty figuring out all the suffixes, assist them first by giving them more examples (refer to the word list on page 133). If they still have particular difficulty with "ness" and "ment," give them the information for these two suffixes. The correct answers are: 1. g; 2. c or f; 3. h; 4. e; 5. f or c; 6. d; 7. b; 8. a.

❖ PRACTICING WITH INDIVIDUAL WORDS

Select a manageable number of words from the word list provided on page 133 for your students to spell.

◊ PRACTICING SPELLING IN CONTEXT

Select a manageable number of sentences from the following list for your students to write. Since your students have now been writing the words "to," "of," and "said" for the past eleven lessons, assume your students know how to spell them. These words will no longer be underlined in the text. If your students continue to have difficulty with these words, provide a written model for them.

Tom is skillful at his job.

Beth and Jane went fishing in the lake.

"Put the boxes in the basement," Jill said.

His illness made him rest in bed.

Bob put his glasses on and then drove the van to the shop.

The homeless man sat on the bench and ate a muffin.

Fred can run the fastest mile in this state.

"It is shameful that Ron is acting like that," Pam said.

The band had saxes, flutes, trumpets, and a base drum.

The shipment of red glasses did not get to Wisconsin.

◉ REINFORCING ACTIVITIES

Allow your students to choose from the following list of activities:

1. Find pairs of words that have the same suffix; for example, "dampness" and "sadness," or "inches" and "lunches." Make sentences with these pairs of words. An example for the last pair is, "He didn't care that he was gaining inches, so he ate both the lunches." If you wish, illustrate one or more of your sentences.

2. Play Suffix Bingo. Make bingo cards by drawing a 5″ × 5″ square on a piece of paper. Draw lines at inch intervals, so that you finish with 25 one-inch squares. Ask each player to write a suffix in each square. The players can use any suffix that has been studied, and can repeat them in any order desired.

   Make a bunch of caller cards, one suffix to a card. Cut some inch squares out of colored paper for bingo chips, or you can use colored beads if you have them.

   Once the materials are prepared, players sit with their cards in front of them. The caller picks the top card and calls out the suffix and its meaning. If players have that suffix on their cards, they cover one of them with a bingo chip. The first person who gets either a horizontal, vertical or diagonal line covered, calls out "Bingo!" and wins.

3. Have you ever heard the expression, "He has time on his hands"? It means that he's got a lot of free time, but the words have quite a different literal meaning. Draw a picture that illustrates the literal meaning of this cliché.

4. LITERATURE CONNECTION: You have discovered eight suffixes in this lesson. There are other suffixes that are closed syllables that you can now spell; for example, the suffix "ish" which means "somewhat like" or "belonging to a group of people."

   By reading books, we can learn a lot about groups of people. One such group is the Jewish people.

Anne Frank was a young Jewish girl who, with her family, hid from the Nazis in Amsterdam during the Second World War. Her diary, published as *The Diary of a Young Girl* (Pocket Books, 1952) tells us much about her and the struggles of her people. Read this book to learn about the Jewish people.

Spanish-speaking people also have rich literature that helps us know about their history and their feelings. One such story is *The Red Comb* by Fernando Picó, illustrated by Maria Antonia Ordonex (adapted and published in English by BridgeWater Books, copyright by Ediciones Huracán of Puerto Rico in 1991 and Ediciones Ekaré of Venezuela in 1991). *The Red Comb* tells of how a young girl and an older woman save a runaway slave in Puerto Rico. Although it is fiction, it is based on historical facts.

⊟ EXTRA INTERESTING FACTS

Have your ever wondered where our suffixes come from? It is believed that the suffix "less" originated in the Indo-European languages (those are the languages spoken throughout Europe and some of those from southwestern Asia and India), and that it began as "loiso," meaning "small." Old German borrowed this word and changed it into "laisiz," which then became the Old English "less."

The suffix "less" follows the "ff, ll, ss" spelling generalization you discovered several lessons ago. But the suffix "ful" does not. Since "ful" literally means "full of," this is surprising. The following theory is unsubstantiated, but it is an interesting and fun way to think of this change of spelling.

The first written records and books were made by people carefully writing down words by hand. Do you think that one of these scribes got tired and just didn't feel like adding the second "l" to "ful"?

You have discovered that there are two ways of making words plural: add either "s" or "es." The suffix "es" is generally added to words ending in the letters "z," "x," "ss," "sh," and "ch."

WORD LIST

EIGHT COMMON SUFFIXES

Words ending in "ful"

bashful	shameful
grateful	skillful
helpful	spiteful
hopeful	stressful
restful	wishful

Words ending in "ing"

acting	rocking
fishing	rushing
helping	standing
locking	testing
printing	trusting

Words ending in "ment"

basement	investment
enchantment	pavement
engagement	placement
enrichment	shipment
entrapment	statement

Words ending in "est"

dampest	grandest
dullest	richest
fastest	softest
fondest	strongest
freshest	swiftest

Words ending in "es"

brushes	glasses
classes	inches
dishes	lunches
dresses	taxes
foxes	waltzes

Words ending in "less"

blameless	nameless
endless	restless
helpless	shameless
homeless	spotless
jobless	tireless

Words ending in "s"

bugs	pets
cats	ships
flutes	shells
homes	tops
names	tribes

Words ending in "ness"

dampness	likeness
fondness	madness
freshness	rudeness
gladness	sadness
illness	swiftness

✤ ✤ ✤ ✤ ✤ ✤ ✤ ✤ ✤ ✤ ✤ ✤ ✤ ✤ ✤ ✤ ✤

FINISH IT!

Fill in the blanks with words from the word list.

1. The two boys collected _____ at the beach.

2. Jan was the _____ runner in the state.

3. He cleaned for three hours and, therefore, the kitchen was

   _____.

4. The painting was a perfect _____ of the woman and her dog.

5. Letetia was _____ a lot of questions because she wanted to understand the assignment.

6. The child was _____ and didn't want to tell the story to everyone.

7. The politician made a _____ to the press.

8. There was no cafeteria at the new school, so the students brought their

   own _____.

9. "I am so lucky," Malcolm said, "that I feel like the _____ person in the world."

10. The woman's _____ did not win her any friends.

WORD LIST

likeness	shells
statement	bashful
swiftest	richest
rudeness	spotless
asking	lunches

Name _____   **Date** _____

A GAME OF CATEGORIES

Choose words from your word list that belong in each category.

ANIMALS

_____

_____

_____

_____

_____

FOUND IN THE KITCHEN

_____

_____

_____

_____

_____

POSITIVE CHARACTERISTICS OR FEELINGS

_____

_____

_____

_____

ACTIONS

_____

_____

_____

_____

WORD LIST

packing	rushing
pups	helpful
glasses	cats
skillful	dishes
rocking	chickens
picking	grateful
kittens	napkins
hopeful	cups
plates	rabbits

Name _____   Date _____

LOOK IT UP!

Look up the listed words in your dictionary. Then match each word with its correct definition.

1.	baseless	a.	the state of not being fit or able
2.	ineptness	b.	the state of being too quick
3.	fateful	c.	doing what one wants to do even in the face of opposition
4.	bluntness	d.	having no factual foundation
5.	rashness	e.	very angry
6.	daftest	f.	having the quality of showing what is going to happen
7.	ireful	g.	a share or portion of something
8.	muteness	h.	the state of not talking
9.	willful	i.	not having a sharp point
10.	allotment	j.	the most foolish

Now choose five words from the above list and use each one in a sentence.

1. _____

_____

2. _____

_____

3. _____

_____

4. _____

_____

5. _____

_____

Name _____ **Date** _____

LIST IT!

Names are important things about which all of us feel strongly. Make a list of names. You can do a general list of names of people you know or you can be more specific; for example, you can write girls' names or even names of pets. If you wish, you can list names that, to you, sound beautiful.

_____

_____

_____

_____

_____

_____

_____

_____

_____

_____

_____

_____

_____

_____

Name _____   **Date** _____

WRITE ON!

Poetry can take many forms, from free expressions of images to structured works. Use the following structure to create a four-line poem.

1. First, choose a word that names something.

2. Next, write three words ending with the suffix "ing" that tell what your word can do.

3. Then, write a short sentence about your word.

4. Last, choose a second word that describes your first word in an unusual way.

The following is an example of such a poem:

Wind
whispering, laughing, howling
it chases everything it can
Bully

Write one or more poems in the space below.

_____

_____

_____

_____

_____

_____

_____

_____

© 1996 by Cynthia Stowe

Name _____   **Date** _____

SUFFIX
"-ed"

▣ GETTING STARTED

Ask your students to tell you about suffixes. Together, list the eight suffixes studied so far and think of words that include these suffixes. Then ask your students to make a page for suffixes in their notebooks.

◖● INTRODUCING NEW INFORMATION

"Today, we are going to work with another suffix. Listen to this: I jump. What does that mean?"

"That's right, it tells you that I am jumping right now." Stand up and jump and say, *"I jump."* Write "I jump." on a piece of paper.

"Listen to this: I jumped. What does that mean?"

"Yes, I jumped before." Jump once or twice, wait a few moments and then say, *"I jumped."* Write "I jumped." on a piece of paper.

Show your students the two written sentences. *"What is added to the word 'jump'?"*

"That's correct, the suffix 'ed.'"

"How does the suffix 'ed' change a word?"

"Yes, it changes it from the present to the past tense."

"Listen to the endings of these words: yelled, smelled, fished, packed, hunted, rested. Do the endings sound the same?"

"You're right. The endings sound different." Record the following words: yelled, smelled, fished, packed, hunted, rested. *"Are the endings the same?"*

"Yes, all these words end with the 'ed' suffix, and are in the past tense."

"How do 'yelled' and 'smelled' end?"

"I agree, they end with the /d/ sound. How do 'fished' and 'packed' end?"

"Yes, they end with the /t/ sound."

"How do 'hunted' and 'rested' end?"

"That's right, they end with the /ed/ sound. The suffix 'ed' is a little difficult, because it has three different sounds."

❖ PRACTICING WITH INDIVIDUAL WORDS

Select a manageable number of words from the word list provided on page 142 for your students to spell.

⑤ PRACTICING SPELLING IN CONTEXT

Select a manageable number of sentences from the following list for your students to write.

"Fire! Fire!," yelled Jim.

Fran rushed to get to the film at nine.

Don missed Steve at the bike shop.

Beth packed six boxes of glasses and five boxes of plates.

Mike wished that his mom had not left on that plane.

When the class ended, Ben went home.

The waves swelled, and Jill jumped in and swam.

Nat trusted June, and June did the job well and on time.

Dave spilled milk on his tan pants.

Meg grunted five times and then lifted the trash can.

◼ REINFORCING ACTIVITIES

Allow your students to choose from the following list of activities:

1. Select pairs of words with the "ed" suffix that end with the same sound; for example, "filmed" and "pulled," or "ended" and "printed." Make sentences with these words. An example for the last pair is, "He ended his letter and then printed it out on his printer." If you wish, illustrate one or more of your sentences.

2. Play the WHO-DID-WHAT? game. Gather some blank cards; pieces of paper at least 1″ × 3″ are fine. Either by yourself or with friends, make a word bank for your game. First, write the name of a person or an animal (burglar, Ben, dog, elephant), one per card, on at least ten cards. Next, write an action word with the suffix "ed" (lifted, kicked, yelled, tricked), one per card, on at least ten cards. Last, write a word that names a thing (table, bone, flowers, T.V.), one per card, on at least ten cards.

Place your three types of words in their own separate boxes so that you cannot see the writing. Find one or two friends who want to play.

The first player takes one card from each pile. Her job is to make up a sentence with the three words she gets and then to explain the sentence so that it makes sense. For example, if she picks the words "dog," "yelled," and "T.V," she could say, "The dog yelled at the T.V., because, you see, this is a talking dog and because he could talk, he could also yell. The dog didn't like what was on T.V., so he yelled at it."

Then, the next player gets a turn to pick three cards. Enjoy all of the unusual and interesting stories that you and your friends create.

3. The cliché "He's all washed up" means that someone is not being very successful. The literal meaning of these words, however, is quite different. Illustrate the literal meaning of this cliché.

4. LITERATURE CONNECTION: Throughout history, people have been tricked by others. One example is the Native Americans being tricked out of much of their land by the people who came from Europe to America.

Read *Morning Girl* by Michael Dorris (Hyperion Books for Children, 1993) to learn about Native Americans before the newcomers arrived. Another excellent book is *Dawnland Encounters, Indians and Europeans in Northern New England* by Colin Calloway (University Press of New England, 1991). This book contains selected texts translated from primary sources and gives a fascinating picture of how Native Americans and Europeans interacted in northern New England from their first encounters to the end of the eighteenth century.

EXTRA INTERESTING FACTS

There are many words in the English language that were inspired by the sounds they represent. For example, listen for a sound when you hear the sentence, "The snake hissed." Other words inspired by sounds are "clicked," "clucked," "crashed," "fizzed," and "splashed." Can you think of others?

You may have noticed that most of the words presented in this lesson that end with the suffix "ed" (as in /d/), have two "l"s before the suffix, as in "spilled" and "pulled." There will be many other words that will be presented in future lessons that will end in "ed" (as in /d/) that will not have two "l"s before the "ed." Some examples are: "grinned," "enjoyed," "sailed," "bugged," "covered," and "grabbed."

WORD LIST

WORDS ENDING IN "ED" AS /D/

billed	killed	swelled
chilled	pulled	thrilled
drilled	shelled	willed
filled	smelled	yelled
filmed	spelled	
grilled	spilled	

WORDS ENDING IN "ED" AS /ED/

acted	hunted	ranted
blasted	landed	rented
blended	lasted	rested
chanted	lifted	rusted
drifted	listed	sanded
dusted	melted	sifted
ended	mended	tested
funded	nested	trusted
granted	panted	twisted
grunted	planted	wilted
hinted	printed	

WORDS ENDING IN "ED" AS /T/

asked	helped	picked
brushed	hissed	pressed
bumped	jumped	risked
camped	kicked	romped
checked	kissed	rushed
dressed	limped	shocked
ducked	locked	stamped
dumped	missed	tracked
fished	mocked	tricked
fussed	packed	wished
gulped	passed	

✣ ✣ ✣ ✣ ✣ ✣ ✣ ✣ ✣ ✣ ✣ ✣ ✣ ✣ ✣ ✣

FINISH IT!

Fill in the blanks with words from the word list.

1. Jess _____ the delicious odor of onions frying.

2. Jared _____ in his house for his lost car keys.

3. The two friends went to the lake and _____ from their rowboat.

4. Because it hadn't been watered for days, the plant _____.

5. Pat hiked during the day and _____ at night in the White Mountains.

6. Vladimir _____ the gallon of milk all over the kitchen floor.

7. "Look out! It's a bear!" _____ Jack.

8. Liz bent down and _____ the puppy up and gave him a hug.

9. Sondra _____ her sister Meg because she had been gone so long.

10. Mike was happy that he had _____ the word correctly.

WORD LIST

wilted   hunted
yelled   missed
smelled   spilled
fished   lifted
camped   spelled

Name _____   **Date** _____

A GAME OF CATEGORIES

Choose words from your word list that belong in each category.

RELATING TO COMMUNICATION

_____

_____

_____

_____

_____

JOBS PERFORMED BY HANDS AND ARMS

to have _____

to have _____

to have _____

to have _____

to have _____

ACTIONS PERFORMED BY FEET

to have _____

to have _____

to have _____

to have _____

RELATING TO FEELINGS

_____

_____

_____

_____

WORD LIST

dusted	sanded
trusted	asked
picked	jumped
yelled	shocked
mended	thrilled
kicked	ranted
called	limped
wished	hinted
packed	stamped

Name _____   **Date** _____

LOOK IT UP!

Look up the listed words in your dictionary. Then match each word with its correct definition.

1. ranted   a. to have been too economical

2. minted   b. to have stopped something from growing

3. hacked   c. to have printed money

4. scrimped   d. to have struck something or someone and made a heavy sound

5. culled   e. to have spoken loudly and with great feeling

6. stunted   f. decorated with a bunch of thin things such as grass or feathers

7. thumped   g. to have roughly cut

8. tufted   h. to have shined, as with a gleam

9. jelled   i. to have selected out or separated

10. glinted   j. to have caused to take a definite form

Now choose five words from the above list and use each one in a sentence.

1. _____

_____

2. _____

_____

3. _____

_____

4. _____

_____

5. _____

_____

Name _____   **Date** _____

LIST IT!

Imagine a person who is standing outside of your door. That person has just yelled. Make a list of possible reasons the person has yelled. Some examples are:

He yelled because he saw a very large bug.

He yelled because an elephant just stepped on his toe.

Enjoy making your list. Be as imaginative as you can.

_____

_____

_____

_____

_____

_____

_____

_____

_____

_____

_____

_____

Name _____ **Date** _____

WRITE ON!

Have you ever seen a skit that can be acted without words? The challenge for the actors is to be expressive with their faces and their movements. Props can be helpful to let the audience know what is happening.

Write a skit for yourself or for you and your friends to perform. Make the directions simple and easy to follow in a sequenced way. An example follows:

Henry hunted for his lost dog.

He called and called.

He hunted in his home.

Henry hunted around his neighborhood.

He walked for miles and hunted in the city.

All of a sudden, Henry's dog came to him and jumped on him.

The hunt ended.

_____

_____

_____

_____

_____

_____

_____

_____

_____

_____

_____

Name _____   **Date** _____

THE E RULE

🔲 GETTING STARTED

Ask your students to look through their notebooks and to tell you anything they wish about the structure of the English language. Discuss what they introduce.

Ask your students to tell you what they remember about the suffix "ed." Provide time for your students to make a notebook page for this suffix.

🌑 INTRODUCING NEW INFORMATION

"Today, you are going to discover your first spelling rule."
Record the following words: bake, drive, hope, make, smile, tune.
"What type of syllable do you see in all of these words?"
"Yes, they all contain vowel-consonant-e syllables. What letter do they all end with?"
"It's obvious: they all end with the letter 'e.'"
Record the following formulas:

chase + ed = chased

vote + ing = voting

brave + est = bravest

148

"What happened when a suffix was added to these words?"
"That's right, the 'e' was dropped and the suffix was added."
Record the following formulas:

home + less = homeless

like + ness = likeness

plate + ful = plateful

"What happened when a suffix was added to these vowel-consonant-e words?"
"I agree, nothing happened. The 'e' was not dropped and the suffix was added."
Place the two sets of formulas in front of your students. *"Can you figure out why, in some cases, the 'e' was dropped, and in other cases it was not?"*
"That is correct. When a suffix that begins with a vowel is added to a word ending in 'e,' the 'e' is dropped. When a suffix that begins with a consonant is added to a word ending in 'e,' the 'e' remains."

❖ PRACTICING WITH INDIVIDUAL WORDS

Select a manageable number of words from the word list provided on page 151 for your students to spell.

⑤ PRACTICING SPELLING IN CONTEXT

Select a manageable number of sentences from the following list for your students to write.

Ben is driving home to Memphis.

"This film is exciting," Pam said.

The graceful actress waved to them.

The convict escaped and ran up the hillside.

Meg and Beth hiked and then camped next to the lake.

Bob hoped that Jane had saved the sick rabbit.

"It is shameful that the man is homeless," Jim said.

As she smiled, Fran said, "Mike is joking."

Dave disliked the man and accused him of making a rude statement to the press.

"It is not taking Steve much time to run six miles," Bruce said.

▣ REINFORCING ACTIVITIES

Allow your students to choose from the following list of activities:

1. Select pairs of words, one in which the "e" is dropped when a suffix is added, and one in which the "e" remains; for example, "saved" and "graceful," and "hoping" and "lateness." Make sentences with these words. An example for the last pair is, "She was hoping that her lateness would not be a problem." If you wish, illustrate one or more of your sentences.

2. Play charades. Make a pack of at least ten cards, each of which has either an action word or phrase written on it. Some examples are: "skating," "escaping," "riding a bike," "driving a bus," or "baking a cake." Then get some friends together and divide them into two groups. One player selects one card and acts out the word or phrase for her group to guess. If the group guesses successfully within a given time period, they get a point, and the other group tries its luck with a new card. The group with more points at the end wins the game.

3. The cliché "all fired up" means that a person is full of enthusiasm and excitement. As you can tell, however, the literal meaning of this phrase is quite different. Illustrate the literal meaning of "all fired up."

4. LITERATURE CONNECTION: Sometimes, the bravest people among us start out afraid. This is the case with Albert Brooks, the hero in *The Contender* by Robert Lipsyte (Harper Keypoint Book, 1967). Albert has dropped out of high school and is struggling with fear—fear of the bullies around him and fear of his own lack of opportunity in life.

But Albert takes positive action. He joins a gym and begins to train to be a boxer. Read *The Contender* and discover how Albert becomes one of the bravest people on his block.

⅔ EXTRA INTERESTING FACTS

Some English words come from two words being pushed together; for example, the word "smog" comes from the combination of "smoke" and "fog." In this case, not only the "e" was dropped, but also the "k" and the "f."

Other English words are the result of two words being connected; for example, "baseball," "bareback," "driveway," and "fireplace." In these cases, no letters are dropped. It's interesting to think about how both old words contribute to the meaning of the new word.

There is one main exception to the "E" rule you have discovered in this lesson. When a word ends with a soft "c" or a soft "g," usually the "e" is kept, even if the suffix begins with a vowel. Examples of such words are "traceable" and "manageable."

WORD LIST

ONE-SYLLABLE WORDS—THE "E" IS DROPPED

baked	probed
bravest	riding
chased	ripest
dining	saved
driving	shaking
faded	shining
framed	smiled
hated	taking
hiked	traded
hoped	voted
joking	waved
making	widest
named	

ONE-SYLLABLE WORDS—THE "E" REMAINS

apes	muteness
blameless	pavement
cuteness	plateful
graceful	rudeness
grateful	rules
homeless	shameful
hopeful	spiteful
hopeless	statement
hugeness	themes
jokes	timeless
lateness	tireless
likeness	wakeful
miles	

MULTISYLLABLE WORDS—THE "E" IS DROPPED

accusing	exciting
admired	exploded
dictated	invading
disliked	invited
engaged	inviting
escaped	misplaced
escaping	stampeded
excited	

MULTISYLLABLE WORDS—THE "E" REMAINS

athletes	hillsides
bagpipes	hotcakes
basement	placement
confinement	potholes
cupcakes	trombones
engagement	vampires
flagpoles	wishbones
gemstones	

FINISH IT!

Fill in the blanks with words from the word list.

1. The little girl _____ her friend around the schoolyard.

2. The townspeople _____ the mayor for his honesty and courage.

3. "I am still _____ that I will be able to come to the party," Brianna said.

4. On election day, Fred left home early and _____ before he went to work.

5. Jose _____ his best hat and was upset that he could not find it.

6. "You are _____ when you wear your seat belt," Mike told his son.

7. Peg has been _____ horses in shows since she was eight years old.

8. At the Halloween costume party, there were several _____.

9. On Saturday, we _____ ten loaves of bread.

10. They went to the _____ room for supper.

WORD LIST

hopeful	voted
misplaced	riding
vampires	baked
admired	chased
dining	safest

Name _____   **Date** _____

A GAME OF CATEGORIES

Choose words from your word list that belong in each category.

RELATING TO FIRE AND HEAT

_____

_____

_____

_____

RELATING TO MOVEMENT

_____

_____

_____

_____

RELATING TO HAPPY FEELINGS

_____

_____

_____

WORDS THAT DESCRIBE FOOD

_____

_____

_____

WORD LIST

fires	ripest
admired	smoked
flames	hiked
hoping	boneless
riding	baked
stalest	excited
blazing	biked
smiled	glazed
sliding	driving

Name _____   **Date** _____

LOOK IT UP!

Look up the listed words in your dictionary. Then match each word with its correct definition.

1. anecdotes
2. pruning
3. crazed

4. meted
5. glazed
6. alluded
7. enslavement

8. imbibing
9. truncated
10. aspiring

a. to have referred to
b. to have given out a certain portion
c. to have been cut short, or to look as if this has happened
d. to be trimming a plant
e. to want success or what success can buy
f. to have been put into bondage
g. to have covered a surface with a smooth finish
h. little stories, often of a personal nature
i. to be drinking
j. to become frantic over something

Now choose five words from the above list and use each one in a sentence.

1. _____

_____

2. _____

_____

3. _____

_____

4. _____

_____

5. _____

_____

Name _____ **Date** _____

LIST IT!

People are all different, but our sameness is more compelling than our differences. Make a list that deals with the sameness of all people. For example:

1. We all need air to breathe.

2. We experience feelings such as joy or anger.

3. People all need to be cared for when they are born and very young.

See how many ways you can think of that illustrate the sameness of all people.

_____

_____

_____

_____

_____

_____

_____

_____

_____

_____

_____

_____

Name _____ Date _____

WRITE ON!

SMOKING IS HAZARDOUS TO YOUR HEALTH!

Have you ever seen or heard that slogan? What do you think about smoking cigarettes? Do you feel it is fair for a business to restrict the right of people to smoke? Do you feel nonsmokers have more rights than smokers because of the danger of breathing in second-hand smoke?

Write your opinion about smoking. You can discuss one of the questions mentioned above, or you can write about a different issue that relates to smoking.

Name _____ **Date** _____

OPEN SYLLABLE
"a"

▣ GETTING STARTED

Talk with your students about the "E" rule. Take one or two words with the "e" already dropped, such as "driving" or "baked," and write out the formulas used to get the final spellings (drive + ing = driving and bake + ed = baked). Assist your students as they make a page for the "E" rule in their notebooks.

◖● INTRODUCING NEW INFORMATION

"Today, you are going to discover a third, new type of syllable."
Say the following words: agent, April, canine, label, native, vacate.
"What do you hear in the first syllable of these words?"
"Yes, long 'a.'"
Record the following words: agent, April, canine, label, native, vacate.
"What do you see in the first syllable of all of these words?"
"I agree, you see an 'a' with no letter after it for that syllable. This type of syllable is called an open syllable. It is a syllable where a single vowel is the last letter in the syllable."

"In the words that have been presented so far, the vowel 'a' is long. In some words, however, something unusual happens, and the 'a' does not represent the expected long 'a' sound in an open syllable."

Say the following words: Alaska, alone, amaze, arose, canal, charade.

"What do you hear in the first syllable of these words?"

"That's what I hear, too, a short 'u' sound."

Record the following words: Alaska, alone, amaze, arose, canal, charade.

"What vowel do you see in the first syllable of these words?"

"Yes, there is an 'a' followed by no other letter. This makes these syllables all open syllables. But in these words, the 'a' represents the short 'u' sound. I need to give you some information to help you understand when open syllable 'a' respresents the short 'u' sound.

"When we say multisyllabic words in English, we put more emphasis on some syllables than on others."

Say: ta'-ble.

"Which syllable has more emphasis?"

"That's right, the first syllable 'ta.'"

Say: a-lone'.

"Which syllable has more emphasis?"

"Yes, the second syllable 'lone.'"

Practice with words until your students can clearly hear accented (emphasized) versus non-accented (not emphasized) syllables. For some students, this requires more than one session.

Record the following words: agent, April, David, hatred, label, native.

"What syllable is emphasized in all of these words?"

"Yes, the syllable with the open syllable 'a.' Is the vowel long or does it represent the short 'u' sound?"

"I agree, the vowel is long."

Record the following words: adrift, alike, along, amend, amuse, aside.

"Is the open syllable with 'a' the syllable that is emphasized?"

"That's right, it's not, and it also represents the short 'u' sound. Can you think of a generalization to help you remember this?"

"Great, in words with an open syllable with 'a,' the 'a' is long if the syllable is emphasized. The 'a' represents the short vowel 'u' if the syllable is not emphasized. This is true regardless of the placement of the syllable in the word; for example, the last syllables in 'extra' and 'delta' have open syllables with 'a' which represents the short 'u' sound."

❖ PRACTICING WITH INDIVIDUAL WORDS

Select a manageable number of words from the word list provided on page 161 for your students to spell.

◐ PRACTICING SPELLING IN CONTEXT

Select a manageable number of sentences from the following list for your students to write.

Edna is a native of Alabama.

"Montana is a nice state," Pat said.

Jim awoke at six but did not get up until ten.

In April, Ned will vacate his cabin and take a trip to Alaska.

Don is giving his extra cash to the victims of the fire.

"Let's sit and rest next to that majestic elm," Jan said.

His naked hatred did not amuse the class.

"This time, Beth will pass Basic Math," Peg said.

"The ship is adrift in this fog?" Jane asked.

David did not tell his dad that Atlanta did not win the baseball game.

◘ REINFORCING ACTIVITIES

Allow your students to choose from the following list of activities:

1. Select pairs of words, one with the open syllable "a" in an emphasized syllable and one with the open syllable "a" in a syllable that is not emphasized; for example, "nature" and "awake," and "April" and "amuse." Make sentences with these pairs. An example for the last pair is, "In April, Tom amused himself by making and flying beautiful kites." Notice that in this sentence, the "E" rule has been used to change the spelling of the word "amuse." If you wish, illustrate one or more of your sentences.

2. Have you noticed that there are many place names that contain the open syllable with "a"? Select one of these places and make a mobile map for it. Get a piece of oaktag and a map of your place to copy. Outline your map, as large as you wish, and cut the oaktag around the border.

   Within the border, indicate important rivers, landmarks or cities or anything else that interests you about your place. An encyclopedia is usually helpful in discovering this type of information. Color your map on both sides and hang it from the ceiling for people to learn from and enjoy.

3. "Amazing Grace" is a gospel song with a fascinating history. It was composed by John Newton (1725–1807) who was the captain of a slaveship. On one voyage with many slaves on board, John Newton realized the wickedness of what he was doing and turned his ship around. He brought the people back to Africa and freed them.

   John Newton composed "Amazing Grace" as a response to his new-found life. Many artists have recorded this song, including Judy Collins on her *Whales and Nightingales* album and Willie Nelson on *The Sound in Your Mind.* You can also find the words to this song in the *Rise Up Singing* book, edited by Peter Blood-Patterson (A Sing Out Publication, 1988).

4. LITERATURE CONNECTION: There are many stories of amazing canines in literature. One favorite is *Stone Fox* by John R. Gardiner (Crowell Publications, 1980).

This story tells of a dog that gives all he has for the love of a boy. It is a story that stays with you long after you have read the book.

Try to find other stories about amazing canines in your library. There are many excellent ones.

⧉ EXTRA INTERESTING FACTS

One of the factors that keeps the English language vital is that new words are constantly being introduced. One new word is "ninja" which refers to someone who practices martial arts and who is particularly good at being elusive and, in fact, almost seeming invisible.

Did "ninja" gain its popularity from ninja movies? Or do you think that the "Mutant Ninja Turtles" helped fix this word in American culture?

WORD LIST

OPEN SYLLABLE "A," EMPHASIZED SYLLABLE

agent	David	nature
apex	hatred	rabid
April	label	raven
basic	latent	sacred
basin	latex	Salem
basis	matrix	saline
canine	naked	stamen
craven	native	vacate

OPEN SYLLABLE "A," NOT EMPHASIZED SYLLABLE

abide	along	Edna
abode	amaze	extra
abolish	amazing	Gabon
abuse	amend	gala
abut	amid	Japan
adapt	amuse	Kenya
adept	arise	Libya
adopt	arose	majestic
adrift	aside	Montana
adult	Atlanta	ninja
agenda	atone	parole
Alabama	awhile	stanza
Alaska	awake	stigma
alfalfa	awoke	Tampa
alike	Canada	trapeze
aline	canal	tundra
alive	charade	ultra
aloft	delta	vista
alone	dogma	

FINISH IT!

Fill in the blanks with words from the word list.

1. The dog was sick, but, fortunately, he was not _____.

2. _____ is a country bordering the U.S. where French and English are spoken.

3. Kim _____ the stray puppy.

4. "David is going to study lions in _____," Francis said.

5. The movie was about a secret _____ who stole important defense plans.

6. Slavery in the United States was _____ in the 1800s.

7. "That magician does such _____ tricks," Isaac said.

8. "I like to hike outside and enjoy _____," Shaniqua said.

9. The rooster _____ before the sun came up.

10. The _____ listed the ingredients of the canned stew.

© 1996 by Cynthia Stowe

WORD LIST

abolished	rabid
Canada	agent
label	nature
Kenya	adopted
amazing	awoke

Name _____ **Date** _____

A GAME OF CATEGORIES

Choose words from your word list that belong in each category.

COUNTRIES

_____

_____

_____

_____

_____

CITIES AND STATES

_____

_____

_____

_____

_____

ASPECTS OF LANDSCAPE

_____

_____

_____

_____

OUT OF THE ORDINARY

_____

_____

_____

_____

WORD LIST

Tampa	Montana
Libya	sacred
delta	Canada
amazing	tundra
Japan	Atlanta
gala	savanna
Alabama	Alaska
Kenya	ultra
vista	Gabon

Name _____   **Date** _____

LOOK IT UP!

Look up the listed words in your dictionary. Then match each word with its correct definition.

1. adept		a.	a view
2. tundra		b.	the very top of something
3. vista		c.	a treeless plain in a cold land
4. atone		d.	hidden, not apparent
5. stamen		e.	to make amends for a wrong done
6. apex		f.	to be very skilled
7. abut		g.	having salt within it
8. craven		h.	to be cowardly
9. latent		i.	the pollen-bearing part of a flower
10. saline		j.	to join or touch, as with a border

Now choose five words from the above list and use each one in a sentence.

1. _____

   _____

2. _____

   _____

3. _____

   _____

4. _____

   _____

5. _____

   _____

Name _____ **Date** _____

LIST IT!

An abode is another word for a home. People and animals have many different types of homes. People live in houses and tents. Animals live in nests and caves. Some fish probably call the ocean home.

Make a list of as many different kinds of abodes as you can. It's fun to check the encyclopedia for information on where a particular animal rests its head or to do research on the type of abode an unfamiliar group of people call home.

Name _____   **Date** _____

WRITE ON!

"EXTRA! EXTRA! READ ALL ABOUT IT!"

In the past, people selling newspapers would stand on the corner and shout these words when an extra edition of a paper was put out. But extra papers were not published during ordinary times. They were published for extraordinary situations, like the ending of World War II.

Write a front page headline and article for an extra edition of a newspaper. Possible headlines are:

MARTIANS LAND IN PHILADELPHIA!

KING KONG LIVES!

A CURE FOR CANCER DISCOVERED!

_____

_____

_____

_____

_____

_____

_____

_____

_____

_____

_____

Name _____ **Date** _____

OPEN SYLLABLE
"i"

▣ GETTING STARTED

Discuss the syllable types presented thus far. Ask your students to choose one with which they feel most comfortable.

Provide time for your students to make a page for open syllable "a" for their notebooks. Ask them to include information on both "a" in emphasized syllables and "a" in syllables that are not emphasized.

◖ INTRODUCING NEW INFORMATION

"Today, we are going to continue to work with open syllables. We will be working with a new vowel."

Say the following words: China, hi, I, minus, migrate, quiet.

"What vowel sound do you hear in the first syllable of these words?"

"I agree, long 'i.'"

Record the following words: China, hi, I, minus, migrate, quiet.

"What vowel do you see in the first syllable of all these words?"

"Yes, you see an 'i' with no letter after it for that syllable. What type of syllable ends with a single vowel?"

"That's right, an open syllable has a single vowel with no letter after it. In the words presented so far in this lesson, 'i' in an open syllable has the long sound."

"What do you remember about emphasized syllables?"

"Yes, they are syllables that have more emphasis of voice placed on them; for example, the first syllable of 'ta-ble' is emphasized. The second syllable is not."

Say the following words: divide, divine.

"What vowel sound do you hear in the first syllable of these words?"

"Yes, short 'i.'"

Record the following words: divide, divine.

"What vowel do you see in the first syllable of these words?"

"Of course, an 'i.' What type of syllable are they?"

"That's correct. They are open syllables, because they have a single vowel with no letter after it in that syllable."

Record the following words: Africa, confident, estimate, optimistic, sensitive, ventilate.

"Look at these words. Read them to yourself or out loud if you wish, and then tell me when you think an 'i' in an open syllable has the short sound."

"You are right. An 'i' in an open syllable has the short 'i' sound when it is in a syllable that is not emphasized."

❖ PRACTICING WITH INDIVIDUAL WORDS

Select a manageable number of words from the word list provided on page 171 for your students to spell.

❚ PRACTICING SPELLING IN CONTEXT

Select a manageable number of sentences from the following list for your students to write.

"That vanilla cake is divine," Pam said.

At last, the crisis passed.

"Life is complicated," Jeff said.

Dan is confident that Jess will win the race.

The giant sat on the hut and crushed it.

"I just cannot estimate math problems," Rick said.

Edna went to Africa and then to Tibet.

Fran picked an iris and then put it in a vase.

"I estimate that it will take a lot of fabric to make that dress," Ben said.

The quiet man gave Bob a plateful of rice and shrimp.

◼ REINFORCING ACTIVITIES

Allow your students to choose from the following list of activities:

1. Select pairs of words, one with the open syllable "i" in an emphasized syllable and one with the open syllable "i" in a syllable that is not emphasized; for example, "hifi" and "compliment," and "giant" and "confident." Make sentences with these pairs. An example for the last pair is, "The giant was confident he could lift the car." If you wish, illustrate one or more of your sentences.

2. The English language is based on an alphabet where letters represent sounds. Chinese writing, however, is based on pictures. For every Chinese word, there is a different picture.

    Sometimes, these pictures are drawings that are based on what the word means; for example, the ancient character for "water" is , and the ancient character for "eye" is . If the word represents an abstract concept, a symbol was developed; for example, the character for "up" is , and the character for "down" is . Sometimes, a character for a word is made up of two or more smaller pictures put together; for example, when "woman" and "child" are combined, the new word is "love."

    To learn more about Chinese writing, read a book like *Chinese Writing* by Diane Wolff (Holt, Rinehart and Winston, 1975).

    Make up a few of your own pictures that represent words. Try to write a sentence or even a paragraph. Do you think you can write a short story using pictures? This is particularly enjoyable if you give your picture writing to a friend to translate.

3. Play the "Investigate" game. Each player gets five blank cards. Agree on a subject area; for example, you could agree to work in the area of "Information about Africa." Each player gets ten minutes to write out five questions about the selected subject. Examples of questions are "How many countries are there in the continent of Africa?" and "What is a favorite food in one of the countries of Africa?"

    When the ten-minute question time is up, exchange questions, and players get ten minutes to investigate the subject area and find the answers. The player with the most correct answers wins.

It is helpful to gather resource materials once you have decided on the subject area. Then decide on a plan regarding who gets to use which resources for how long once the game begins.

4. LITERATURE CONNECTION: People who investigate a great deal are scientists. They investigate how animals live, the secrets that are hidden in the deepest oceans, the laws that govern energy. Go to your library and see what kinds of books on science you can find.

Two interesting series for elementary school-age students are: *Growing Up with Science, the Illustrated Encyclopedia of Invention* (H. S. Stuttman, Inc, 1984) and *The Marshall Cavendish Science Project Books*, written by Steve Parker, illustrated by David Parr (The Marshall Cavendish Library of Science Projects, 1988).

∃ EXTRA INTERESTING FACTS

The word "investigate" has a fascinating history. It comes from the Latin "in" and "vestigo," which means to follow a footprint. "Vestigo" is derived from "vestigium" or footprint.

When we investigate something, we follow a path where clues lead us. If we're lucky, those clues are as obvious as footprints clearly marked out in snow, mud, or sand.

WORD LIST

OPEN SYLLABLE "I," EMPHASIZED SYLLABLE

biped	hifi	nitric
biplane	I	quiet
bisect	ibex	shining
china	icon	silent
China	Iran	sinus
climax	iris	siren
crisis	Irish	stipend
dialect	item	tirade
digest	libel	tripod
dilute	mica	vibrate
disquiet	migrate	vitamin
giant	minus	widen
hi	nitrate	

OPEN SYLLABLE "I," NOT EMPHASIZED SYLLABLE

altitude	estimate	obligate
Africa	fabricate	optimistic
antidote	illicit	optimum
candidate	indicate	platinum
captivate	imitate	sanitize
complicate	immigrate	sensitive
compliment	implicate	sentiment
confident	implicit	silicon
cultivate	inhibit	silicone
diligent	instigate	stabilize
divide	investigate	subdivide
dividend	litigate	substitute
divine	medicate	ventilate
dominate	mobilize	

FINISH IT!

Fill in the blanks with words from the word list.

1. The machinery stopped working and, suddenly, it was _____.

2. If you _____ a pie in half, you will have two equal parts.

3. Steve turned on his _____ and began to dance.

4. _____ is one of the continents.

5. Fifteen _____ five equals ten.

6. Liu's tooth hurt and was _____ to hot and cold.

7. Ms. Rodriguez was sick, so the fourth grade had a _____ teacher.

8. "Can you wait at least an hour for your meal to _____ before you go swimming?" Jim asked.

9. "I am _____ that everything will be fine," Ben said.

10. Many _____ people use chopsticks to eat their food.

WORD LIST

hifi	quiet
Chinese	optimistic
divide	substitute
sensitive	minus
Africa	digest

Name _____   Date _____

A GAME OF CATEGORIES

Choose words from your word list that belong in each category.

RELATING TO NUMBERS

_____

_____

_____

_____

_____

CHEMICAL ELEMENTS

_____

_____

_____

_____

_____

PLACES

_____

_____

_____

_____

RELATING TO FEELINGS

_____

_____

_____

_____

WORD LIST

nitrate
platinum
Africa
biped
nitric
optimistic
tripod
sentiment
silicone

China
tirade
trisect
Tibet
silicon
trident
disquiet
bisect
Iran

Name _____   **Date** _____

LOOK IT UP!

Look up the listed words in your dictionary. Then match each word with its correct definition.

1. implicit   a. a certain amount of money given to a person

2. biped   b. a type of wild goat with curved horns

3. condiment   c. to take away or deprive

4. illicit   d. a spice or sauce that seasons food

5. stipend   e. to finish, often by reaching a high point

6. divest   f. not allowed, not lawful

7. strident   g. to take conflict to court

8. ibex   h. a two-footed animal

9. litigate   i. something that is not directly stated, but is implied

10. culminate   j. to make a harsh, grating sound

Now choose five words from the above list and use each one in a sentence.

1. _____

_____

2. _____

_____

3. _____

_____

4. _____

_____

5. _____

_____

Name _____ **Date** _____

LIST IT!

Make a list of occurrences, each of which can be considered a crisis. You can be serious in your list or you can be humorous. For example, you can say:

- The roof of the school fell in during the night.

- Thomas was having a good time until he noticed the large rhinoceros at the door.

Once you have finished your list, be sure to save it. Your list of "crisis ideas" can give you ideas for stories you may wish to write.

_____

_____

_____

_____

_____

_____

_____

_____

_____

_____

_____

_____

Name _____   **Date** _____

WRITE ON!

The following places all contain open syllable "i" in their names: Africa, China, and Iran. Choose one of these places that you would like to study.

Find some resource material and read about your place. Then, write about your place, but don't write as an outsider. Rather, pretend you are a person who lives in that place. Give yourself a name, an age, a physical description, a home, a family. Include as many details as you wish about this new character you are discovering. If you wish, you can also do an oral presentation, pretending you are the character you have developed.

_____

_____

_____

_____

_____

_____

_____

_____

_____

_____

_____

_____

_____

Name _____   **Date** _____

OPEN SYLLABLE
"O"

▣ GETTING STARTED

Ask your students to tell you what they remember about the vowel "i" in open syllables. Give them time to make a page for "i" in open syllables for their notebooks. Ask them to include information on both "i" in emphasized syllables and "i" in syllables that are not emphasized.

◖● INTRODUCING NEW INFORMATION

"Today, we are going to work with a new vowel in open syllables."
Say the following words: bonus, coconut, frozen, locate, open, tomato.
"What vowel sound do you hear in the first syllable of these words?"
"Yes, long 'o.'"
Record the following words: bonus, coconut, frozen, locate, open, tomato.
"What vowel do you see in the first syllable of these words?"
"I agree, long 'o.' What type of syllable are all those first syllables?"
"That's right. They are open syllables because the single vowel ends the syllable."
Record the following words: absolute, banjo, halo, omit, polite, violin.

177

"Say these words to yourself or read them aloud if you wish. Then tell me if the open syllables with 'o' are emphasized."

"No, they're not. Does the 'o' still have the long 'o' sound?"

"That's correct. Open syllables with 'o' generally have the long 'o' sound whether or not they are the emphasized syllable."

❖ PRACTICING WITH INDIVIDUAL WORDS

Select a manageable number of words from the word list provided on page 180 for your students to spell.

⑤ PRACTICING SPELLING IN CONTEXT

Select a manageable number of sentences from the following list for your students to write.

Peg ate a baked potato.

"Open wide and take these vitamins," Bruce said.

Stephen spends a lot of time with his banjo and his violin.

"At the moment, the hotel is full," the man at the desk said.

The robot helped to run the printing press.

"Joseph is so polite," Jan said.

Janet went to visit Fran in Toronto, Canada.

"It is an absolute shame that Jim is sick," Pete said.

At lunch, the students set up a picket line and protested.

"I am hoping that I can go to Oklahoma," Edna said.

◼ REINFORCING ACTIVITIES

Allow your students to choose from the following list of activities:

1. Select pairs of words that end with the open syllable "o"; for example, "go" and "solo," and "ago" and "photo." Make sentences with these pairs of words. An example for the last pair is, "Four years ago, I took a prize-winning photo of the moon." If you wish, illustrate one or more of your sentences.

2. A diorama is a three-dimensional representation of a place. Often, people turn a shoebox on its side and "landscape" the sides of the box and then include objects to depict a scene.

   Choose a place that has an open syllable "o" in its name; for example, Arizona, Ohio, Toronto, Oslo, Angola, Morocco, Poland, or Samoa. Then do research on what the place is like in terms of landscape and climate.

You can look in encyclopedias or books, or you can try to find a person who has lived in or visited your selected place. Then make a diorama of your place.

3. Play a geography riddle game. Find a large world map or a globe. Then, if you don't know them, learn some words that relate to geography like "longitude" and "latitude."

   The next step is to find as many place names as you can that have the open syllable "o" in their names. Include cities, states, countries, islands, and continents. Write your list of names on either a large piece of paper or the chalkboard.

   Find at least one friend with whom to play "Geography Riddle." The player who is "it" mentally selects a place from the list of names. Then, she gives clues to the other players. For example, she can say, "My place is a city. It is north of Denmark." She continues to give clues until someone guesses the place, and then that player selects the next mystery place.

4. LITERATURE CONNECTION: Poems are expressions of all aspects of human experience: relationships, nature, our innermost feelings. Poems are created in all cultures and reflect our diverse experiences. They can be lyrical and serious, or they can be humorous.

   The following are interesting books of poetry. *Birches* by Robert Frost, illustrated by Ed Young (Henry Holt and Co., text copyright 1944, illustrations copyright 1988) presents Mr. Frost's poem in a picture-book format. *The Dragons Are Singing Tonight* by Jack Prelutsky, pictures by Peter Sis (Greenwillow Books, 1993) offers funny poems about dragons that are hard to resist, even if you don't believe in dragons. *Miracles, Poems by Children of the English-Speaking World,* collected by Richard Lewis (Simon and Schuster, 1966), gives a fascinating collection of poems by children.

⊇ EXTRA INTERESTING FACTS

The word "potato," as well as the vegetable, shows how interconnected our world is. The potato is native to the Andes area of South America. People believe that the Spanish invaders learned about the potato and then brought it back to Europe. Irish immigrants brought the potato to the United States in 1719.

People believe that the word "potato" comes from the Spanish "patata." This, in turn, is derived from the Haitian word "batata." The Taino language is spoken in Haiti and other Caribbean islands, and "batata" is this language's word for sweet potato.

WORD LIST

OPEN SYLLABLE "O," ONE- AND MULTI-SYLLABLE WORDS

abdomen	hotel	potent
absolute	Idaho	profile
ago	Indo-China	program
Angola	Iowa	prolong
annotate	isolate	protect
aristocrat	limbo	protest
Arizona	locate	proton
banjo	locust	provide
bingo	lotus	robot
bonus	moment	rodent
broken	motel	rotate
coconut	nitro	Samoa
coma	nitrogen	silo
crocus	no	sloping
diagnosis	oasis	so
diorama	Ohio	soda
diploma	Oklahoma	solo
dislocate	omen	spoken
donate	omit	tempo
Eskimo	open	tomato
focus	ozone	Toronto
frozen	photo	totem
go	poem	violent
gusto	Polish	violin
halo	polite	
hoping	potato	

FINISH IT!

Fill in the blanks with words from the word list.

1. Arthur put sour cream on his baked _____.

2. The machine was _____ and could not be fixed.

3. "I was _____ that you could come to my party," Pat said.

4. Rats and mice are _____.

5. The cake recipe called for chopped dates and _____.

6. Juan liked to play his _____ in the school orchestra.

7. Anna went to _____ and saw the Pacific Ocean for the first time.

8. "Please _____ that drawer and take out my notebook," Sam said.

9. Four years _____ Aric visited Mexico.

10. _____ is in the midwestern part of the U.S.

WORD LIST

coconut	hoping
potato	San Francisco
open	broken
Ohio	ago
rodents	violin

Name _____   Date _____

A GAME OF CATEGORIES

Choose words from your word list that belong in each category.

STATES IN THE U.S.

_____

_____

_____

_____

_____

CITIES

_____

_____

_____

_____

_____

COUNTRIES IN AFRICA

_____

_____

_____

_____

**COUNTRIES OR ISLANDS
NOT IN AFRICA**

_____

_____

_____

_____

WORD LIST

Ohio	Oslo
Congo	Mexico
Toronto	Idaho
Oman	San Francisco
Copenhagen	Togo
Poland	Arizona
Iowa	Samoa
Morocco	Sacramento
Oklahoma	Angola

Name _____   **Date** _____

LOOK IT UP!

Look up the listed words in your dictionary. Then match each word with its correct definition.

1. asphodel
2. cogent
3. trilobate
4. stiletto
5. isometric
6. accolade
7. thorax
8. disoblige
9. mimosa
10. annotate

a. to not do what someone wants you to do
b. a little dagger
c. herbs, shrubs, and trees that belong to the pea family
d. indicating that the measure is equal
e. a flower of the lily family
f. a ceremony in which a person is made a knight
g. to have three lobes, as some leaves do
h. to make notes, often about literary works
i. the human chest
j. forceful, compelling

Now choose five words from the above list and use each one in a sentence.

1. _____

_____

2. _____

_____

3. _____

_____

4. _____

_____

5. _____

_____

Name _____ **Date** _____

LIST IT!

Mexico is the United States' neighbor to the south. Mexico is a fascinating and beautiful country with much rich history and culture. Find some books that tell you about Mexico or find some people who know things about this country. If you are from Mexico, and if you already know a lot about the country, try to learn some new information. Then, make a list of interesting facts about Mexico.

_____

_____

_____

_____

_____

_____

_____

_____

_____

_____

_____

_____

_____

_____

Name _____ Date _____

△△△△△△△△△△△△△△△△△△△

WRITE ON!

Photographs capture poignant, important, and sometimes silly moments in our lives. Find a photo that you would like to write about. You can use a photo from home, or from a magazine or newspaper. The book *The Family of Man,* published for the Museum of Modern Art in New York (Maco Magazine Corporation, 1955), contains photos of people from 68 different countries in the world.

Once you have selected your photo, you can write about what is happening in the picture, or you can make up a story about the people in the photograph. You can make up a story about what happened before or after the photograph was taken. Let the photo inspire your imagination.

_____

_____

_____

_____

_____

_____

_____

_____

_____

_____

_____

_____

_____

Name _____   **Date** _____

OPEN SYLLABLE "u" AND OPEN SYLLABLE "e"

▣ GETTING STARTED

Discuss the three types of syllables discovered so far: closed syllables, vowel-consonant-e syllables, and open syllables. Provide time for your students to make a page in their notebooks for the open syllable with "o."

☾ INTRODUCING NEW INFORMATION

"Today, we are going to work with two different vowels in open syllables."
Say the following words: Cuba, Cupid, fuel, humid, unit, unite.
"What vowel sound do you hear in the first syllable of these words?"
"That's right, you hear a long 'u.'"
Record the following words: Cuba, Cupid, fuel, humid, unit, unite.
"What vowel do you see in the first syllable of these words?"
"Yes, long 'u.' What type of syllable are all these first syllables?"
"That's correct. They are open syllables because the single vowel ends the syllable."
Say the following words: duel, duo, student, tuba, tunic, Zulu.
"What vowel sound do you hear in the first syllable of all of these words?"
"Yes, the sound is an /oo/ as in 'tool.'"

186

Record the following words: duel, duo, student, tuba, tunic, Zulu.

"What vowel and syllable type do you see in all these first syllables?"

"I agree that all these syllables have the 'u' in open syllables. What can you say about this difference in sound?"

"That's right, in some open syllables with 'u,' the 'u' has the long 'u' sound. In other open syllables with 'u,' the 'u' represents the /oo/ sound as in 'tool.'"

"Now let's work with our second vowel."

Say the following words: begin, even, me, refresh, secret, veto.

"What sound do you hear in the first syllable of all these words?"

"Yes, I hear a long 'e' also."

Record the following words: begin, even, me, refresh, secret, veto.

"What vowel do you see in the first syllable of all of these words?"

"It's an 'e.' What type of syllable are these first syllables?"

"Yes, all these syllables are open syllables because they end with a single vowel."

❖ PRACTICING WITH INDIVIDUAL WORDS

Select a manageable number of words from the word list provided on page 189 for your students to spell.

⚊ PRACTICING SPELLING IN CONTEXT

Select a manageable number of sentences from the following list for your students to write.

He will take a trip to Sweden.

The reruns went on and on.

She regrets that she misbehaved.

"Even so, it is time to go home," Mom said.

He revised his plans so that he got to go to Munich.

In the U.S., we elect a president and a vice president.

The student sat at his desk and rested.

"It is futile to resist me," Beth said with a smile.

"Music helps me relax," Steve said.

"I predict that it will be hot and humid," Liz said.

◼ REINFORCING ACTIVITIES

Allow your students to choose from the following list of activities:

1. Select pairs of words that have either "e" in an open syllable or "u" in an open syllable; for example, "demand" and "secret," and "human" and "future." Make

33333

sentences with these pairs of words. An example for the last pair is, "In the future, humans will probably discover fascinating things about the universe." If you wish, illustrate one or more of your sentences.

2. "He (or she) is driving me up the wall!" is a cliché many of us have heard quite often. It means that someone is bothering us. The literal meaning of this cliché, however, is quite different and unique. Enjoy illustrating the literal meaning of this cliché.

3. Music is something that enriches all our lives. Carole King, a songwriter and singer, wrote a song that puts spelling into a song. Try to find Aretha Franklin's recording of Carole King's song "Respect." Once you have heard Ms. Franklin sing out R . . . E . . . S . . . P . . . E . . . C . . . T . . . , spelling will never again seem like a lifeless task!

4. LITERATURE CONNECTION: *To Be a Slave* by Julius Lester, illustrated by Tom Feelings (Dial Press, Inc., 1968) is a book that tells us what slavery was really like, because it is a compilation of what people who were slaves said and wrote about it. Read this book to learn about the auction block, plantation life, resistance to slavery, and many other aspects of slave life. Read *To Be a Slave* mostly, however, to gain a sense of the great courage of the people who were enslaved.

Ashanti to Zulu by Margaret Musgrove, illustrated by Leo and Diane Dillon (Dial Press, 1976), is an unusual alphabet picture book that tells of different groups of African people. The groups are arranged by names placed alphabetically. For each group, a beautiful painting and interesting information are presented.

⧛ EXTRA INTERESTING FACTS

Sometimes, a modern word is derived directly from an ancient source. Such is the case with "video." We all recognize this as the word for the taped movies we enjoy. But did you know that "video" is a Latin word that means "see"? It is fun to speculate how this very old word entered our modern language with no changes made to its form.

Our word "pupil" has a less direct derivation. This word comes from the Latin word "pupilla," which means a small doll. It is speculated that people thought that a group of young students looked like little dolls and, therefore, they called them "pupils."

WORD LIST

OPEN SYLLABLE "U," MULTISYLLABIC WORDS

accumulate	futile	puma
aluminum	future	pupil
calculate	human	student
Cuba	humid	stupid
cubic	impudent	tuba
Cupid	menu	tulip
duplex	music	tunic
duel	mutant	unit
duo	mutate	unite
fuel	peninsula	Zulu

OPEN SYLLABLE "E," ONE- AND MULTI-SYLLABLE WORDS

be	event	refund
begin	evil	regret
behave	feline	reject
belong	female	relax
beyond	frequent	remote
decide	he	rerun
defend	hero	respect
define	heroic	respond
demand	Korea	result
depend	me	revise
deposit	misbehave	secret
devote	predict	she
ego	pretend	veto
elect	prevent	we
elope	rebate	
even	refresh	

✣ ✣ ✣ ✣ ✣ ✣ ✣ ✣ ✣ ✣ ✣ ✣ ✣ ✣ ✣ ✣ ✣

FINISH IT!

Fill in the blanks with words from the word list.

1. "It is a _____ that Jack will not tell to anyone," Peg said.

2. Michael played his _____ in the marching band.

3. It was so cold, it felt like ten degrees below _____.

4. Manuel wrapped the potatoes in _____ foil and put them in the oven.

5. If a volcano is active, it can _____.

6. "I'm glad you have made up your mind and have _____ what to do," Dave said.

7. Many scientific advances will be made in the _____.

8. Sonia _____ money in the bank.

9. The _____ of his fall was a hurt knee.

10. In past times, men sometimes fought _____.

WORD LIST

erupt	tuba
zero	decided
secret	aluminum
result	deposited
future	duels

Name _____ **Date** _____

A GAME OF CATEGORIES

Choose words from your word list that belong in each category.

PLACES

_____

_____

_____

_____

_____

RELATING TO FEELINGS

_____

_____

_____

_____

RELATING TO MATHEMATICS

_____

_____

_____

_____

PEOPLE

_____

_____

_____

_____

WORD LIST

tabulate	elated
Cuba	Pasadena
zero	regret
respect	he
cubic	Korea
we	calculate
detest	repent
Munich	me
she	Sweden

Name _____ **Date** _____

LOOK IT UP!

Look up the listed words in your dictionary. Then match each word with its correct definition.

1. depot   a. a disturbance

2. cumulus   b. a stone used for polishing

3. edict   c. a warehouse or a railroad station

4. impudent   d to stop

5. pumice   e. an official proclamation

6. defunct   f. a bone in the leg of a person

7. betroth   g. a type of cloud

8. tumult   h. promise to be married

9. desist   i. bold and offensive, not modest

10. fibula   j. extinct, no longer existing

Now choose five words from the above list and use each one in a sentence.

1. _____

_____

2. _____

_____

3. _____

_____

4. _____

_____

5. _____

_____

Name _____ **Date** _____

LIST IT!

Menus are lists people sometimes make when they are planning a special meal, or when they are letting other people know what they will be eating. Make a menu of a special meal you would like to have. Include all of your favorite foods. Remember to include an appetizer as well as salad and soup, bread, vegetable(s), main dish, and dessert.

If you wish, you can invent some special foods; for example, a chocolate cake with five layers of frosting: vanilla, butterscotch, fudge, maple walnut, and coconut. You can also choose to write a humorous menu. For example, how would you like a slice of pizza with salamanders and toads?

_____

_____

_____

_____

_____

_____

_____

_____

_____

_____

_____

Name _____ **Date** _____

WRITE ON!

Write a *Famous Person and Me* story. This activity is inspired by the book *Ben and Me: An Astonishing Life of Benjamin Franklin by His Good Mouse Amos,* discovered, edited and illustrated by Robert Lawson (Little, Brown and Company, 1939).

In *Ben and Me,* Benjamin Franklin's longtime friend and companion, Amos the mouse, tells the true story: it was Amos—not Mr. Franklin—who was responsible for much of the good man's famous inventions. Amos's record may not agree with most historians, but his account is, nonetheless, most inspiring to read.

Choose a famous person whom you would like to study. Check encyclopedias and other sources to gather information. Then, write a story about the person from an animal's point of view.

Here are two ideas:

1. Write a story about Alexander the Great from the point of view of his horse.

2. Write a story about Amelia Earhart from the point of view of her cat.

_____

_____

_____

_____

_____

_____

_____

_____

_____

_____

Name _____   **Date** _____

OPEN SYLLABLE AT THE END OF WORDS "y"

▣ GETTING STARTED

Ask your students to tell you about open syllables. Spend a little time looking around the room and even checking in books to find some open syllables with the five vowels studied. Ask your students if they have noticed any open syllables outside of school; for example, in a brand name such as "Volvo."

Give your students time to make two pages in their notebooks, one for open syllable with "u" and one for open syllable with "e."

◖ INTRODUCING NEW INFORMATION

"Today, we are going to study an open syllable with a sixth vowel. Can you think of a sixth vowel?"

"That's right. Sometimes, the letter 'y' is used as a vowel."

Say the following words: cry, dry, fly, my, sky, try.

"What vowel sound do you hear in these words?"

"Yes, I also hear a long 'i.'"

Record the following words: cry, dry, fly, my, sky, try.

"What vowel do you see in these words?"

195

"Right, you see a 'y' in an open syllable. How many syllables does each of these words have?"

"I agree that each word has one syllable."

Say the following words: chilly, dusty, happy, industry, penny, twenty.

"What vowel sound do you hear at the end of these words?"

"Yes, you hear a long 'e.'"

Record the following words: chilly, dusty, happy, industry, penny, twenty.

"What vowel do you see at the end of all of these words?"

"That's correct, there is a 'y.' What type of syllables are they?"

"I agree, they are open syllables, because a single vowel ends the syllable. In these words, are there more than one syllable?"

"Yes, there are."

Present the lists of one syllable and multisyllabic words.

"Can you make up a generalization for words that end with 'y'?"

"Very good. When a one-syllable word ends with 'y,' the word ends with the long 'i' sound. When a multisyllabic word ends with 'y,' the word usually ends with the long 'e' sound."

❖ PRACTICING WITH INDIVIDUAL WORDS

Select a manageable number of words from the word list provided on page 199 for your students to spell.

⑤ PRACTICING SPELLING IN CONTEXT

Select a manageable number of sentences from the following list for your students to write.

Henry likes sticky candy.

Patty got the red ruby glass at the shop.

"It is my duty to ask," said the sentry.

Sixty times ten is six hundred.

"That lamp is so ugly, it is disgusting," Jeff said.

"Why is the baby upset?" Kate asked.

"I am so hungry. Let's go and get lunch," Lucy said.

The student had twenty funny poems in his desk.

Bruce put lumpy gravy on his baked potato.

Jan picked up the rusty can and put it on the shelf.

◼ REINFORCING ACTIVITIES

Allow your students to choose from the following list of activities:

1. Select pairs of words, one of which is a one-syllable word ending in "y," and the other being a multisyllabic word ending in "y"; for example, "fly" and "silly," and "shy" and "kitty." Make sentences with these pairs of words. An example for the last pair is, "The kitty was happy and definitely not shy." If you wish, illustrate one or more of your sentences.

2. Play a "Quick-Match" card game. Make up a deck of cards, each card having a one-syllable word written on it. Make sure you write words with all three syllable types discovered so far: closed, vowel-consonant-e, and open. For this game, it is best to have a big deck of cards.

   Find a friend or two who would like to play this game. Give each player at least twenty cards. All players sit with their cards in front of them, face down on the table. When the leader says "Go!" all players pick up their cards and place them in three piles: one pile has closed syllable words, the second has vowel-consonant-e words, and the third has open syllable words. The first player who finishes arranging all her or his cards, wins the game.

3. Make a "Tiny Twenty" picture. Cut a piece of paper, no larger than 5″ × 8″. You can also use the blank side of a 5″ × 8″ index card for your drawing. You arc going to make a picture that contains twenty of the same object. You can make your drawing be realistic, as of a forest that has twenty trees or a garden that has twenty flowers. If you wish, you can create a design, as with twenty stars all overlapping or twenty representations of the letter "y."

4. LITERATURE CONNECTION: A biography tells the story of a person's life. A biography usually contains more than just dates and facts about what a person did and when he or she did it. Good biographies usually attempt to show what a person was like, so that the reader feels that he or she has a "sense" of the person.

   Lincoln: A Photobiography by Russell Freedman (Clarion Books, Ticknor and Fields, a Houghton Mifflin Company, 1987) is a fascinating account of Abraham Lincoln. Read this book to feel that you have had a personal encounter with the man.

   If there are historical figures in whom you are particularly interested, go to your library and try to find a biography of him or her. Biographies are usually in their own separate section of the library.

▧ EXTRA INTERESTING FACTS

"Merry-go-sorry" is an expression that has "died" in the English language. Can you figure out what it meant? It had a logical meaning. "Merry-go-sorry" used to represent a story that made the reader feel both happy and sad.

The letter "y" is fascinating because it represents or "borrows" so many different sounds in English. First, as you know, it can be a consonant, as in "yellow" and "yes."

The letter "y" is often used as a vowel. In this lesson, you have discovered its two sounds at the ends of words. But the letter "y" is also used in two other ways as a vowel. First, it represents the short "i" sound in closed syllables such as in "myth" and "Olympics." Second, it represents the long "i" sound in open syllables in some multi-syllabic words such as "cyclone" and "hydrogen."

Don't worry about remembering all these different sounds of "y." You can always check your dictionary if you are unsure of a correct spelling. Also, if you spell a word incorrectly with an "i" in place of a "y," a spell check on a computer can also point out the correct spelling.

WORD LIST

OPEN SYLLABLE "Y," ONE-SYLLABLE WORDS

by	ply	spy
cry	pry	thy
dry	shy	try
fly	sky	why
fry	sly	
my	spry	

OPEN SYLLABLE "Y," AT THE END OF MULTISYLLABIC WORDS

baby	hilly	rusty
belly	hobby	sentry
bumpy	holly	seventy
bunny	holy	shabby
candy	hungry	shady
chilly	icy	shiny
clumsy	ivy	silly
copy	jelly	sixty
cozy	Judy	skinny
dusty	lady	sloppy
duty	lazy	sticky
empty	lucky	sunny
enemy	nasty	taffy
entry	navy	tidy
envy	ninety	tiny
fifty	pantry	truly
funny	Patty	twenty
gravy	penny	ugly
grumpy	plenty	wavy
happy	pony	windy
hazy	risky	
Henry	ruby	

FINISH IT!

Fill in the blanks with words from the word list.

1. Carlotta's _____ is collecting stamps.

2. Ten times five is _____.

3. The _____ was too young to be ridden.

4. "It must be wonderful to be able to _____ like a bird," Lucy said.

5. The laundry on the line blew all around because it was so

   _____.

6. Luis joined the _____ so that he could be a sailor.

7. "You can boil, bake, or _____ potatoes," Henry told Maria.

8. Helen waxed her car until it was _____.

9. The stranger was accused of being a _____.

10. The poem was so _____ that all the people laughed.

© 1996 by Cynthia Stowe

WORD LIST

fly	windy
shiny	pony
fifty	spy
silly	fry
navy	hobby

Name _____   **Date** _____

A GAME OF CATEGORIES

Choose words from your word list that belong in each category.

NUMBERS

_____

_____

_____

_____

_____

HOW OR WHAT YOU CAN FEEL

_____

_____

_____

_____

WORDS THAT DESCRIBE THE WEATHER

_____

_____

_____

RELATING TO APPEARANCE

_____

_____

_____

WORD LIST

angry	sixty
sultry	happy
shiny	chilly
twenty	dusty
fifty	silly
shabby	sunny
grumpy	seventy
windy	envy
ninety	filthy

Name _____   **Date** _____

LOOK IT UP!

Look up the listed words in your dictionary. Then match each word with its correct definition.

1.	ruddy	a.	full of surprises, sly
2.	spry	b.	a little song
3.	scanty	c.	too small an amount, barely enough
4.	amnesty	d.	being of reddish color
5.	wily	e.	a ravine created by water flow
6.	giddy	f.	a pardon, often of an official nature
7.	cranny	g.	to be dizzy, to feel whirled about
8.	gully	h.	something that is made from used or poor quality material
9.	ditty	i.	active, full of energy
10.	shoddy	j.	tiny opening or crack, as in a huge rock

Now choose five words from the above list and use each one in a sentence.

1. _____

_____

2. _____

_____

3. _____

_____

4. _____

_____

5. _____

_____

Name _____   Date _____

LIST IT!

Think about what it would be like if all people could live in a Land of Plenty. Would all people have enough to eat? Would there be homes for everyone?

Make a list of what you would like to see in the Land of Plenty. You can list things of the material world; for example, everyone will have a warm winter coat. You can also list things related to feelings; for example, all people will be good to each other.

_____

_____

_____

_____

_____

_____

_____

_____

_____

_____

_____

_____

_____

_____

Name _____   **Date** _____

WRITE ON!

Do you know what it feels like to be grumpy about something you have bought, something that has not been of the quality that you expected? Express these feelings. Write a letter of complaint.

It can be especially fun to invent a purchase. Then your letter of complaint is not bound by the laws of truth.

There are several words that end in open syllable "y" that express negative qualities; for example: filthy, shoddy, nasty, rusty, sticky, sloppy. Try to use a few of these in your letter.

The following is a short example of such a letter (a fictional one).

January 3, 19XX

Dear Sirs,

Two weeks ago, I purchased from you what I believed to be a fine pair of snowshoes. They looked shiny. They looked new. They weren't rusty or sloppy. As soon as it snowed last weekend, I set out to explore the forest.

I was a mile out when disaster struck. My snowshoes fell apart! Obviously, they were of shoddy construction and of sloppy workmanship. All I know is, I had to trudge home, without snowshoes, through deep snow.

I want my money back!

A Very Grumpy Customer

Name _____   **Date** _____

THE
DOUBLING RULE

▣ GETTING STARTED

Tell your students to look through their notebooks and to find some information that they wish to share about the English language. Then ask if they remember the six vowels that are present in open syllables. Discuss these six vowels. Provide time for your students to make a page for their notebooks for "y" in open syllables.

◖● INTRODUCING NEW INFORMATION

"In today's study, we are going to work with an important spelling rule."
Record the following words: big, drop, grin, plan, sit, stop.
"Tell me what you notice about these words."
"That's correct. They are all closed syllable words that end with a single consonant. They each have one syllable."
Keep your previous list on the table where your students can see it. Then record the following words: biggest, dropped, grinning, planned, sitting, stopped.
"What do you notice about these words?"
"Yes, in each case, a suffix has been added to the smaller or 'root' word."
"Is that all that has happened?"

205

"Good, the consonant at the end of the root word has been doubled."

Record the following words: flat, glad, job, sad, ship, spot.

"Are these all closed syllable words that end in a single consonant?"

"I agree."

Keep this list of words on the table where your students can see it. Then record the following words: flatness, gladness, jobless, sadness, shipment, spotless.

"What do you notice about these words?"

"That's right, a suffix has been added to all the root words, but the last consonant has not been doubled. Can you figure out why?" Place all four lists on the table in clear view.

"Great, you've figured it out. The last consonant in a closed syllable word is doubled when a suffix that begins with a vowel is added. When a suffix that begins with a consonant is added, no doubling occurs."

Record the following words: camp, dress, fish, plant, sell, trust.

"Let's look for a minute at closed syllable words that end in more than one consonant. Do you think the last consonant will be doubled when a suffix beginning with a vowel is added?"

"Let's check." Record the following words: camped, dressed, fishing, planting, selling, trusted.

"Are the last consonants doubled?"

"No, they are not. Can you figure out a simple way of remembering when to double the last consonant of a closed syllable word?"

"That's correct. You double the last consonant of a closed syllable word when the word has one syllable, ends in one consonant, and the suffix begins with a vowel."

❖ PRACTICING WITH INDIVIDUAL WORDS

Select a manageable number of words from the word list provided on page 209 for your students to spell.

ⓢ PRACTICING SPELLING IN CONTEXT

Select a manageable number of sentences from the following list for your students to write. For the sentence that contains the word with the apostrophe, assess if your students know how to use this punctuation mark. If they do not, provide a model for the word.

The man acted restless.

"I was just kidding," Peggy said.

Janet and David went shopping at the mall.

Pete dropped the glass and spilled his milk.

"It is getting hot, so let's go swimming," Pam said.

The rabbit hopped past the potato plants but then stopped and ate a radish plant.

"It is getting late and we cannot stop to rest," Judy said.

Jack is used to winning at chess.

She is digging a well, so she is tired.

Nick chopped up a big tomato and put it in a pot on the stove.

◼ REINFORCING ACTIVITIES

Allow your students to choose from the following list of activities:

1. Challenge yourself to write sentences that each have more than two words in which the final consonant of the root word is doubled. An example of such a sentence is, "When Helen stopped being careful, she tripped and dropped her book." If you wish, illustrate one or more of your sentences.

2. Play a "Quick Act" game. For this game, you will need a pair of dice, a stopwatch or a watch with a good second hand, and some blank cards. Make a deck of ten to fifteen cards, each of which has an action word that illustrates the doubling rule written on it. Good words are: jumping, ripping, swimming, dragging, clapping, hugging, hopping, chopping, spinning, digging, grabbing, jogging, trotting, tapping, sagging.

   Gather together at least four other people to play this game. Show all the players the cards with the words written on them. Then place the cards face side down on the table.

   Select a person who will be responsible for keeping time. Then form two teams. Roll a pair of dice to determine which team will start the game. Then select a player on each team who will be the "actor."

   When the game begins, each team gets one minute for each round. The first "actor" picks a card off the table, keeps it secret, and acts out the word. If his team guesses the correct word, he can keep the card and select another and then another, until the team's time is up. Then the second team has a turn. The team that has the most cards at the end, wins the game.

3. The cliché "My nose is running" means that you have a cold or a sinus infection. The literal meaning of this cliché is very different, however, and quite amusing. Draw a picture that illustrates the literal meaning of this cliché.

4. LITERATURE CONNECTION: In the book *The Cat Who Came for Christmas* by Cleveland Amory (Penguin Books, 1988), we read the true story of how Mr. Amory helped rescue his cat Polar Bear from a New York City alley. He only intended to shelter the cat in his apartment temporarily, but the cat had other ideas. Thus, their relationship began.

   The Cat Who Came for Christmas begins at Christmas time, but it is not truly a Christmas tale. It is a story of bragging about Polar Bear. In the midst of this bragging (and Polar Bear certainly deserves every sentence), there is a tale full of great warmth and humor.

⧈ EXTRA INTERESTING FACTS

It is believed that the word "zip," which becomes "zipped" in the past tense, comes from a very unique sound that people tried to describe: the sound of a bullet flying by. The word "zipper" is also believed to have originated when people tried to express what it sounded like when the fastener was connected. Do you hear a sound in this sentence, "She zipped up her jacket"?

WORD LIST

CLOSED SYLLABLE WORDS ENDING IN ONE CONSONANT FOR THE DOUBLING RULE

beg + g + ed

big + g + est

brag + g + ing

chop + p + ed

clap + p + ing

dig + g + ing

drag + g + ed

drop + p + ed

flat + ness

fret + ful

get + t + ing

glad + ness

grin + n + ed

hit + t + ing

hop + p + ed

hot + t + est

hug + g + ed

job + less

kid + d + ing

map + p + ed

pet + t + ed

plan + n + ed

rap + p + ed

rip + p + ed

rub + b + ing

sad + ness

ship + ment

shop + p + ing

sit + t + ing

slam + m + ed

snap + p + ed

spin + n + ing

spot + less

stop + p + ed

swim + m + ing

thin + n + est

trap + p + ed

trip + p + ed

wag + g + ed

win + n + ing

CLOSED SYLLABLE WORDS ENDING IN TWO CONSONANTS FOR THE DOUBLING RULE

act + ed

bash + ful

camp + ed

crush + ed

damp + est

dress + ing

fill + ed

fish + ing

fond + ness

fresh + est

gasp + ed

hand + ful

help + less

hunt + ing

ill + ness

jump + ing

land + ed

lift + ed

limp + ing

melt + ed

miss + ed

pass + ing

plant + ed

print + ed

rent + ing

rest + ful

rich + est

rush + ing

self + less

sell + ing

send + ing

skill + ful

soft + est

stamp + ed

thrill + ing

toss + ed

trust + ed

vast + ness

wish + ed

yell + ed

❄ ❄ ❄ ❄ ❄ ❄ ❄ ❄ ❄ ❄ ❄ ❄ ❄ ❄ ❄ ❄ ❄ ❄

FINISH IT!

Fill in the blanks with words from the word list.

1. Fran was hungry, so she ate the _____ piece of pizza.

2. The audience _____ loudly because they liked the show.

3. "Why are you _____ your car?" Eduardo asked.

4. Tom _____ that it was easy for him to lift one hundred pounds.

5. Mulugeta _____ the scrap paper into the recycling bin.

6. The policeman _____ traffic.

7. The dog was so happy, he couldn't stop _____ his tail.

8. They hiked into the woods and then _____ for two days.

9. "I'm tired of _____ at this desk all day," Brenda said, "so let's take a walk."

10. Jim _____ butter for the popcorn.

WORD LIST

selling	stopped
wagging	biggest
tossed	melted
sitting	bragged
clapped	camped

Name _____   **Date** _____

A GAME OF CATEGORIES

Choose words from your word list that belong in each category.

RELATING TO COMMUNICATION

_____

_____

_____

_____

TO HAVE HIT

_____

_____

_____

_____

_____

RELATING TO THE PREPARATION OF FOOD

_____

_____

_____

RELATING TO MOVEMENT

_____

_____

_____

WORD LIST

telling

stepping

bashed

chopping

thrashed

spinning

mashing

bragging

jumping

melting

calling

hopping

smashed

chatting

clubbed

cutting

begging

jabbed

Name _____   **Date** _____

LOOK IT UP!

Look up the listed words in your dictionary. Then match each word with its correct definition.

1. wafted
2. glutted
3. tamped
4. whetting
5. flitting
6. hulled
7. chugged
8. gushing
9. sopped
10. lilting

a. to have put too many of a product on the market
b. to have taken off the outside protective covering, as of a seed or a nut
c. a sudden outpouring
d. to have a light and happy quality
e. to have pounded down
f. to have made a repetitive sound
g. to have absorbed liquid
h. to have traveled on the air, as with a smell
i. to make more intense, as with an appetite
j. to make a quick movement

Now choose five words from the above list and use each one in a sentence.

1. _____

_____

2. _____

_____

3. _____

_____

4. _____

_____

5. _____

_____

Name _____   **Date** _____

LIST IT!

Make a list of things that will keep you grinning. Three possible examples are:

1. having no homework assignment

2. watching a friend be successful

3. being invited to a special event

Perhaps, even making this list will keep you grinning!

_____

_____

_____

_____

_____

_____

_____

_____

_____

_____

_____

_____

Name _____ **Date** _____

WRITE ON!

Write a "Just Kidding" poem. This is a special kind of poem where you write down the words JUST KIDDING, one letter to a line, like the following:

J
U
S
T

K
I
D
D
I
N
G

Then write a sentence starting with each letter, as with the following:

Jelly fish are made of raspberry jam.

Unicorns are tired of not being noticed.

Sensational Martians are living in my kitchen.

Trees are green umbrellas created for birds.

. . . and so on with KIDDING.

Because this is a "Just Kidding" poem, you can make up silly or imaginative lines. It's helpful to use a dictionary to find excellent words for the first words of your sentences.

Use the back of this sheet for your "Just Kidding" poem.

Name _____   **Date** _____

SIX COMMON PREFIXES

▣ GETTING STARTED

Ask your students to tell you about the two spelling rules they have discovered: the "E" rule and the Doubling rule. Work with some vowel-consonant-e words, such as "drive," and add endings to them; for example, "drive" + "ing" = "driving." Then, work with some closed syllable words such as "sit," and add endings to them; for example, "sit" + "ing" = "sitting." Discuss how a person can know when to use the "E" rule and when to use the Doubling rule.

Provide time for your students to make a page in their notebooks for the Doubling rule.

◖ INTRODUCING NEW INFORMATION

"Today, we will be working with prefixes. Prefixes are beginnings that are added to words to change their meanings. Prefixes are little syllables like 'un' and 'sub.'

"There are many prefixes in the English language, many of which come from Latin, Anglo-Saxon, and Greek. Today, we're going to focus on six of them."

Write the following on either a large piece of paper or the chalkboard. Then say, *"You already know a lot about prefixes. Match the prefixes with their correct meanings in the chart below."*

215

1. un- (unlike)	a. under
2. mis- (misplace)	b. into
3. sub- (subtropics)	c. across
4. trans- (transmit)	d. not
5. in- (inland)	e. back + again
6. re- (rebate + rerun)	f. wrong

If your students have difficulty figuring out all the prefixes, give them more examples (refer to the word list on page 219).

The correct answers are: 1. d; 2. f; 3. a; 4. c; 5. b; 6. e.

Prefixes sometimes confuse students because one prefix can have more than one meaning, as in "re-" meaning "back" and "again." The prefix "in" can also mean "not" as in "ingrate," but this meaning is not presented in this lesson.

One goal of this lesson is to help students gain the understanding that words can be built upon, and that prefixes are an important addition to the English language. A second goal is to help students become interested in prefixes. Memorizing many prefixes and their meanings is not necessary, and can, in fact, be counter-productive.

❖ PRACTICING WITH INDIVIDUAL WORDS

Select a manageable number of words from the word list provided on page 219 for your students to spell.

Ⓢ PRACTICING SPELLING IN CONTEXT

Select a manageable number of sentences from the following list for your students to write.

Patty instructed Beth in math.

Don misplaced his pen and pencil.

"I will transplant this rose bush into a sunny spot," Jeff said.

The quiet pond reflected the sun.

"It is unlike Tom to not let us help him," Janet said.

Sandy invited Mike to go shopping at the mall.

Tim made the mistake of trusting Luke with his secret.

Jane lived in the subtropics last fall.

"This writing is French, but I can translate it," Peggy said.

Judy will replace the glass vase she broke.

◼ REINFORCING ACTIVITIES

Allow your students to choose from the following list of activities:

1. Challenge yourself to write sentences that each have more than two words with prefixes you have studied. An example is, "Inside the prison, the inmates mistrusted everyone." If you wish, illustrate one or more of your sentences.

2. Do you think the prefix "un" is a common one? Can you guess how many words there are in the dictionary that begin with "un"? Write down your guess on a piece of paper, and then ask other people for their estimates, also.

   When all the guesses are collected, look up "un" in your dictionary and count the words. How close did you get? If you wish, guess how many words begin with "mis," and then try the other prefixes with which you have worked.

3. Play "Prefix Concentraton." For this game, you will need twenty blank pieces of paper (3 × 5 index cards work well) and a pair of dice.

   Select ten words that contain root words and prefixes. Write down the prefixes, one to a card, and the root words on the others. Place all twenty cards face down on the table in a random order.

   Find a friend to play "Prefix Concentration," and then roll the dice to select the first player. That person turns over two cards. If she has selected a prefix and a root word that combine to create a real word (like "re" + "run" = "rerun"), she keeps the cards and gets another turn. If she has not selected such a word, she replaces the cards face down, and the next player gets a turn. The player with more cards at the end, wins the game.

4. LITERATURE CONNECTION: Some prefixes refer specifically to numbers. "Bi" means two, as in "bicycle," or "a cycle that has two wheels." "Tri" refers to the number three.

   The Tripods Trilogy by John Christopher (Collier Books, Macmillan Publishing Company, 1967) is a set of three science fiction books. The story begins long after most men have forgotten what it is like to live free on Earth. Instead, they are used to the domination of the Tripods, three-legged machines that, long ago, took control.

   The three books in the series are: *The White Mountains, The City of Gold and Lead* and *The Pool of Fire*. Read these books for wonderful stories of courage, resistance, and escape. The stories are fast paced, but also filled with interesting and thoughtful characters.

⧓ EXTRA INTERESTING FACTS

Some root words have more than one prefix that can be added to them. One such root word is "duct." It is easy to see how "duct," which means a tube or channel, is derived from the Latin "ductus" (something that leads). "Ductus" is a form of the Latin word "ducere," which means "to lead."

When the prefix "in" is added to "duct," the new word "induct" is created. This refers to leading someone in, as when a new person is officially invited to join a new organization. When the prefix "ab," which means "away," is added to "duct," the new word "abduct" is created. This means to lead away, as when a person is captured and taken away against his or her will.

WORD LIST

SIX COMMON PREFIXES

Words with the prefix "un"

uneven	unrest
unfit	unripe
unjust	unsafe
unlike	unspoken
unlock	unwise

Words with the prefix "in"

indent	inside
inflate	intake
inhale	intrude
inland	invade
inmate	invite

Words with the prefix "mis"

misconduct	misprint
misfire	misquote
misfit	misspell
mishap	mistake
misplace	mistrust

Words with the prefix "trans"

transact	transmit
transatlantic	transpose
transfuse	transplant
transit	translate
translucent	transcribe

Words with the prefix "sub"

subclass	subplot
subcontinent	subside
subject	subsist
sublet	subtract
submit	subtropics

Words with the prefix "re"

(meaning "back")	*(meaning "again")*
rebate	refill
recall	replace
reflect	reprint
	rerun
	resell

FINISH IT!

Fill in the blanks with words from the word list.

1. Jan went on the _____ voyage to Europe.

2. Tae watched _____ on TV all afternoon.

3. Ted had such a bad sinus infection, it was hard for him to

   _____.

4. The waters _____ after the flood.

5. The words were _____, so the secret was not revealed.

6. The senator was angry because he had been _____ in the newspaper.

7. Thomas Edison _____ an early phonograph.

8. "That puppy _____ strangers and runs away from them," Sophia said.

9. The bridge was _____, so they did not cross it.

10. The _____ of the book is the Civil War.

WORD LIST

receded	unsafe
mistrusts	reruns
misquoted	transatlantic
invented	subject
inhale	unspoken

Name _____   **Date** _____

A GAME OF CATEGORIES

Choose words from your word list that belong in each category.

HAVING NEGATIVE CHARACTERISTICS

_____

_____

_____

_____

_____

THINGS YOU DO WITH WORDS

_____

_____

_____

_____

_____

RELATING TO MOVEMENT

_____

_____

_____

_____

RELATING TO GEOGRAPHY

_____

_____

_____

_____

WORD LIST

translate	unjust
repel	reprint
unsafe	transatlantic
misfit	subcontinent
transit	invade
unwise	inland
transcribe	subtropics
inscribe	recede
rewrite	unfit

Name _____   Date _____

LOOK IT UP!

Look up the listed words in your dictionary. Then match each word with its correct definition.

1. misapprehend   a. to excel above all normal limits

2. rebuff   b. to publicly withdraw a previously held belief

3. uncanny   c. to cut across

4. recant   d. to not understand

5. unwitting road   e. the layer that forms the foundation, as of a

6. subjugate   f. to rudely refuse

7. transcend   g. to gain power over another person or group of people

8. inequity   h. to be unaware

9. subgrade   i. having a mysterious quality

10. transit   j. an injustice

Now choose five words from the above list and use each one in a sentence.

1. _____

_____

2. _____

_____

3. _____

_____

4. _____

_____

5. _____

_____

Name _____ **Date** _____

LIST IT!

The word "reflect" can mean to give back an image, as a mirror reflects our likenesses. "Reflect" can also mean to think seriously about something important.

Take some time and reflect on the work you have been doing with spelling. Then make a list of some of your thoughts. You can include your ideas about:

1. what you have enjoyed learning

2. what you have not enjoyed about spelling

3. what has been easiest to learn

4. what has been difficult to learn

5. what you feel your progress has been

6. what you would like to accomplish for the rest of this year

7. suggestions you would like to give to your teacher for helping you to learn in the future

_____

_____

_____

_____

_____

_____

_____

_____

Name _____ **Date** _____

WRITE ON!

This activity is called: "It's All a Big Mistake!" First, select a character from folk literature who does not have a good reputation, such as Cinderella's stepmother. Write a story from the point of view of this character, telling why all the recorded facts are wrong. For example, the stepmother might start by saying:

"Complain! Complain! That's all she ever does these days. I was teaching Cinderella how to cook and clean for her own good. How did I know she'd end up with a Prince?

"But let me tell you my side of the story."

_____

_____

_____

_____

_____

_____

_____

_____

_____

_____

_____

_____

_____

_____

Name _____ **Date** _____

VOWEL COMBINATION SYLLABLE
"ai"

▣ GETTING STARTED

Discuss the three syllable types discovered so far. Ask your students to talk about short vowels and long vowels. Then ask them to tell you how many ways they could spell the long "a" sound if they heard it in a word. If they have difficulty with this, tell them to check their notebooks for assistance.

Once they have realized that they now can spell long "a" with either a vowel-consonant-e syllable, as in "game," or with an open syllable, as in "ta-ble," discuss some words from both syllable types. The most important aspect of this discussion is to help your students understand that a long vowel sound can be spelled more than one way.

Spend a few minutes talking about prefixes with your students. Then give them time to make a page for their notebooks.

◖ INTRODUCING NEW INFORMATION

"Today, you are going to discover a fourth type of syllable."
Say the following words: aim, braid, paint, rain, tail, wait.
"What vowel sound do you hear in these words?"
"Yes, you hear long 'a.'"

225

Record the following words: aim, braid, paint, rain, tail, wait.
"What vowels do you see in these words?"
"That's right, you see an 'a' and an 'i' together. Do they make one sound?"
"I agree. You have just discovered your fourth type of syllable. When two vowels that are together make one vowel sound, the syllable is called a vowel combination syllable."
Record the following words: explain, inlaid, plainspoken, raisin, retail, waitress.
"Do you see any vowel combination syllables in these multisyllabic words?"
"Yes, each of these words has a vowel combination syllable with 'ai.' Therefore, we see that this syllable type also occurs in multisyllabic words."

❖ PRACTICING WITH INDIVIDUAL WORDS

Select a manageable number of words from the word list provided on page 228 for your students to spell.

⑤ PRACTICING SPELLING IN CONTEXT

Select a manageable number of sentences from the following list for your students to write.

Steve claims that he can stand on his hands.

Beth felt sick and then she fainted.

The cat chased his tail.

Amy and Ben painted the cabin red.

"Wait until ten and then go shopping," Jack said.

It got quiet and then, all of a sudden, the wind and the rain came.

Jeff paid the man, got his ticket, and then went on the train.

"I will explain it all when I get home," Kate said.

Beth liked the landscape painting and the painting of the black cat.

"I still maintain that that puppy has a pain in his leg," Pete said.

▣ REINFORCING ACTIVITIES

Allow your students to choose from the following list of activities:

1. Select some words with "ai" vowel combination syllables, such as "claim," "painting," and "quaint," and say them slowly to yourself. How do these words sound to you? How does it feel to say them slowly and to listen carefully to their sounds?

Select some favorite words and write sentences with them. Make your sentences simple; for example, "The old inn was quaint." Then say your sentences slowly and listen to the sounds of the words. If you wish, illustrate one or more of your sentences.

2. Challenge yourself with the "Train Game." Begin with an initial statement, which is the "engine" of your train; for example, "I went to the store." Then add "cars" on your train by adding statements that begin with "because." To illustrate:

   I went to the store . . .

   because I wanted to buy some bread . . .

   because I wanted to make toast . . .

   because I was hungry . . .

   because I hadn't eaten since yesterday . . .

   because (and so on).

   The challenge is to make as long a "train" as you can.

3. We all know that the cliché "It's raining cats and dogs" means that it's raining hard outside. The literal meaning, however, is quite different. Illustrate the literal meaning of this cliché.

4. LITERATURE CONNECTION: Rain is necessary for our survival. Places where a great deal of rain falls are the rain forests. Over the past decade, we have come to learn how essential these places are for maintaining the health of the Earth.

   Two good picture books that help people gain understanding of rain forests are *The Giant Kapok Tree* by Lynne Cherry (Gulliver Books, Harcourt Brace Jovanovich, 1990) and *Rain Forest Secrets* by Arthur Dorros (Scholastic Inc., 1990).

⊡ EXTRA INTERESTING FACTS

There is much controversy about where the expression "It's raining cats and dogs" comes from. One popular belief is that it originates in Norse folklore, where cats had magical powers that could bring rain and dogs could call forth wind.

There is no record in history of it ever actually raining cats and dogs. An Associated Press article printed in *The Recorder* of Greenfield, Massachusetts on September 24, 1994, reports that there *have* been many recorded cases of other strange creatures and objects "raining" to the earth.

Greek historians recorded fish and frogs coming from the skies. In 1947, Marksville, Louisiana received a shower of bass, shad and other fish. In 1953, Leicester, Massachusetts had frogs "raining" down. A hailstone approximately the size of a volleyball fell on Coffeyville, Kansas in 1970. And pennies fell on Hanham, England in 1956.

Tornadoes and other natural phenomenon account for some of these occurences. But where did the money come from? Or the frogs?

WORD LIST

VOWEL COMBINATION SYLLABLE "AI," ONE-SYLLABLE WORDS

aid	jail	rain
aim	maid	sail
bait	mail	saint
braid	main	sprain
brain	nail	stain
chain	paid	strain
claim	pail	tail
drain	pain	trail
fail	paint	train
faint	plain	trait
frail	quail	wait
gain	quaint	waist
grain	raid	
hail	rail	

VOWEL COMBINATION SYLLABLE "AI," MULTISYLLABIC WORDS

abstain	explain	plainsman
ailment	faithful	prevail
aimless	ingrained	proclaim
attain	inlaid	raisin
attainment	maiden	regain
derail	mainland	remain
detail	maintain	restrain
detain	monorail	retail
disclaim	obtain	retain
disdain	painful	stainless
disdainful	painless	sustain
domain	painting	topsail
exclaim	pigtail	upbraid

❋ ❋ ❋ ❋ ❋ ❋ ❋ ❋ ❋ ❋ ❋ ❋ ❋ ❋ ❋ ❋ ❋

FINISH IT!

Fill in the blanks with words from the word list.

1. Dimitri hammered the _____ into the wall.

2. "Look at that beautiful sunset!" Judy _____.

3. Anna _____ her ankle when she fell off her bike.

4. He filled his _____ with soapy water and then washed the floor.

5. The bruise looked like it was _____.

6. Edna picked up her _____ at the post office.

7. "Please _____ seated," the speaker said.

8. Reyna and Liz were careful to stay on the _____ on their hike in the mountains.

9. The _____ they saw was a beautiful bird.

10. Meg took a _____ ride across Canada.

WORD LIST

painful   sprained
quail   remain
nail   train
trail   exclaimed
pail   mail

© 1996 by Cynthia Stowe

Name _____   **Date** _____

A GAME OF CATEGORIES

Choose words from your word list that belong in each category.

RELATING TO THE MAIL

_____

_____

_____

_____

THINGS DEFINED AS "NOT SOMETHING"

_____

_____

_____

_____

TO DO SOMETHING AGAIN

_____

_____

_____

_____

WAYS TO RESPOND TO FEELINGS

_____

_____

_____

_____

WORD LIST

mailbag	repaint
bewail	mailbox
unafraid	regain
retrain	unpaid
mailman	unexplained
exclaim	reclaim
mailing	wail
explain	postpaid
unpainted	unchained

Name _____ Date _____

LOOK IT UP!

Look up the listed words in your dictionary. Then match each word with its correct definition.

1. gait   a. a fold of fabric

2. upbraid   b. to fight against change, to be conservative

3. plait   c. the way one walks

4. acclaim   d. to harm or spoil

5. prevail   e. to not allow to leave

6. ingrained   f. to praise with great energy

7. staid   g. to criticize or scold

8. taint   h. wood paneling, especially on the lower portion of a wall

9. wainscot   i. to be completely established

10. detain   j. to overcome odds, to be successful

Now choose five words from the above list and use each one in a sentence.

1. _____

_____

2. _____

_____

3. _____

_____

4. _____

_____

5. _____

_____

Name _____ **Date** _____

LIST IT!

Write an "It Isn't Easy" list. Think of things that would be extremely difficult to accomplish. You can be serious with your list or you can be humorous, as in the following.

It isn't easy to:

1. lift a red Chevy truck

2. skateboard down Mt. Everest

3. memorize the dictionary

_____

_____

_____

_____

_____

_____

_____

_____

_____

_____

_____

_____

Name _____ **Date** _____

WRITE ON!

Do you get nervous when you have to explain about something you are not proud of? Perhaps all thoughts vanish from your head and you stand there, embarrassed and confused. Don't just wait for this to happen. Just for fun, prepare, in advance, some really ridiculous explanations.

For example, to explain why you were late, you could say:

I was almost here, ten minutes early, when I looked up in the sky and saw a flash of light. All of a sudden, my body felt light, and I noticed that my feet were no longer touching the ground. I was rising . . . rising . . . . Then, suddenly, I was back on the sidewalk. But it was two hours later!

If you wish, you could prepare an explanation for why you did not do your homework!

_____

_____

_____

_____

_____

_____

_____

_____

_____

_____

_____

Name _____   **Date** _____

SPELLING GENERALIZATION
"ai" and "ay"

▣ GETTING STARTED

Talk about the four types of syllables discovered so far. Discuss their special characteristics, and ask your students to choose one they feel is most common.

Direct the discussion to the vowel combination syllable with "ai." When they are ready, have your students record information about "ai" in their notebooks.

◖ INTRODUCING NEW INFORMATION

"Today, you are going to discover a new spelling generalization."
Say the following words: day, gray, May, play, ray, stay.
"What sound do you hear in each of these words?"
"That's right, long 'a.'"
Record the following words: day, gray, May, play, ray, stay.
"What do you notice?"
"Yes, they all have 'ay' in them. What type of syllable is this?"
"I agree that it is a vowel combination syllable, because the 'a' and the 'y' (which is a vowel in this word), stay together and make one sound. Now let's look at how you can figure out whether to use a vowel combination syllable with 'ai' or with 'ay' in a word."

234

Record these words in the following lists:

aid	pay
rain	stray
paid	bay
bait	way

"What do you notice?"
"That's what I see. It's an 'ai' when it's in the beginning or middle of a word and an 'ay' at the end."

Record the following words:

detain	betray
explain	display
painting	Friday
raisin	subway

"Is this generalization also true for multisyllabic words?"
"That's right. When you hear a long 'a' sound in the middle of a word, an option for spelling it is with the vowel combination syllable 'ai.' When you hear a long 'a' sound at the end of a word, it is usually spelled with the vowel combination syllable 'ay.'"

❖ PRACTICING WITH INDIVIDUAL WORDS

Select a manageable number of words from the word list provided on page 237 for your students to spell.

⑤ PRACTICING SPELLING IN CONTEXT

Select a manageable number of sentences from the following list for your students to write.

I will take a ride on the subway.

Tom put the bait in his pail.

Sam felt sad when it rained on Sunday.

He painted his home gray with red trim.

Did you spend time fishing in the bay?

If Jan cannot get tickets, she will stay home.

He cannot sustain himself with just raisins and milk. Can he?

"Fred did not stay at the game," Pete said.

"Will the big rain delay the train?" Fran asked.

Beth's painting is on display until Friday.

◼ REINFORCING ACTIVITIES

Allow your students to choose from the following list of activities:

1. Select some favorite words with "ai" or "ay" in them. Choose words that either sound good to you; for example, "pathway" or "gray," or words that you like for unexplained reasons. Write sentences with your favorite words. If you wish, illustrate one or more of your sentences.

2. See how many "ai" and "ay" words you can find in your dictionary. (*Hint*: Start with "rai" and see what you find.) Then, during the day, challenge yourself to notice as many words with "ai" and "ay" as you can. If you wish, record these words in your notebook.

3. Play syllable rummy. First, make a card deck with one word on each card. Choose one-syllable words from your "ai" and "ay" lists. Choose, also, one-syllable words from your work with closed syllables, vowel-consonant-e syllables, and open syllables.

   Each player starts the game with five cards. The rest of the deck is face down on the table. In turn, players pick a card from the top of the deck and discard one if they wish. If a player has at least three words with the same syllable type, she can place that grouping face up on the table, and she can add to it from future selections from the main deck. The winner is the first person who uses up all her cards to form groups of the same type of syllable.

4. LITERATURE CONNECTION: Plays are fun to perform in, but they are, also, surprisingly interesting to read. One such play is Paul Zindel's *The Effect of Gamma Rays on Man-in-the-Moon Marigolds* (Bantam Books, 1970).

   This play, which won the Pulitzer Prize, shows a young girl's struggle for hope in a less-than-"normal" family. It is a serious work, one full of much sadness and laughter. Once you have met Tillie, the young girl who experiments with the marigolds, it is hard to forget her.

▧ EXTRA INTERESTING FACTS

There are some cases where the "ay" occurs in the middle of words. In a word like "payday," this happens because it is a compound word. "Pay" and "day" could each stand alone but have been fused together by common use.

In words like "payment" and "playful," suffixes have been added to base words, pushing the "ay" back to the middle.

Some "ai" and "ay" words have interesting histories. For example, the word "assail," which means "to attack or hurt," comes from the Latin, "salio." "Salio" means "to jump." If we jump upon someone, we often hurt them. "Assailant" becomes "a person who jumps upon someone."

The word "X-ray" was invented by the famous German physicist Wilhelm Konrad von Roentgen who discovered the phenomenon in 1895. Because he did not know exactly what he had discovered, he called the radiation "X-strahlen," ("X-ray" in English). The "X" meant that he was unsure about what the rays actually were.

WORD LIST

VOWEL COMBINATION SYLLABLE "AY," ONE-SYLLABLE WORDS

bay	may	shay
clay	May	slay
day	nay	spray
fray	pay	stay
gay	play	stray
gray	pray	tray
hay	ray	way
jay	Ray	
lay	say	

VOWEL COMINATION SYLLABLE "AY," MULTISYLLABIC WORDS

ashtray	Friday	pathway
astray	gainsay	prepay
beltway	getaway	raceway
betray	gunplay	railway
bikeway	halfway	relay
Bombay	hallway	repay
castaway	holiday	replay
decay	inlay	runaway
defray	mainstay	runway
delay	midday	safeway
dismay	midway	subway
display	mislay	Sunday
driveway	misplay	teleplay
escapeway	nosegay	today
essay	okay	

FINISH IT!

Fill in the blanks with words from the word list.

1. The day after Saturday is _____.

2. When Jessie fell and broke her leg, it was very _____.

3. If you don't have to work, you can _____.

4. Lots of sun and _____ help a garden grow.

5. She will _____ the house white with blue trim.

6. The cat was a _____ before Pete gave him a home.

7. "I will _____ why I was an hour late," Naomi said.

8. He had to write an _____ for English class.

9. The _____ ride from New York to Washington, D.C. takes only a few hours.

10. "Let's _____ here at the inn and hike in the mountains," Alex said.

WORD LIST

stay   paint

painful   stray

explain   play

rain   train

Sunday   essay

© 1996 by Cynthia Stowe

Name _____   **Date** _____

A GAME OF CATEGORIES

Choose words from your word list that belong in each category.

RELATING TO TRANSPORTATION

_____

_____

_____

_____

_____

PEOPLE

_____

_____

_____

_____

_____

RELATING TO INJURY OR ILLNESS

_____

_____

_____

_____

PARTS OF THE BODY

_____

_____

_____

_____

WORD LIST

Ray	saint
ailment	brain
runway	strain
pigtail	waist
train	maiden
sprain	subway
Fay	maid
braid	railway
faint	pathway

Name _____ **Date** _____

LOOK IT UP!

Look up the listed words in your dictionary. Then match each word with its correct definition.

1. shay
2. attainment
3. splay
4. domain
5. trait
6. fray
7. disdain
8. bray
9. hobnail
10. nosegay

a. a short nail
b. something that is gained, especially a skill
c. a bouquet of flowers
d. a little carriage drawn by a horse
e. to make a loud sound like a donkey
f. a special characteristic
g. to spread out or expand
h. a fight
i. to treat with contempt
j. land that belongs to a person or country

Now choose five words from the above list and use each one in a sentence.

1. _____

_____

2. _____

_____

3. _____

_____

4. _____

_____

5. _____

_____

Name _____   **Date** _____

LIST IT!

When people play, they have fun and enjoy themselves. What some people consider play, others do not; for example, some people enjoy doing crossword puzzles and others find this activity frustrating.

Make a list of different types of play. You can include games such as Connect Four, sports such as playing baseball and jumping rope, or other types of leisure activities such as walking or reading a good book.

If you wish to challenge yourself, choose a group of people you do not know, such as the Navajo or the Swedish people, and do research to find out what types of play these people enjoy.

_____

_____

_____

_____

_____

_____

_____

_____

_____

_____

_____

_____

Name _____ **Date** _____

WRITE ON!

The word "play" also refers to a literary form in which people act out conflicts and issues. The form relies on dialogue and action.

Write a short, one-act play. To do this, think of a situation that is full of drama. Then have your characters talk to each other and see what happens.

Two possible dramatic situations are:

1. Harry and Fred are standing in their empty classroom. Harry has just accidentally let the classroom pet, the mouse Broomhilda, escape from her cage.

2. Meg and Peter are sitting on Meg's front porch. Silently, Meg takes off her engagement ring and hands it to Peter.

_____

_____

_____

_____

_____

_____

_____

_____

_____

_____

_____

_____

Name _____ **Date** _____

VOWEL COMBINATION SYLLABLE "ee"

▣ GETTING STARTED

Ask your students to tell you how they would consider spelling the long "a" sound in a word. Once they tell you that they would decide among an open syllable, a vowel-consonant-e syllable, and a vowel combination syllable with "ai" or "ay," discuss the options. Talk about how dictionaries and spell checks can help them find the common spelling of a given word.

Discuss the spelling generalization with "ai" and "ay." Then give your students time to make a page for this information in their notebooks.

◖ INTRODUCING NEW INFORMATION

"Today, we are going to work with a new vowel combination syllable."
Say the following words: bee, deep, feet, need, speech, three.
"What sound do you hear in all these words?"
"Yes, you hear a long 'e' sound."
Record the following words: bee, deep, feet, need, speech, three.
"What do you notice about these words?"
"I agree that you see two 'e's together. What type of syllable is this?"

243

"That's right, this is a vowel combination syllable. Now let's check if this syllable type with 'ee' occurs in multisyllabic words."

Record the following words: agree, beehive, chickadee, freeway, sixteen, treetop.

"What do you notice about these words?"

"Good. The vowel combination syllable with 'ee' does occur in multisyllabic words. Also, in these words, we see examples of closed, open, vowel-consonant-e and the vowel combination syllable with 'ay.'"

❖ PRACTICING WITH INDIVIDUAL WORDS

Select a manageable number of words from the word list provided on page 246 for your students to spell.

☯ PRACTICING SPELLING IN CONTEXT

Select a manageable number of sentences from the following list for your students to write:

We all need to sleep.

The baby has three teeth.

"It is not safe to play in the street," Jake said.

Kathy planted grass seed next to the stone wall.

"When we spend the week in Tennessee, we will visit Tom and Janet," Abe said.

Betty will be sixteen on April 19.

Ben put on his dungarees and went to weed the tomato patch.

"I can see that David still seems mad," Sally said.

Ted put on sunscreen and then rested in the sun all day.

Joseph drove on the freeway all the way to San Francisco.

▣ REINFORCING ACTIVITIES

Allow your students to choose from the following list of activities:

1. Select some favorite words with "ee" in them. Choose words that either sound good to you when you say them slowly; for example, "speech" or "seventeen," or words that intrigue you for other reasons. Write sentences with these words. If you wish, illustrate one or more of your sentences.

2. Find a partner with whom you can write challenge poems. Each person gives the other a set of rhyming words; for example, "green" and "sheen," or "sleet" and

"meet." The challenge is to make a rhyming couplet out of these words. An example of a couplet for the second set of words given here is:

> I would rush through rain or sleet,
>
> If it were you whom I was going to meet.

Obviously, the couplets can be silly! If you and your partner wish to challenge each other more, you can give each other two sets of rhyming words to put into one poem.

3. The cliché "She's got two left feet" means that someone is clumsy. The literal meaning of this cliché, however, is quite different, and it is quite humorous. Illustrate the literal meaning of "She's got two left feet."

4. LITERATURE CONNECTION: Unfortunately, many people are currently being forced to live on the streets of our cities. *Slake's Limbo* by Felice Holman (Charles Scribner's Sons, 1974), tells of a boy named Aremis Slake who runs away from a very difficult home to live on the streets. Actually, Aremis creates a home for himself under the streets in the New York City subway system. Even though *Slake's Limbo* deals with very painful issues, the book also shows how a boy can respond to kindness, and how he can begin to heal himself.

⧩ EXTRA INTERESTING FACTS

Have you ever seen anyone turn green with envy? Probably not, but you may have heard the expression, "He turned green with envy." Where did this expression come from?

The early Greeks felt that when a person became jealous, his liver released a large amount of greenish fluid into the body. Thus, if he became very envious, he would develop a greenish tint to the skin. Since early times, famous authors such as Shakespeare have made references to green being the color of jealousy, and this has kept the connection between the color and the feeling alive.

WORD LIST

VOWEL COMBINATION SYLLABLE "EE," ONE-SYLLABLE WORDS

bee	green	speech
beet	greet	speed
bleed	keep	street
creep	meet	sweet
deep	queen	teeth
eel	see	three
feed	seed	tree
feel	seem	weed
feet	sheep	week
free	sleep	weep

VOWEL COMBINATION SYLLABLE "EE," MULTISYLLABIC WORDS

agree	dungarees	proceed
agreed	esteem	redeem
agreement	exceed	seventeen
asleep	feedback	sheepdog
beechnut	feeling	sixteen
beehive	fifteen	succeed
beeline	freestanding	sunscreen
between	freeway	teenage
cheekbone	Greenland	Tennessee
chimpanzee	Halloween	toffee
coffee	indeed	treetop
coffeecake	keepsake	unseen
coffeepot	meeting	upkeep
decree	midweek	velveteen
deepest	misdeed	weekday
degree	nosebleed	weekend
disagree	preteen	

FINISH IT!

Fill in the blanks with words from the word list.

1. Meg made a fifteen-minute _____ in front of an audience of two hundred people.

2. Adam was so tired, he was _____ before his head hit the pillow.

3. "I have to go home to _____ my dog his supper," Jim said.

4. Tameesha walked over to the _____ to collect the honey.

5. The _____ of the owl frightened Harry.

6. The teacher held a class _____ every day at the beginning of school.

7. "I like ice cream and candy, and just about anything that is _____," Jill said.

8. The _____ blew his whistle and stopped the game.

9. "Do you _____ bad that you can't go to the party?" Rick asked.

10. Liz is glad she doesn't have to go to school on the _____.

WORD LIST

feed   beehive
meeting   weekend
feel   sweet
referee   speech
asleep   screech

Name _____ **Date** _____

A GAME OF CATEGORIES

Choose words from your word list that belong in each category.

THINGS THAT PEOPLE CAN BE

_____

_____

_____

_____

_____

TYPES OF WEEDS

_____

_____

_____

_____

_____

NUMBERS

_____

_____

_____

_____

FROM THE ANIMAL KINGDOM

_____

_____

_____

_____

WORD LIST

nominee	sheepdog
chickadee	milkweed
fifteen	trainee
chickweed	chimpanzee
bee	ragweed
refugee	sixteen
duckweed	trustee
seventeen	pigweed
escapee	nineteen

Name _____   Date _____

LOOK IT UP!

Look up the listed words in your dictionary. Then match each word with its correct definition.

1. nankeen   a. a North American Algonquin people

2. banshee   b. an herb that can flavor curry

3. settee   c. a place protected from the wind

4. lee   d. fancy and delicate decoration

5. wee   e. a type of cloth that comes from China

6. Cree   f. a type of money

7. weevil   g. a type of beetle

8. filigree   h. a wailing creature from folklore

9. fenugreek   i. a small amount, tiny

10. greenback   j. a sofa or couch for two or three people

Now choose five words from the above list and use each one in a sentence.

1. _____

_____

2. _____

_____

3. _____

_____

4. _____

_____

5. _____

_____

Name _____ **Date** _____

LIST IT!

People who are lucky enough to be able to walk sometimes take their legs and their feet for granted. Think about how it would feel if you had to cross a street or road, but you could not let your feet touch the ground. Make a list of some ways you could get across. You can be serious with your list, as with:

Go in a wheelchair.

Ride a bicycle.

You can also be humorous, as with:

Walk on my hands.

Train a giant bird to fly me across.

_____

_____

_____

_____

_____

_____

_____

_____

_____

_____

Name _____ **Date** _____

WRITE ON!

We perform certain actions every day, like brushing our teeth, but do we really think about what we are doing? Write a series of directions for how to brush your own teeth. Make each direction as specific as you can; for example:

1. Close fingers around the handle of my toothbrush.

2. Lift the toothbrush into the air in front of me.

Bring your directions home with you and then follow them with your own toothbrush. This is fun to do and it will also show you how carefully you need to think when writing directions. *Hint:* Don't forget to include opening and closing your mouth in your directions!

_____

_____

_____

_____

_____

_____

_____

_____

_____

_____

_____

_____

Name _____ **Date** _____

VOWEL COMBINATION SYLLABLE "oa"

🔲 GETTING STARTED

Talk with your students about how the same sound can be spelled different ways in English. Ask them how they would consider spelling the long "e" sound. If they have problems with this, tell them to refer to their notebooks for help.

Once they tell you that they would consider spelling a long "e" sound with either an open syllable, with a vowel-consonant-e, or with the vowel combination syllable with "ee," discuss the options. Provide time for your students to make a page for the vowel combination syllable with "ee" for their notebooks.

◖ INTRODUCING NEW INFORMATION

"Today, we are going to work with a new vowel combination syllable."
Say the following words: boat, coach, foam, loan, oath, roast.
"What sound do you hear in all these words?"
"That's right. You hear a long 'o' sound."
Record the following words: boat, coach, foam, loan, oath, roast.
"What do you notice about these words?"

"Good. You see an 'o' and an 'a' together, and these two vowels make one sound. What type of syllable is this?"

"Yes, it's a vowel combination syllable. Let's see if this syllable with 'oa' occurs in multisyllabic words."

Record the following words: coastline, foamy, presoak, railroad, speedboat, unload.

"Do these words have vowel combination syllables with 'oa'?"

"I agree that they do. These words also contain closed, open, vowel-consonant-e, and vowel combination syllables with 'ai' and 'ee.'"

❖ PRACTICING WITH INDIVIDUAL WORDS

Select a manageable number of words from the word list provided on page 255 for your students to spell.

⑤ PRACTICING SPELLING IN CONTEXT

Select a manageable number of sentences from the following list for your students to write.

The boat stayed close to the coastline.

"That cockroach was huge!" Pam said.

The coach asked Tom to sit on the bench.

Joan put coal in the stove and lit the fire.

"The goat ate the grass, and then he ate all the stuff in the trash can," Amy said.

Don liked to put his hands in the soapsuds.

The bandits stopped the stagecoach and then robbed it.

Mike put on his black coat and his silk tophat.

The oak tree provided a lot of shade on the hot day.

Peggy groaned, and then she got up to finish washing the pots and pans.

▣ REINFORCING ACTIVITIES

Allow your students to choose from the following list of activities:

1. Select favorite words with "oa" in them. Perhaps you will select words that sound good to your ear, but you are unsure of their meanings and you wish to learn them; for example, "shoal" and "oafish." Write sentences with these words. If you wish, illustrate one or more of your sentences.

2. Compound words are created by adding two separate and complete words together; for example, "soapsuds" is a combination of "soap" and "suds." Often (but not always) the meaning of the compound word is a combination of its two smaller words.

   Surprisingly, there are a great number of words with the vowel combination syllable with "oa" that are compound words; for example, "boatman," "coastline," and "planeload." Try to find as many of these compound words with "oa" as you can. (*Hints:* Look up "road" in your dictionary and see how many of these words there are. Don't forget about different types of boats and coats.)

3. A catboat is a particular type of sailboat that has one sail close to the front of the boat. Where do you think this boat's special name came from?

   You can check books and encyclopedias to see a picture of a catboat, or you can make up your own imaginary image of the boat that reflects its name. Where will you place the "cat's" tail in your drawing?

   If you wish, also draw illustrations (either true or reflecting the literal meaning) of a fireboat and an iceboat.

4. LITERATURE CONNECTION: The Underground Railroad was not a railroad at all. It wasn't even a road. It was a group of people (conductors) who helped slaves escape in the years before slavery was outlawed in the United States.

   Harriet Tubman spent a lot of time in the Underground Railroad. She escaped slavery herself and then returned to the South nineteen times between 1850 and 1861. She led more than three hundred people to freedom. Read more about Harriet Tubman in *Go Free or Die* by Jerri Ferris, illustrations by Karen Ritz (Carolrhoda Books, Inc., 1988).

▧ EXTRA INTERESTING FACTS

Have you ever heard the expression "He gets my goat"? This expression means that someone is annoying the speaker, but where could this expression have come from? Most people in the United States don't own goats at this time.

Surprisingly, this expression has its origins in the field of horse racing. It was common practice to put a goat in a horse's stall as a companion animal. The horse would soon become very attached to his goat friend.

A competitor would sometimes steal the goat from the horse's stall the night before an important race. The belief was that this would upset the horse so much that he would not be able to race so well as he normally would. Thus, the competitor "got his goat."

WORD LIST

VOWEL COMBINATION SYLLABLE "OA," ONE-SYLLABLE WORDS

boast	foam	oat
boat	goal	oath
cloak	goat	poach
coach	groan	road
coal	load	roast
coast	loaf	soak
coat	loan	soap
coax	moan	throat
float	oaf	toad
foal	oak	toast

VOWEL COMBINATION SYLLABLE "OA," MULTISYLLABIC WORDS

afloat	gunboat	roadway
approach	iceboat	scapegoat
bemoan	inroad	shipload
boatman	loaded	soapbox
caseload	loadstone	soapsuds
cloaking	oatcake	soapy
coaching	payload	speedboat
coachmen	planeload	stagecoach
coastline	presoak	tailcoat
coating	railroad	topcoat
cockroach	raincoat	trainload
cocoa	redcoat	truckload
cutthroat	reload	tugboat
fireboat	reproach	uncloak
foamy	roadbed	unload
freeload	roadblock	waistcoat
goatskin	roadside	

FINISH IT!

Fill in the blanks with words from the word list.

1. Chang had a sore _____ and a fever.

2. The Boston Bruins scored four _____ and won the game.

3. Kate _____ the truck with boxes of books.

4. Jana and Lucy _____ marshmallows over the campfire.

5. The _____ helped the big ship into the harbor.

6. Henry put butter and jam on his _____.

7. "Wear your _____ because it's cold outside," Dave said.

8. The _____ was covered with ice, so the driving was hazardous.

9. The man stood on the _____ and made a speech.

10. "I'll _____ you ten dollars until Monday," Helen said.

WORD LIST

roasted	loaded
coat	soapbox
throat	toast
loan	road
tugboat	goals

Name _____   **Date** _____

A GAME OF CATEGORIES

Choose words from your word list that belong in each category.

TYPES OF BOATS

_____

_____

_____

_____

_____

TYPES OF COATS

_____

_____

_____

_____

_____

RELATING TO ROADS

_____

_____

_____

_____

RELATING TO SOAP

_____

_____

_____

_____

WORD LIST

raincoat	topcoat
roadbed	speedboat
gunboat	soapsuds
redcoat	roadside
soapbox	tugboat
waistcoat	tailcoat
roadblock	soapflakes
lifeboat	soapy
roadway	sailboat

Name _____   **Date** _____

LOOK IT UP!

Look up the listed words in your dictionary. Then match each word with its correct definition.

1. goatee   a. to bring up a subject

2. shoal   b. hatred

3. broach   c. a type of silver money

4. roan   d. a beard that is short and pointed

5. loam   e. to slowly take over property or rights

6. bemoan   f. a fertile soil

7. loathing   g. a color, often used to describe a horse

8. encroach   h. a type of mustard plant

9. woad   i. a shallow section of a sea or river

10. groat   j. to express sadness

Now choose five words from the above list and use each one in a sentence.

1. _____

_____

2. _____

_____

3. _____

_____

4. _____

_____

5. _____

_____

Name _____ **Date** _____

LIST IT!

Foals are baby horses. Often, the babies of animals have special names that signify their young age.

Make a list of baby animals. When you have written down all the animals with whom you are familiar, check the encyclopedia or other books to discover more names of young ones.

Challenge yourself. Do you know what a baby elephant is called? If you discover that she or he is called a baby elephant, write that on your list.

_____

_____

_____

_____

_____

_____

_____

_____

_____

_____

_____

_____

_____

_____

Name _____   **Date** _____

WRITE ON!

Sometimes, it's good to boast. It can help you think about the accomplishments you have made and the obstacles you have overcome.

Write a BOAST POEM. Follow this format:

I am proud because

I can spell "soapstone" and "seventy," and

I can keep my room clean (at least sometimes) and

I can . . . .

If you wish, you can do a humorous BOAST POEM with boasts that are slightly exaggerated. For example:

I am proud because

I can hit a baseball right out of the city, and

I can eat more pizza than a hungry gorilla, and

I can . . . .

_____

_____

_____

_____

_____

_____

_____

_____

Name _____   **Date** _____

VOWEL COMBINATION SYLLABLE
"ea"

▣ GETTING STARTED

Ask your students to tell you how many ways they now know to spell the long "o" sound. Discuss these options: open syllable with "o," vowel-consonant-e with "o," and the vowel combination syllable with "oa." Give your students time to make a page for "oa" for their notebooks.

◖ INTRODUCING NEW INFORMATION

"Today, we are going to work with a new vowel combination syllable."
Say the following words: beach, cream, heat, lead, mean, sea.
"What sound do you hear in all these words?"
"Good. You hear a long 'e' sound."
Record the following words: beach, cream, heat, lead, mean, sea.
"What do you notice about these words?"
"That's right. They all have the letter 'e' and 'a' together, and these two vowels together make one sound. What type of syllable is this?"
"Yes, it's a vowel combination syllable. Let's see if this syllable with 'ea' occurs in multisyllabic words."

261

Record the following words: beneath, defeat, easy, leaflet, mislead, teacup.

"Do these words have vowel combination syllables with 'ea'?"

"That's correct, they do. Therefore, we know that the vowel combination syllable with 'ea' occurs in multisyllabic words. Now we need to discover something else about this 'ea' combination."

Say the following words: bread, deaf, health, meant, sweat, thread.

"What do you hear in all these words?"

"Yes, you hear a short 'e' sound."

Record the following words: bread, deaf, health, meant, sweat, thread.

"What do you see in all these words?"

"I agree that there is the vowel combination syllable with 'ea.' In these words, however, this vowel combination represents the short 'e' sound. Now let's see if 'ea' can represent short 'e' in multisyllabic words."

Record the following words: already, bedstead, healthy, instead, pleasant, ready.

"Does the vowel combination syllable with 'ea' represent the short 'e' sound in these words?"

"Yes, it does. We also see open syllables and closed syllables in these words. Can you summarize what you have discovered today?"

"That's correct. The vowel combination syllable with 'ea' occurs in single and multisyllabic words. It can represent the long 'e' sound or the short 'e' sound."

"Now, I am going to give you some information. The vowel combination syllable with 'ea' usually represents the long 'e' sound. Words with 'ea' that represent the short 'e' sound are primarily of Anglo-Saxon origin."

❖ PRACTICING WITH INDIVIDUAL WORDS

Select a manageable number of words from the word list provided on page 264 for your students to spell.

☉ PRACTICING SPELLING IN CONTEXT

Select a manageable number of sentences from the following list for your students to write.

Bruce ate a peach and had a cup of tea.

The flea bit the cat on his belly.

It is easy to spell "peanut."

"Henry will not cheat on his math test," Jean said.

The heat of the day made David sweat.

"I will eat a slice of bread with jam and then I will go home," Janet said.

Sally will lead the way to the bus stop.

"I will see Tom when he has finished cleaning," Jack said.

Steve is a wise and healthy man at seventy-three.

Instead of going to Alaska, Pam is going to go to Africa.

◼ REINFORCING ACTIVITIES

Allow your students to choose from the following list of activities:

1. Select pairs of rhyming words, such as "steal" and "squeal," "feast" and "beast," and "speak" and "squeak." Make pairs of couplets with these words; for example, a couplet for the last pair presented is:

    I would not speak

    If I heard a strange squeak.

    If you wish, illustrate one or more of your couplets.

2. Have you ever read aloud to someone else? Select either a short story or poem, or a portion of a novel. This can be your own writing or you can choose a published work. Literature that contains drama and/or humor is effective when read aloud. Then practice reading by yourself until you can read with good tone and expression.

    When you are ready, read your passage aloud to either your class or a smaller group. It is sometimes very enjoyable to read to young children.

3. When we say that someone is bullheaded, we mean that he or she is very stubborn. The literal meaning of this word is quite different, however. Illustrate the literal meaning of "bullheaded."

    People have other derogatory terms that focus on the head; for example: egghead, fathead, blockhead, and bonehead. Illustrate one or more of the literal meanings of these words.

4. LITERATURE CONNECTION: Much rich literature has been written about the sea. A favorite of many people is the classic book *Treasure Island* by Robert Louis Stevenson (Scribner's, 1938). Read this book to enjoy high adventure and intrigue. Also, notice the changes in literary style that have occurred in the past fifty years.

⧈ EXTRA INTERESTING FACTS

Do you think the word "blockhead" was invented recently by a person who wanted to say that someone else was extremely foolish? Blockhead does seem like a modern word, but, alas, the first known record of it comes from 1549!

At that time, hatmakers and wigmakers used blocks of wood (either carved to resemble the human head or not carved at all) to show off their wares. We do not know if people who were angry shouted "You blockhead!" to each other in the 1500s, but my guess is that there was at least one person who did.

In this lesson, you discovered that the vowel combination "ea" usually represents the long "e" sound, and less frequently represents the short "e" sound. It does, however, also represent the long "a" sound in a few words. Three common words in which this occurs are: "break," "great," and "steak."

WORD LIST

VOWEL COMBINATION SYLLABLE "EA" AS LONG "E," ONE-SYLLABLE WORDS

beach	heal	read
bean	heat	scream
cheap	lead	sea
clean	leaf	seam
cream	leap	seat
dream	mean	speak
each	neat	tea
eat	pea	teach
feast	peach	team
flea	reach	weak

VOWEL COMBINATION SYLLABLE "EA" AS LONG "E," MULTISYLLABIC WORDS

beneath	greasy	retreat
cheaply	impeach	reveal
cheapskate	meanness	seaweed
daydream	meanwhile	sneaky
defeat	mislead	steamboat
drumbeat	oatmeal	streamline
eaglet	peanut	teacup
easel	peacock	teammate
easy	really	treatment
feasting	repeat	treaty

VOWEL COMBINATION SYLLABLE "EA" AS SHORT "E," ONE-SYLLABLE WORDS

bread	health	thread
breath	head	threat
dead	meant	
deaf	sweat	

VOWEL COMBINATION SYLLABLE "EA" AS SHORT "E," MULTISYLLABIC WORDS

ahead	heaven	ready
already	instead	steady
healthy	peasant	
heavy	pleasant	

❋ ❋ ❋ ❋ ❋ ❋ ❋ ❋ ❋ ❋ ❋ ❋ ❋ ❋ ❋ ❋ ❋

FINISH IT!

Fill in the blanks with words from the word list.

1. "I'll be _____ in ten minutes," Sabrina said.

2. The _____ finally learned to fly.

3. "It's fun to go to the _____ to collect seashells!" Ben said.

4. Alfred _____ his needle and began to sew on his buttons.

5. In the past, baby _____ have been hunted for their fur.

6. Napoleon's army was eventually _____.

7. Joan woke up anxious from her bad _____.

8. "Good _____ is more important than great wealth," Stephen said.

9. The sun rises in the _____.

10. Betty played on the varsity basketball _____.

WORD LIST

beach	health
defeated	seals
eaglet	ready
east	team
dream	threaded

Name _____   **Date** _____

A GAME OF CATEGORIES

Choose words from your word list that belong in each category.

FROM THE ANIMAL KINGDOM

_____

_____

_____

_____

_____

FOOD

_____

_____

_____

_____

SOUNDS

_____

_____

_____

_____

**TO USE WORDS
TO COMMUNICATE**

_____

_____

_____

_____

WORD LIST

flea	scream
plead	bread
oatmeal	seal
squeal	appeal
peacock	peanut
preach	creak
peach	speak
squeak	eaglet
weasel	bean

Name _____   **Date** _____

LOOK IT UP!

Look up the listed words in your dictionary. Then match each word with its correct definition.

1. bream
2. stealth
3. glean
4. impeach
5. sheath
6. ream
7. measly
8. bleat
9. realm
10. teak

a. a type of tree that is valued for its hard timber
b. a protective covering for a sword
c. not generous, an overly cheap amount
d. a self-contained area that has its own laws
e. a type of fish
f. to cry like a goat or sheep
g. a secretive and hidden maneuver
h. a large amount of paper
i. to accuse a person, especially a public official, of wrongdoing
j. to gather the food leftover after a harvest

Now choose five words from the above list and use each one in a sentence.

1. _____

_____

2. _____

_____

3. _____

_____

4. _____

_____

5. _____

_____

Name _____   **Date** _____

LIST IT!

A few lessons ago, you wrote an "It Isn't Easy" list. Now write an "It Is Easy" list. Think of skills you have in many areas of your life; for example:

It is easy to make an interesting collage.

It is easy to bake muffins.

It is easy to kick a football.

If you wish, think of things that are now easy for you that used to be difficult. Use this time to examine many of the strengths you have.

_____

_____

_____

_____

_____

_____

_____

_____

_____

_____

_____

_____

Name _____ **Date** _____

WRITE ON!

A tiny bean causes a great deal of difficulty in the classic folk tale *Jack and the Beanstalk.* Find a copy of this story and then read it to remind yourself of this tale in which a poor boy gets the best of an evil giant.

But wait! We have only heard this story from the boy's point of view. We don't know how the giant feels about what happened.

Rewrite *Jack and the Beanstalk* from the giant's point of view. Or, you can rewrite the story from the point of view of a newspaper reporter who lives in the giant's town.

_____

_____

_____

_____

_____

_____

_____

_____

_____

_____

_____

_____

Name _____ **Date** _____

VOWEL COMBINATION SYLLABLES
"ie" and "ei"

◨ GETTING STARTED

Talk with your students about how many ways they know to spell the long "e" sound in a word. Once they have stated that a long "e" sound can be spelled with an open syllable with "e," with an open syllable with "y" at the end of a word, with a vowel-consonant-e syllable with "e," and with vowel combination syllables with "ee" and "ea," ask them to list the options and to give examples of each possibility. Do this together and offer assistance if needed. This task should be approached as an interesting way to look at spelling. Students do not need to memorize these options.

Provide time for your students to make a page for the vowel combination syllable with "ea" for their notebooks. Include the three sounds that "ea" can represent.

◖ INTRODUCING NEW INFORMATION

"Today, we are going to work with two vowel combination syllables that are quite confusing. The only thing that can be said about them is that they are not regular for spelling."
Record the following chart on a large piece of paper or on the chalkboard.

Groups of Words	Sounds That the Vowel Combination Syllables Represent
1. pie, lie, tie	a. "ie" represents the short "e" sound
2. friend, befriend	b. "ie" represents the long "e" sound
3. chief, thief, belief	c. "ie" represents the long "i" sound
4. ceiling, conceit, deceit	d. "ei" represents the long "a" sound
5. vein, rein, veil	e. "ei" after a "c" represents the long "e" sound
6. protein, sheik, weird	f. "ei" represents the long "e" sound

Then ask, *"What vowel combination syllables are we working with today?"*

"Yes, we're going to become more familiar with the vowel combination syllables 'ie' and 'ei.' Say these groups of words out loud, and try to match the groups with the proper sounds listed on the right."

Assist your students with this task if they experience difficulty. The correct answers are: 1. c; 2. a; 3. b; 4. e; 5. d; 6. f.

"Can you make a generalization about the vowel combination syllables 'ie' and 'ei'?"

"Good. These two syllables are so erratic that it is difficult to make a generalization about when they will occur. Do you wish to make a guess about which one of these groups occurs most commonly in English? Think about words you know or have seen in books."

"That's right. The most common is the vowel combination syllable with 'ie' that represents the long 'e' sound as in 'brief' and 'grief.'

"Because there is no consistent pattern when you put 'i's and 'e's together, just be aware that this is a confusing letter combination, and refer to your dictionary or spell check on your computer to find the standard spelling of a specific word."

❖ PRACTICING WITH INDIVIDUAL WORDS

Select a manageable number of words from the word list provided on page 274 for your students to spell.

❸ PRACTICING SPELLING IN CONTEXT

Select a manageable number of sentences from the following list for your students to write. If your students are not familiar with the use of an apostrophe to show possession, give them help with this punctuation mark in the fifth sentence.

Jack likes to tie-die clothing.

Beth made a pumpkin pie.

Janet and Keith painted the ceiling.

"Help! Help!" Annie shrieked.

The thief stole Bonnie's black coat.

Christie got dressed up as a zombie for Halloween.

Connie kicked a field goal in the game.

Ron and his friend Bob spent the day at the beach.

"That cake has hundreds of calories and lots of fat," Alex said.

"It is a relief that James is safe at home and is not driving on the icy roads," David said.

◼ REINFORCING ACTIVITIES

Allow your students to choose from the following list of activities:

1. Select pairs of words, one with the vowel combination syllable "ie" and one with the vowel combination syllable "ei"; for example, "belief" and "conceit," and "chief" and "ceiling." Write sentences with these pairs of words. An example for the last pair given is, "'My chief complaint is that the ceiling is falling down!' Tom said." If you wish, illustrate one or more of your sentences.

2. Make a pie. Check in your library for a good recipe, or ask your teacher or a parent to help you select one. If you do not have access to an oven, you can make a pie with a crushed graham cracker crust, instant pudding, and a whipped cream topping. If you do have access to an oven, you can make an apple, blueberry, walnut, peach, rhubarb, or any type of pie you wish. If you use a stove or other cooking utensils, make sure that an adult who is knowledgeable about cooking helps you with this project.

3. Play "Word Thief." For this card game, you will need two sets of dice and a pack of one hundred cards that you will make yourself. Three by five index cards make excellent cards for this game.

   On each card, write one word. Select words that have the vowel combination syllables of "ie" and "ei," and also use words with other vowel combination syllables you have discovered. Use approximately one-third of your deck for words like this.

   For the next third of your deck, write important words like "and," "the," "a," "but," "is," and "was," one per card. Repeat these words several times.

   The last third of your card deck will remain blank. Players will be able to use whatever word they wish when they have one of these blank cards.

   Find a friend who wishes to play "Word Thief." The object of the game is to create as many good sentences with the words from the card deck as you can. Any player can place a sentence on the table whenever she or he wishes. Sentences can be added to at any time. Each card on the table is worth one point, and the winner is the player who has the most cards on the table at the end of the game. For this game, rules of capitalization and punctuation will not be used.

Give your friend and yourself each five words from the deck. Then each of you roll your set of dice. The person who gets the higher number takes a new card from the card deck. If you and your friend roll the same number, you simply repeat the roll. If one of you rolls a seven, the person "steals" all the cards in the other player's hand! If you both roll a seven on the same roll, you exchange cards.

Good luck! And enjoy playing "Word Thief."

4. LITERATURE CONNECTION: "The Ransom of Red Chief," is a short story by the American writer O. Henry. This humorous story is about a little boy who calls himself Red Chief, and who creates a great deal of stress and turmoil for the two men who kidnap him. As with many of O. Henry's other stories, there is a surprise twist to the ending.

O. Henry led a life full of surprises. Challenge yourself to do research in your library and to discover some of them.

"The Ransom of Red Chief" can be found in many short story collections. One of them is Bennett Cerf's *Houseful of Laughter* (Random House, 1963).

⊟ EXTRA INTERESTING FACTS

Anyone who has ever made a pie will question where the expression "easy as pie" comes from. Pies are fun to make, but they are not made without effort. Besides, instead of "easy as pie," why don't people say "easy as mashed potatoes"?

The expression "easy as pie" originated in the late 1800s. In those days, people said, "easy as eating pie." Over the years, the word "eating" was just dropped.

WORD LIST

VOWEL COMBINATION SYLLABLE "IE" AS LONG "E," ONE-SYLLABLE WORDS

brie	fiend	shriek
brief	grief	thief
chief	priest	wield
field	shield	yield

VOWEL COMBINATION SYLLABLE "IE" AS LONG "E," MULTISYLLABIC WORDS

Annie	calorie	grieving
backfield	chiefly	rabies
belief	Connie	relief
Bonnie	diesel	zombie
briefcase	genie	
caddie	goalie	

VOWEL COMBINATION SYLLABLE "IE" AS LONG "I"

die	lie	tie
fie	pie	vie

VOWEL COMBINATION SYLLABLE "IE" AS SHORT "E"

befriend	friend

VOWEL COMBINATION SYLLABLE "EI" AS LONG "A"

feint	rein	veil
lei	skein	vein

VOWEL COMBINATION SYLLABLE "EI" AFTER "C" AS LONG "E"

ceiling	conceit	deceit

VOWEL COMBINATION SYLLABLE "EI" AS LONG "E"

Keith	sheik
protein	weird

✠ ✠ ✠ ✠ ✠ ✠ ✠ ✠ ✠ ✠ ✠ ✠ ✠ ✠ ✠ ✠

FINISH IT!

Fill in the blanks with words from the word list.

1. Helen's class took a _____ trip to the Museum of Science.

2. "I could eat that apple _____ all by myself!" Hakeem declared.

3. The movie was _____ because it did not reflect real life.

4. The meeting was _____, so everyone got home early.

5. Jeff and Wanda have been best _____ for years.

6. The _____ made three spectacular saves at the soccer game.

7. Hector got all dressed up in a suit and _____.

8. John used the trash can cover as a _____ from the rain.

9. "Trickery and _____ do not pay," Rick agreed.

10. He felt great _____ when the test was over.

WORD LIST

brief	pie
tie	relief
field	deceit
friends	goalie
shield	weird

Name _____   **Date** _____

A GAME OF CATEGORIES

Choose words from your word list that belong in each category.

THINGS PEOPLE CAN BE

_____

_____

_____

_____

_____

RELATING TO A FIELD

_____

_____

_____

_____

_____

FEMALE NAMES

_____

_____

_____

_____

RELATING TO THE SUPERNATURAL

_____

_____

_____

_____

WORD LIST

field day	weird
caddie	field glass
Annie	fiend
field gun	Christie
zombie	field hand
Bonnie	thief
goalie	Connie
genie	field music
bailie	chief

Name _____   **Date** _____

LOOK IT UP!

Look up the listed words in your dictionary. Then match each word with its correct definition.

1. skein   a. a large necklace of Hawaiian flowers

2. brie   b. a negative expression

3. vie   c. to care deeply for

4. lief   d. a specified amount of yarn or thread

5. feint   e. a person's way of presenting herself or himself

6. lei   f. to compete or struggle with another

7. bowie   g. a type of knife

8. fie   h. a type of cheese

9. belie   i. to present false information

10. mien   j. a pretended action

Now choose five words from the above list and use each one in a sentence.

1. _____

_____

2. _____

_____

3. _____

_____

4. _____

_____

5. _____

_____

Name _____   **Date** _____

LIST IT!

When you reach down and pick up the old blue bottle on the beach, you do not expect a genie to appear.

"This just happens in fairy tales!" you exclaim.

"Not really," the genie answers, "because here I am."

Your genie informs you that you have an unlimited number of wishes. The only requirement? Every wish has to benefit not only you, but someone else as well.

Make a list of these wishes. Two examples are:

I wish someone would donate ten large pizzas to my class.

I wish that today's science class will be outdoors.

_____

_____

_____

_____

_____

_____

_____

_____

_____

_____

_____

_____

Name _____   **Date** _____

WRITE ON!

FIND THE LIE

Write a paragraph about yourself. Include information about your hobbies, your pets, your family, or anything else you wish. Also include one lie. This can be a little lie, such as a false name for one of your pets, or it can be a large lie. For example, you can talk about living in California when you, in fact, have never stepped foot outside of Minnesota.

Read your paragraph to a small group of classmates or to your teacher. Challenge them to find your lie.

_____

_____

_____

_____

_____

_____

_____

_____

_____

_____

_____

_____

Name _____   **Date** _____

VOWEL COMBINATION SYLLABLE "OO"

▣ GETTING STARTED

Ask your students to tell you what they remember about the "ie" and "ei" vowel combination syllables. Discuss the irregularities of these syllables, and present words that illustrate many of the possible sounds and letter combinations. Provide time for your students to make two pages for their notebooks: one for the vowel combination syllable "ie," and another page for "ei."

◖ INTRODUCING NEW INFORMATION

"Today, we are going to work with a new vowel combination syllable."
Say the following words: cook, foot, good, look, stood, wool.
"What vowel sound do you hear in all these words?"
"That's right, you hear the /oo/ sound as in 'cook.'"
Record the following words: cook, foot, good, look, stood, wool.
"What vowel combination do you see in all these words?"
"I agree that these words have the vowel combination 'oo.' Now let's see if this vowel combination syllable occurs in multisyllabic words."
Record the following words: Bigfoot, cookie, driftwood, football, precook, woolen.

"Do you see the vowel combination syllable 'oo' in these words?"

"Yes. These words also contain closed and open syllables and the vowel combination syllable with 'ie.' Let's work more with the 'oo' combination."

Say the following words: broom, food, hoop, moon, room, too.

"What vowel sound do you hear in these words?"

"That's correct. You hear /oo/ as in 'moon.'"

Record the following words: broom, food, hoop, moon, room, too.

"What vowel combination syllable do you see?"

"Good, you see the /oo/ combination again, but in these words, it represents a different sound. Let's see if /oo/ as in 'moon' occurs in multisyllabic words."

Record the following words: bridegroom, gloomy, lunchroom, noonday, raccoon, seafood.

"Do you see the /oo/ as in 'moon' in these words?"

"Yes. And there are also closed, open, and vowel-consonant-e syllables, and vowel combination syllables with 'ay' and 'ea.' Can you make a general statement about the vowel combination syllable 'oo'?"

"Very good. The vowel combination syllable with /oo/ can represent the sound 'oo' as in 'cook,' or the sound /oo/ as in 'moon.' This vowel combination occurs in single and multisyllabic words."

❖ PRACTICING WITH INDIVIDUAL WORDS

Select a manageable number of words from the word list provided on page 283 for your students to spell.

Ⓢ PRACTICING SPELLING IN CONTEXT

Select a manageable number of sentences from the following list for your students to write. If your students are not familiar with contractions, give them assistance with the words "It's" and "I'm" in these sentences.

David likes to cook.

Jeff went to his room and cleaned it.

Janet stood at the base of the tree and looked up.

"It's foolish to eat that mushroom," Tom said.

Betty took three good books to read at the beach.

Russ and Don played football in the open field until sunset.

"I'm in a funny mood," Fran said, " so just go away and let me be alone."

The class had cookies and milk in the lunchroom.

Ben shook his head and said, "No, I will not chop all that wood!"

Meg took food and clothing to the fire victims.

◼ REINFORCING ACTIVITIES

Allow your students to choose from the following list of activities:

1. Select pairs of single syllable words with the vowel combination "oo." Each word in the pair should have the same vowel sound; for example, "book" and "stood," and "moon" and "spoon." Make sentences with these pairs of words. An example for the last pair presented is, "I ate my chocolate ice cream with my silver spoon under the full moon." If you wish, illustrate one or more of your sentences.

2. Make a very personal cookbook. If you have special recipes, write them down. You can also ask people you know to give you their favorite recipes. If there is a dish you particularly enjoy, ask the chef to tell you how he made it.

   You can record your recipes on regular sheets of paper, or you can put them on index cards. If you wish to make a copy of your cookbook, this can make a very special present for someone. Remember to give credit to the book or person who has contributed each recipe.

3. About one hundred years ago, a man named Dr. William Spooner had an odd habit. He transposed the first letters of words in his speech. For example, if he wanted to say, "That is a frisky kitten," he would by accident say, "That is a kisky fritten." Dr. Spooner made this type of mistake so often that the mistake began to be called a spoonerism.

   Write some spoonerisms. Start with a simple sentence and then transpose the first letters of two of the words. When you have written a few examples, read your spoonerisms to a friend and enjoy how silly they sound.

4. LITERATURE CONNECTION: How would it feel to be marooned on a deserted island? *The Swiss Family Robinson*, written by a Swiss man in 1813 for his children, tells the tale of such an event. Many of the book's translations, such as *The Swiss Family Robinson* by Johann Wyss, edited by G. E. Mitton (Macmillan, 1907), have been somewhat altered. It is reported that the language has been simplified.

   In *The Swiss Family Robinson,* the family not only survives on its deserted island, but in many ways flourishes there in spite of pirates and other grave dangers. Find this classic tale and enjoy reading about a fantastic adventure.

▤ EXTRA INTERESTING FACTS

Our modern word "book" comes from the Old English "boc," which meant "beech," as in "beech tree." Not surprisingly, people in those days scratched their words either on the bark of the beech tree or on the wood. It's very easy to see how the word derived its meaning.

The term "fast food" also has an interesting history, mostly because it has very little history at all. This is a modern term, created by our culture where people can drive up to a restaurant and be fed very quickly. Fifty years ago, people would have shaken their heads in confusion at the term "fast food."

WORD LIST

VOWEL COMBINATION SYLLABLE "OO" AS IN "COOK," ONE-SYLLABLE WORDS

book	foot	hook	stood
brook	good	look	took
cook	hood	shook	wood
crook	hoof	soot	wool

VOWEL COMBINATION SYLLABLE "OO" AS IN "COOK," MULTISYLLABIC WORDS

Bigfoot	daybook	footprint	scrapbook
bookcase	driftwood	hooded	textbook
bookend	firewood	notebook	uncooked
bookplate	fishhook	passbook	woodblock
cookbook	football	precook	woodpile
cookie	foothill	rosewood	woolen

VOWEL COMBINATION SYLLABLE "OO" AS IN "MOON," ONE-SYLLABLE WORDS

broom	mood	roof	spoon
cool	moon	room	too
food	pool	root	tooth
hoop	proof	shoot	zoo

VOWEL COMBINATION SYLLABLE "OO" AS IN "MOON," MULTISYLLABIC WORDS

bamboo	lunchroom	noontime	shampoo
bridegroom	monsoon	raccoon	tattoo
foolish	moody	rooftop	toolshed
gloomy	moonbeams	roommate	tycoon
igloo	mushroom	roomy	uproot
kazoo	noonday	seafood	voodoo

FINISH IT!

Fill in the blanks with words from the word list.

1. Jane put two heaping _____ of sugar in her hot chocolate.

2. Dominic was so nervous, his hands _____.

3. The full _____ made the night bright.

4. Henry and May went fishing in the _____.

5. There were no _____ in the freshly fallen snow.

6. Abe swept the floor with his _____.

7. "It is _____ that you are eating well," Sam said.

8. The clown carried big red _____ in the parade.

9. "Do you have _____ that Liz took your book?" Steve asked.

10. Shakira wrote down all the information in her _____.

WORD LIST

shook	spoonfuls
broom	good
proof	notebook
balloons	brook
moon	footprints

Name _____   **Date** _____

A GAME OF CATEGORIES

Choose words from your word list that belong in each category.

TYPES OF ROOMS

_____

_____

_____

_____

_____

TYPES OF BOOKS

_____

_____

_____

_____

_____

TYPES OF WOODS

_____

_____

_____

_____

RELATING TO THE FOOT

_____

_____

_____

_____

WORD LIST

boxwood

checkbook

bedroom

splayfoot

deadwood

bathroom

clubfoot

cookbook

driftwood

clubroom

dogwood

chapbook

lunchroom

copybook

flatfoot

playroom

footprint

daybook

Name _____   **Date** _____

LOOK IT UP!

Look up the listed words in your dictionary. Then match each word with its correct definition.

1. rook   a. a curved decoration such as a wreath of flowers or foliage
2. cheroot   b. a small section of a room, often set apart
3. festoon   c. a type of vine with flowers
4. croon   d. a small book, often of poetry
5. bandicoot   e. a kind of cigar
6. nook   f. a wind that consistently blows during a certain time of year
7. monsoon   g. a type of crow
8. woodbine   h. a hair decoration that holds the hair
9. snood   i. a rat found in Australia or India
10. chapbook   j. to sing pleasantly and softly

Now choose five words from the above list and use each one in a sentence.

1. _____

_____

2. _____

_____

3. _____

_____

4. _____

_____

5. _____

_____

Name _____   **Date** _____

LIST IT!

When most people think about Eskimos (the Inupiat or more commonly known as the Inuit), igloos come to mind. Many people believe that igloos were the traditional homes for the Inuit.

Igloos were, in fact, only shelters made during hunting trips. In ancient days, the Inuit lived in sod houses. Now, they live in wooden houses.

Do research on the Inuit people. Look at books like *Arctic Hunter* by Diane Hoyt-Goldsmith, photographs by Lawrence Migdale (Holiday House, 1992) or *An Eskimo Family* by Bryan and Cherry Alexander (Lerner Publications Company, 1985). Then make a list of interesting facts about the Inuit people.

_____

_____

_____

_____

_____

_____

_____

_____

_____

_____

_____

_____

Name _____   **Date** _____

WRITE ON!

For this activity, make sure you are able to eat the cookie your teacher provides. If you are allergic to any food, or have any restrictions on your diet, give your teacher that information.

Write directions on how to eat a cookie. You may think this is simple and that, "Pop the cookie in my mouth!" will be enough. But that is not so. You need to describe all the details involved in opening the container the cookie is placed in, transporting the cookie to your open mouth, and so on.

Once you are finished, follow your own directions. Remember that you must follow them exactly, so be careful what you write. And enjoy your cookie!

_____

_____

_____

_____

_____

_____

_____

_____

_____

_____

_____

_____

Name _____ **Date** _____

VOWEL COMBINATION SYLLABLE "OW"

🔲 GETTING STARTED

Talk with your students about the two main sounds the vowel combination "oo" represents. Ask them to provide words that contain both these sounds. Then give your students time to make a page for the vowel combination syllable "oo" for their notebooks.

🌗 INTRODUCING NEW INFORMATION

"Today, we are going to work with a new vowel combination syllable."
Say the following words: crow, glow, low, row, shown, tow.
"What vowel sound do you hear in all these words?"
"Good. You hear a long 'o' sound."
Record the following words: crow, glow, low, row, shown, tow.
"What letter combination do you see in all these words?"
"That's right. You see an 'o' combined with a 'w.' Is 'w' a vowel?"
"No, it's not. In this syllable, however, it functions with the 'o' as a team, so we still call the syllable a vowel combination syllable. Now let's see if this syllable occurs in multisyllabic words."

289

Record the following words: below, fishbowl, grownup, pillowcase, rowboat, window.

"Do you see the vowel combination syllable with 'ow' in these words?"

"That's correct. This syllable also occurs in multisyllabic words. Now let's work more with this syllable."

Say the following words: brown, cow, crowd, frown, plow, town.

"What vowel sound do you hear in all these words?"

"I agree that you hear the /ow/ as in 'cow' sound."

Record the following words: brown, cow, crowd, frown, plow, town.

"What vowel combination syllable do you see in these words?"

"Yes, once again you see an 'o' and a 'w' together, but this time, the combination makes a different sound. Let's see if this new sound occurs in multisyllabic words."

Record the following words: brownie, cowpoke, downhill, hometown, towel, vowel.

"Do you see the vowel combination syllable 'ow' as in 'cow' in these words?"

"Yes, you do. Can you make a generalization about the vowel combination syllable with 'ow'?"

"That's right. The vowel combination syllable with 'ow' occurs in single and multisyllabic words. It represents two main sounds: the long 'o' sound as in 'grow,' and the /ow/ sound as in 'cow.'"

❖ PRACTICING WITH INDIVIDUAL WORDS

Select a manageable number of words from the word list provided on page 292 for your students to spell.

⑤ PRACTICING SPELLING IN CONTEXT

Select a manageable number of sentences from the following list for your students to write.

Nick fell down and broke his elbow.

Fred put the bowl he made in the shop window.

"The puppy has grown so much this fall!" Andy said.

Patty will row the boat to the end of the lake.

The king put on his crown and sat on the throne.

Mike painted his cabin brown with white and yellow trim.

"Now look," Kate said, " just sit down and stop that!"

On Friday, Kathy and Dan made a six-foot snowman.

Peggy did not say a lot at the meeting but, instead, she kept a low profile.

At snack time, Joseph ate a brownie and had a glass of milk.

◨ REINFORCING ACTIVITIES

Allow your students to choose from the following list of activities:

1. Select pairs of rhyming words, such as "clown" and "town," and "mow" and "grow." Make pairs of couplets with these words; for example, a couplet for the last pair presented is:

    The lawn is something I always have to mow,

    Because every day, the grass seems to grow.

    If you wish, illustrate one or more of your couplets.

2. Play the "Follow" game. In this game, you have to listen carefully to what people say before you. It is best to play this game with at least three or four people.

    The first player says, "I was frowning because I had to carry a crow." The second player follows with, "I was frowning because I had to carry a crow and a bowl." The third player continues, "I was frowning because I had to carry a crow and a bowl and a snowman." Each player that follows must add one new burden to the list. All of the objects' names must contain the vowel combination syllable with "ow."

    A player drops out of the game if she forgets any of the list of objects, or says them in the wrong order, or if she can't think of a new object to add. The winner is the last person in the game.

3. The expression "He's afraid of his own shadow" means that someone is extremely fearful, often to the point that people can't tell why he or she is afraid. The literal meaning of this cliché, however, is very specific in its meaning and is, also, humorous to think about. Illustrate the literal meaning of "He's afraid of his own shadow."

4. LITERATURE CONNECTION: The novel *Sing Down the Moon* by Scott O'Dell (Yearling Book, Dell Publishing Co., Inc., 1970) tells of Bright Morning, a young Navaho girl who lives happily with her family until she is kidnapped by Spanish slavers. She escapes and returns home, only to be forced to go on The Long Walk, the forced journey of the Navahos from their homes to Fort Sumner, where they were kept prisoner until 1868.

    Read *Sing Down the Moon* to enjoy an excellent story, but, also to learn about a little known aspect of American history.

⊰ EXTRA INTERESTING FACTS

To "kowtow" to someone means to be extremely respectful, even submissive. There is an underlying assumption that the person who is "kowtowing" would prefer not to do so.

The word "kowtow" comes directly from the Chinese k'o-t'ou. It is a word from ancient days when a person kneeled on the ground in front of another, bent over, and touched his forehead to the floor. At that time, this action was intended as one of reverence and respect.

WORD LIST

VOWEL COMBINATION SYLLABLE "OW" AS LONG "O," ONE-SYLLABLE WORDS

blow	glow	mow	slow
bow	grow	row	snow
crow	growth	show	tow
flow	low	shown	throw

VOWEL COMBINATION SYLLABLE "OW" AS LONG "O," MULTISYLLABIC WORDS

below	hollow	rowboat	snowflake
elbow	meadow	shadow	snowman
fellow	mellow	shallow	widow
fishbowl	pillow	showboat	willow
follow	pillowcase	showcase	window
grownup	rainbow	sideshow	yellow

VOWEL COMBINATION SYLLABLE "OW" AS IN "COW," ONE-SYLLABLE WORDS

bow	crowd	frown	owl
brow	crown	gown	plow
brown	down	growl	prowl
clown	drown	how	town
cow	fowl	now	yowl

VOWEL COMBINATION SYLLABLE "OW" AS IN "COW," MULTISYLLABIC WORDS

brownie	downcast	letdown	splashdown
brownstone	downhill	powwow	towel
cowbell	downtown	rowdy	uncrowded
cowpoke	drowsy	rubdown	unplowed
dishtowel	hometown	rundown	vowel

✣ ✣ ✣ ✣ ✣ ✣ ✣ ✣ ✣ ✣ ✣ ✣ ✣ ✣ ✣

FINISH IT!

Fill in the blanks with words from the word list.

1. At the party, the _____ made everyone laugh.

2. The _____ was falling steadily, so Helen got out her skis.

3. Dan did not like the way the dog was _____ at him.

4. The _____ flew away over the rooftop.

5. Latoya went _____ to go to the post office.

6. "Hand me that _____ and I'll help dry the dishes," Pat said.

7. The donkey sat _____ and would not get up.

8. Hector opened the _____ to let in some fresh air.

9. "That coat is too good to _____ away," Rick said.

10. Jim put the two goldfish in his brand new _____.

WORD LIST

crow	dishtowel
down	fishbowl
clown	snow
throw	growling
downtown	window

© 1996 by Cynthia Stowe

Name _____   **Date** _____

A GAME OF CATEGORIES

Choose words from your word list that belong in each category.

FROM THE ANIMAL KINGDOM

_____

_____

_____

_____

_____

RELATING TO SNOW

_____

_____

_____

_____

_____

CITIES

_____

_____

_____

_____

RELATING TO GOING DOWN

_____

_____

_____

_____

WORD LIST

cow	snowdrift
Glasgow	downshift
Allentown	owl
snowflake	snowball
blowfish	Moscow
downhill	snowcap
minnow	downgrade
snowman	crow
downfall	Cape Town

Name _____   Date _____

LOOK IT UP!

Look up the listed words in your dictionary. Then match each word with its correct definition.

1. oxbow   a. a purplish glow on top of mountains at sunrise or sunset

2. frowzy   b. a type of boat

3. sallow   c. the group of plants to which cotton belongs

4. renown   d. a U-shaped curve in a river

5. alpenglow   e. a type of shell sometimes used to represent money

6. avow   f. being a sickly color

7. mallow   g. a hand tool

8. trowel   h. well known

9. scow   i. sloppy and dirty

10. cowrie   j. to make a true statement about yourself or your beliefs

Now choose five words from the above list and use each one in a sentence.

1. _____

_____

2. _____

_____

3. _____

_____

4. _____

_____

5. _____

_____

Name _____ **Date** _____

LIST IT!

Make a list of things that grow. Think of common things, such as rose-bushes, children, and kittens. Also, think of things that "grow" in a broader sense, such as:

1. coral on a coral reef

2. rust on an old, abandoned car

3. friendship among people

_____

_____

_____

_____

_____

_____

_____

_____

_____

_____

_____

_____

_____

Name _____ **Date** _____

WRITE ON!

HOW NOW BROWN COW

People continue to use the expression "How now brown cow" because it's fun to say and it sounds good. But how would it feel to really ask a cow, "How are you now, brown cow?" What answer would you get?

Write an interview with a cow or with another animal if you prefer. Of course, for the purposes of this interview, we will assume that you are fluent in the animal's language!

Here are some sample questions:

1. *(for a cow)* What do you do when you're stuck in the barn all winter?

2. *(for a dog)* Do you feel it is fair that you get fed only occasionally, especially when your human can eat whenever he wishes?

_____

_____

_____

_____

_____

_____

_____

_____

_____

_____

_____

Name _____ **Date** _____

THE Y RULE

▣ GETTING STARTED

Discuss the two sounds the vowel combination syllable "ow" represent. Ask your students to present words that illustrate these two sounds. Then provide time for your students to make a page for the vowel combination syllable "ow" for their notebooks.

☾ INTRODUCING NEW INFORMATION

"Today, we are going to work with our third spelling rule. What other spelling rules have we studied so far?"
"That's correct, the "E" rule and the Doubling rule."
Present the following chart:

> baby + es = babies
>
> chilly + est = chilliest
>
> duty + ful = dutiful
>
> happy + ness = happiness
>
> pony + es = ponies
>
> ugly + ness = ugliness

"What do you notice about all the root words in this list?"

"I agree that they all end in 'y.' What happens to the 'y' in all these words?"

"Yes, the 'y' is changed to an 'i' before the suffix is added. Does it matter whether the suffix begins with a vowel or a consonant?"

"No, it does not."

Present the following chart:

```
betray  +  ed  =  betrayed

display  +  ing  =  displaying

play  +  ed  =  played

relay  +  ed  =  relayed

stay  +  ing  =  staying

sway  +  ed  =  swayed
```

"What do all these root words end with?"

"That's right. They also end with a 'y.' What happens to the 'y' when the suffix is added?"

"That's correct, nothing happens to it. The 'y' remains and the suffix is added."

Place the two charts already presented side by side. *"When do you think the 'y' is changed to an 'i,' and when does it remain?"*

"Great. When a suffix is added to a word that ends with 'y,' the 'y' is changed to an 'i' when the letter before the 'y' is a consonant. If the letter before the 'y' is a vowel, the 'y' remains. Now let's look at the one main exception to this rule."

Present the following chart:

```
baby  +  ish  =  babyish

betray  +  ing  =  betraying

cry  +  ing  =  crying

play  +  ing  =  playing

stay  +  ing  =  staying

study  +  ing  =  studying
```

"Did any of the 'y's in the root words change?"

"No, they did not. In this case, it did not matter if the letter before the 'y' was a consonant or a vowel. What do you notice about all of these suffixes?"

"That's right, the suffixes begin with an 'i.' When you add a suffix that begins with an 'i' to a word that ends with a 'y,' the 'y' remains the same. Can you summarize the 'Y' rule?"

"Very good. When a suffix is added to a word that ends in 'y,' the 'y' changes to an 'i' if the 'y' is preceded by a consonant. If the 'y' is preceded by a vowel, the 'y' remains. The only exception is when a suffix beginning with an 'i' is added. In this case, the 'y' always remains the same."

❖ PRACTICING WITH INDIVIDUAL WORDS

Select a manageable number of words from the word list provided on page 302 for your students to spell.

⑤ PRACTICING SPELLING IN CONTEXT

Select a manageable number of sentences from the following list for your students to write.

The skies opened and the rains came.

"Tom is trying to help," Janet said.

Steve spent his ten pennies on candy.

The wet towel dried in the sun.

"I am the luckiest man alive," Jim said.

Jane felt great happiness when she finished the race.

Jennie is flying to San Francisco, and then she is taking a train to Montana.

The puppy played with the ball until he got tired and fell asleep.

"I must admit that Jill's sloppiness is getting to me," Amy said.

Ron stayed in the cabin with his dog Sam until it stopped raining.

◼ REINFORCING ACTIVITIES

Allow your students to choose from the following list of activities:

1. Select words in which the 'y' is dropped when a suffix is added; for example, "happiness," "shiniest," and "plentiful," and say them slowly to yourself. Do you enjoy the sound of these words? Do you like saying them slowly and listening carefully to their sounds?

   Select some favorite words and write sentences with them. One possible sentence is, "It is good when food is plentiful." When you have finished, read your sentences aloud and listen to how your language sounds. If you wish, illustrate one or more of your sentences.

2. Play a "Quick Sort" game. For this game, you will need some pieces of paper, such as 3 × 5 index cards, and a stopwatch. Refer back to your notebook, and select some closed syllable words and some vowel-consonant-e words. For this game, choose one-syllable words only, such as "run" and "time." Then select some words that end with the open syllable "y." These words can be either one syllable or multisyllabic words, such as "cry" and "candy."

Write these words on your cards, one per card. The number you choose to write is up to you, but it is good to have at least a total of thirty cards.

Then play "Quick Sort." The purpose of the game is for one person to divide the pack into three groups: (a) words where the Doubling rule is used when a suffix is added to the root word; (b) words where the "E" rule is used when a suffix is added to the root word; and (c) words where the "Y" rule is used when a suffix is added to the root word. The challenge is to sort your words as quickly as you can. Ask a friend to time you with the stopwatch, or compete with a friend to see who is faster. It's fun to repeat this activity and to see how fast all the players can become.

3. "Pennies from Heaven" is the title song of the 1936 film *Pennies from Heaven*. The lyricist was Johnny Burke, and the composer was Arthur Johnston. The song was originally sung by Bing Crosby, but it has since been recorded by many other singers.

Most of our modern films do not have music woven into them in the same way that the films from the 1930 era did. Ask your teacher or librarian to help you find a film from the 1930s. Sometimes, public libraries have videos to lend, or television stations occasionally show them. Enjoy the film, and also notice how much movies have changed.

4. LITERATURE CONNECTION: *Six Sillies* is a humorous folk tale about a young man who searches for extremely silly people. Find out why he undertakes this strange quest when you read this tale in the collection *The World's Best Fairy Tales*, edited by Belle Becker Sideman, illustrated by Fritz Kredel (The Reader's Digest Association, 1967). Another version of this story is *The Three Sillies* by Kathryn Hewitt (Harcourt Brace Jovanovich, 1986).

⧉ EXTRA INTERESTING FACTS

The term to get "gussied up" illustrates how an expression that begins in one locality can travel widely. People who live in or near Augusta, Georgia, have a fond nickname for their city: Gussy. Therefore, when you get all dressed up to go to the city, you get "gussied up." Somehow, this expression has become well known throughout the United States.

As with all spelling rules, there are always exceptions. Three important exceptions are:

"say" + "ed" = "said"

"pay" + "ed" = "paid"

"day" + "ly" = "daily"

WORD LIST

ONE-SYLLABLE WORDS IN WHICH THE "Y" IS CHANGED TO AN "I" BEFORE A SUFFIX IS ADDED

cry + ed	pry + es
dry + ed	sky + es
fry + es	spy + ed
ply + es	try + ed

MULTISYLLABIC WORDS IN WHICH THE "Y" IS CHANGED TO AN "I" BEFORE A SUFFIX IS ADDED

baby + es	jelly + es
bumpy + est	kitty + es
bunny + es	lady + es
candy + es	lazy + est
chilly + est	lucky + est
clumsy + est	penny + es
cozy + est	plenty + ful
crunchy + est	pony + es
dressy + est	rusty + est
duty + ful	skinny + est
empty + ness	shiny + est
envy + ed	silly + est
fifty + es	sloppy + ness
funny + est	sunny + est
grumpy + est	tiny + est
happy + ness	twenty + es
hilly + est	ugly + ness
hungry + est	witty + est

WORDS IN WHICH THE "Y" REMAINS WHEN A SUFFIX IS ADDED

betray + ed	pray + ed
decay + ing	relay + ed
delay + ed	say + ing
dismay + ed	slay + ing
display + ed	spray + ed
gray + ing	spray + ing
hay + ing	stay + ed
pay + ing	stay + ing
play + ed	sway + ed
play + ing	sway + ing

WORDS IN WHICH THE "Y" REMAINS BECAUSE A SUFFIX BEGINNING WITH AN "I" IS ADDED

baby + ing	fifty + ish
baby + ish	fly + ing
caddy + ing	fry + ing
copy + ing	pry + ing
cry + ing	spy + ing
dry + ing	study + ing
empty + ing	tally + ing
envy + ing	try + ing

❀ ❀ ❀ ❀ ❀ ❀ ❀ ❀ ❀ ❀ ❀ ❀ ❀ ❀ ❀ ❀ ❀ ❀

FINISH IT!

Fill in the blanks with words from the word list.

1. The baby _____ because he was tired and hungry.

2. The geese were already _____ south for the winter.

3. "That puppy was the _____ one at the pound, and that's why I took him home," Tom said.

4. Angelo had a hot dog and french _____ for supper.

5. Edna bought Jeff a box of chocolate _____ for Valentine's Day.

6. Russ _____ three hours for his test.

7. "My room is so clean, I challenge you to find even the _____ speck of dust," Bruce said.

8. Even though it was cold and damp, they still _____ the baseball game.

9. The baby _____ were soft and fluffy.

10. Le Ly was _____ to discover that her favorite book was missing.

WORD LIST

flying	cried
candies	tiniest
played	fries
skinniest	bunnies
dismayed	studied

Name _____   **Date** _____

A GAME OF CATEGORIES

Choose words from your word list that belong in each category.

NEGATIVE DESCRIPTIVE WORDS

_____

_____

_____

_____

_____

POSITIVE DESCRIPTIVE WORDS

_____

_____

_____

_____

FOOD

_____

_____

_____

_____

RELATING TO NUMBERS

_____

_____

_____

_____

WORD LIST

coziest   sloppiest

jellies   sixties

messiest   dandiest

classiest   taffies

twenties   candies

fifties   flimsiest

fries   seventies

shabbiest   spiffiest

tidiest   grubbiest

Name _____   Date _____

LOOK IT UP!

Look up the listed words in your dictionary. Then match each word with its correct definition.

1. tallied (tally + ed)   a. dwellings of poor quality
2. belayed (belay + ed)   b. layers of a material such as cloth or wood
3. shanties (shanty + es)   c. to have recorded an amount
4. affrays (affray + s)   d. channels that allow excess water to run off
5. plies (ply + es)   e. to have harmed by dirtying
6. sullied (sully + ed)   f. strong carts with sides that come off
7. drays (dray + s)   g. to have wound around and made secure, as with a rope
8. glossiest (glossy + est)   h. long blouses with sailor collars
9. spillways (spillway + s)   i. having the most shiny surface
10. middies (middy + es)   j. loud public quarrels

Now choose five words from the above list and use each one in a sentence.

1. _____

_____

2. _____

_____

3. _____

_____

4. _____

_____

5. _____

_____

Name _____   **Date** _____

LIST IT!

Make a list of the funniest books or stories you have read or would like to read. You can include tales such as *The Best Christmas Pageant Ever* by Barbara Robinson and *Lake Wobegon Days* by Garrison Keillor. Once you have finished your list, share it with a friend and tell him or her about your favorite stories.

_____

_____

_____

_____

_____

_____

_____

_____

_____

_____

_____

_____

_____

_____

Name _____   **Date** _____

WRITE ON!

Little children often love stories that include wild exaggeration. Write and illustrate a picture book for young children. Choose from the following made-up titles or make up your own title:

THE GRUMPIEST MAN IN TOWN

SAM'S SLOPPIEST DAY

THE LAZIEST DOG ON OAK STREET

To get started, go to your school or local library, and ask the librarian to show you some picture books that little children enjoy. Read them to gain a sense of how to write your own picture book. And then relax, write, and exaggerate!

_____

_____

_____

_____

_____

_____

_____

_____

_____

_____

Name _____   **Date** _____

CONSONANT-LE SYLLABLES
"ble" and "dle"

▣ GETTING STARTED

Review the "Y" rule with your students. Ask them to tell you about this spelling rule and to illustrate the rule with some examples. Give your students time to make a page for their notebooks for the "Y" rule.

Then ask your students to tell you about the two other spelling rules: the "E" rule and the Doubling rule. Talk about how to decide when to use each rule.

◖ INTRODUCING NEW INFORMATION

"Today, we are going to work with a fourth type of syllable. What types of syllables have we worked with so far?"

"That's right. We've worked with closed, open, vowel-consonant-e, and vowel combination syllables."

Say the following words: able, bubble, edible, mumble, noble, resemble.
"What sound do you hear at the ends of all these words?"
"Yes, you hear a sound like /bull/."

Record the following words: able, bubble, edible, mumble, noble, resemble.
"What do you see at the end of all these words?"

"I agree that you see a 'b' and then an 'l' and then an 'e.' This type of syllable is called a consonant-le syllable. It's unusual because the vowel is at the end of the syllable and does not have a sound of its own. Let's look at one other consonant-le syllable."

Say the following words: bridle, doodle, needle, poodle, riddle, saddle.

"What sound do you hear at the end of these words?"

"Good, you hear a sound that begins with /d/ and rhymes with /bull/."

Record the following words: bridle, doodle, needle, poodle, riddle, saddle.

"What do you see at the end of all these words?"

"Yes, you see a 'd' and then an 'l' and then an 'e.' This, therefore, is a second consonant-le syllable."

Place the two lists of words presented in front of your students. *"What other types of syllables do you see in these words?"*

"Yes, there are closed, open, vowel combination, and consonant-le syllables in these words. The only syllable not represented is the vowel-consonant-e syllable."

❖ PRACTICING WITH INDIVIDUAL WORDS

Select a manageable number of words from the word list provided on page 311 for your students to spell.

⑤ PRACTICING SPELLING IN CONTEXT

Select a manageable number of sentences from the following list for your students to write.

Betty rowed to the middle of the lake.

Mike made banana pancakes on the hot griddle.

"I will run the race if I am able," Helen said.

The man looked feeble and sick.

Ted picked up his fiddle and began to play.

David put the baby in the cradle and rocked him to sleep.

Rob and Liz sat at the table and played Scrabble™.

"Kate can shoot well, and she can dribble," Beth said.

Steve got the white shiny pebbles at the beach.

Joan lit the candle and placed it in the middle of the table.

◼ REINFORCING ACTIVITIES

Allow your students to choose from the following list of activities:

1. Challenge yourself to write sentences that each have more than two words with consonant-le syllables. An example is, "'I am unable to just nibble at a pizza,' Fran

said, 'because I want to gobble it down.'" If you wish, illustrate one or more of your sentences.

2. The game of Scrabble™ (manufactured by Milton Bradley) is a word game people have enjoyed for many years. In this game, you are given individual letters and, together with other players, you create words that interconnect. Each letter is worth a certain number of points (an "x" is worth 8 points), and a player gets all the points in a word he or she creates. The winner is the person with the highest score at the end of the game.

   Ask your teacher or librarian for a copy of Scrabble™. Then enjoy the game.

3. The song "Yankee Doodle" has a fascinating history. It is believed to have been written by Dr. Richard Shuckburg who was a physician for British troops during the French and Indian War. Legend says that he composed the song to ridicule the Yankee soldiers. Many verses of this song were apparently written in the 1750s.

   It is said that at the onset of the Revolutionary War, when British troops set out from Boston in 1775, they sang "Yankee Doodle" as a song of derision. They did not think highly of the army they were about to face. When, however, they were overcome by the colonials at Concord, the song was sung by the latter as a song of pride, and it has since become a well-known patriotic song.

   Check out books in your library that tell about the colonial times. Read about this interesting period of history.

4. LITERATURE CONNECTION: Fables are short tales that have a moral to them. Some famous fables from the past are the Indian *Pancha-Tantra* and the fables of Aesop. These fables intend to teach people important lessons about life.

   In a lighter vein, two books have been written in this century that present fables as humor. These are *Fables for Our Time* by James Thurber (Blue Ribbon Books, 1943) and *Fables* by Arnold Lobel (Harper Trophy, 1980). Read these books and laugh.

⬙ EXTRA INTERESTING FACTS

The word "fadoodle" is a word that has disappeared from common use. From the sound of it, can you guess what it might have meant?

"Fadoodle" meant foolishness. Isn't it a shame that people don't still say, "Now, just sit down and stop that fadoodle!"

"Eating humble pie" is an expression that has survived from the eleventh century. After a hunt, a pie would be prepared from less choice parts (the "umbles," such as the liver) of the animal. The servants ate this pie, while the lord and people in authority ate the "better" cuts of the meat.

Therefore, in the olden times, eating "umble" pie meant that your rank was inferior. Nowadays, we say a person has to eat "humble pie" when he or she has to apologize or otherwise defer to someone else.

Why do you think that "fadoodle" did not survive as a word? Why has "eating humble pie" continued to be in use for almost one thousand years?

WORD LIST

CONSONANT-LE SYLLABLE: BLE

able	excusable	pebble
agreeable	fable	possible
amble	feeble	ramble
available	flammable	reliable
babble	flexible	resemble
Bible	fumble	rumble
bubble	gamble	sable
cable	gobble	Scrabble™
capable	grumble	stumble
credible	incredible	table
crumble	jumble	thimble
dabble	legible	tremble
deniable	mumble	tumble
dependable	nibble	unable
dribble	nimble	usable
edible	noble	visible
enable	notable	

CONSONANT-LE SYLLABLE: DLE

bundle	idle	peddle
candle	kindle	poodle
cradle	ladle	puddle
cuddle	meddle	riddle
doodle	middle	saddle
dwindle	mishandle	sidesaddle
fiddle	needle	straddle
griddle	noodle	swindle
handle	paddle	unsaddle
huddle	panhandle	waddle

FINISH IT!

Fill in the blanks with words from the word list.

1. "That _____ is a beautiful dog," Henry said.

2. Because of the quarterback's _____, the home team lost the game.

3. Tessa put the brand new _____ on the horse.

4. The little girl jumped into the _____ of water.

5. "It is not _____ for a person to pick up an elephant," Joseph said.

6. Dominic bought his mom a beeswax _____.

7. Jane set the _____ with the best dishes.

8. It's almost impossible to find a _____ in a haystack.

9. "That baby _____ his mother," Kate said.

10. A rubber band is very _____.

WORD LIST

saddle	candle
table	possible
poodle	flexible
resembles	fumble
puddle	needle

Name _____ Date _____

A GAME OF CATEGORIES

Choose words from your word list that belong in each category.

THINGS FOUND IN THE KITCHEN

_____

_____

_____

_____

_____

POSITIVE CHARACTERISTICS

_____

_____

_____

_____

_____

RELATING TO MOVEMENT

_____

_____

_____

_____

RELATING TO HORSES

_____

_____

_____

_____

WORD LIST

amble	credible
griddle	ramble
agreeable	noodles
packsaddle	sidesaddle
capable	table
saddle	dependable
skedaddle	soap bubbles
waddle	ladle
bridle	humble

Name _____   **Date** _____

LOOK IT UP!

Look up the listed words in your dictionary. Then match each word with its correct definition.

1. skedaddle		a.	a type of stone used for paving
2. dibble		b.	to coax or flatter in order to gain favor
3. bridle		c.	to be at fault, worthy of blame
4. culpable		d.	to hurry away
5. sidle		e.	a gardening tool used to help plant seeds
6. cobble		f.	that which can be defended, as with a belief
7. rubble		g.	to move in a reluctant manner
8. twaddle		h.	broken and crumbling pieces of stone
9. tenable		i.	a harness for a horse's head
10. wheedle		j.	ridiculous talk

Now choose five words from the above list and use each one in a sentence.

1. _____

_____

2. _____

_____

3. _____

_____

4. _____

_____

5. _____

_____

Name _____ **Date** _____

LIST IT!

DESCRIPTION DOODLES

When we doodle, we scribble little pictures or designs. Generally, we don't take doodles seriously, but instead we have fun with them.

Make a list of some description doodles. These will be word doodles instead of picture ones. Look around and notice objects near you. Then, in a relaxed way, begin to describe what you see.

The following are two examples of description doodles:

1. The plant by the window is a deep green. Its wide leaves look like they are holding the sunlight.

2. The table is long and sturdy. It looks like it has sat in that same spot for ten years.

_____

_____

_____

_____

_____

_____

_____

_____

_____

_____

Name _____ Date _____

WRITE ON!

Riddles are thinking challenges that have been invented by people for over 5,000 years. One way of writing a riddle is to first select an object and then list all of its characteristics that come to mind. For example, if you select "a tooth," you can list: small, white to off-white in color, sharp, can tear meat and other food, chews, works best in a group with others.

The next step is to connect two or more of these characteristics in an interesting way. For example, your riddle could be:

What is smaller than an apple, but with its brothers, can overcome a tiger? (a tooth)

Following these steps, write some riddles of your own.

_____

_____

_____

_____

_____

_____

_____

_____

_____

_____

_____

_____

_____

Name _____   **Date** _____

CONSONANT-LE SYLLABLES
"ple" and "gle"

▣ GETTING STARTED

Talk about the five types of syllables discovered so far: closed, open, vowel-consonant-e, vowel combination, and consonant-le. Ask your students to give examples of each syllable type. Then provide time for your students to make a page for consonant-le with "ble" and "dle" for their notebooks.

◖ INTRODUCING NEW INFORMATION

"Today, we are going to continue to work with consonant-le syllables."
Say the following words: apple, crumple, maple, pimple, steeple, triple.
"What sound do you hear at the end of these words?"
"I agree that you hear a sound like /pull/."
Record the following words: apple, crumple, maple, pimple, steeple, triple.
"What do you see at the end of these words?"
"Yes, you see a 'p' and then an 'l' and then an 'e.' This, therefore, is a third consonant-le syllable. Let's work with one more of this type of syllable today."
Say the following words: bugle, eagle, giggle, jungle, shingle, struggle.
"What do you hear at the end of these words?"

317

"That's right. You hear a sound like /gull/."
Record the following words: bugle, eagle, giggle, jungle, shingle, struggle.
"What do you see at the end of these words?"
"Good, you see a 'g' and then an 'l' and then an 'e.' What type of syllable is this?"
"Yes, it's a consonant-le syllable."
Place both lists of words presented today in front of your students. In addition, present the words: able, bubble, noble, doodle, riddle, saddle.
"Can you make a generalization about where consonant-le syllables occur in words?"
"Good. Consonant-le syllables occur at the end of multisyllabic words. The only time they will occur in the middle of a word is in a compound word such as 'bubblegum,' where two individual words have been combined to make a new word."

❖ PRACTICING WITH INDIVIDUAL WORDS

Select a manageable number of words from the word list provided on page 320 for your students to spell.

◐ PRACTICING SPELLING IN CONTEXT

Select a manageable number of sentences from the following list for your students to write.

Jake made an apple pie.

The beagle sat up and shook hands.

The maple tree provided lots of shade.

Sally went to the jungle to study snakes.

"It is simple to fix that dress so it will fit," Pat said.

David played his bugle at the basketball game.

Sam did not hit a home run, but he did hit a triple.

Jill and Fred put wood shingles on the cabin to make it look nice.

On the day of the play, James got a huge pimple on his nose.

"It will be quite a struggle to untangle all that thread!" Peggy said.

▣ REINFORCING ACTIVITIES

Allow your students to choose from the following list of activities:

1. Write sentences, each of which contains more than two words with consonant-le syllables. You can choose words with "ble," "dle," "ple," or "gle." An example is, "The eagle was clearly visible flying over the maple tree." If you wish, illustrate one or more of your sentences.

2. The game Boggle™ (a Parker Brothers' Hidden Word Game) is a fascinating game that can be enjoyed for many years. In Boggle™ players are presented with six-teen individual letter cubes that are arranged in a square. The arrangement changes each time the game is played.

   Players get three minutes to write down as many words as they can find in the square. The letters must touch each other sequentially.

   Ask your teacher or librarian to help you find a copy of Boggle™. Then enjoy the game!

3. Squiggles are meaningless lines or marks that a person makes on a piece of paper. Find a friend and play a Squiggle Art activity.

   Each person needs to have a piece of unlined paper, such as a sheet of typewriter paper, a pencil, and a piece of lined paper. Once you begin this activity, the basic rule is that you can only communicate in writing, not in spoken language.

   To begin, each player draws a squiggle on her piece of unlined paper. Then play-ers exchange squiggles. The challenge is to make a meaningful picture out of the meaningless squiggle. For example, a curved, twirling line might become a part of a flower. Players can "talk" with each other during this activity, but remember that they can only do so in writing.

4. LITERATURE CONNECTION: There are many books that make us giggle, but one that is sure to do so is *Where the Sidewalk Ends* by Shel Silverstein (Harper Collins Publishers, 1974). This book of poetry and drawings will make people of all ages giggle. It is particularly enjoyable to memorize a favorite poem from this book and present it to others.

⧩ EXTRA INTERESTING FACTS

People do not always know the exact derivation of words. A fascinating example of this is the word "finagle," which means "to cheat or get the better of by trickery." Some people believe this word comes from "fainague," which meant "to cheat or trick, especially at cards."

Other people believe that "finagle" comes from a man's name: Mr. Feinagel, who was a German hypnotist and expert card player in the early 1800s. What do you think? Do you think that, perhaps, "fainague" and "Feinagel" were combined to cre-ate "finagle"?

WORD LIST

CONSONANT-LE SYLLABLE: PLE

ample	maple	sample
apple	multiple	simple
Constantinople	pimple	staple
crabapple	pineapple	steeple
cripple	principle	temple
crumple	quadruple	topple
dimple	quintuple	trample
disciple	ripple	triple
example	rumple	

CONSONANT-LE SYLLABLE: GLE

angle	jangle	snuggle
beagle	jiggle	spangle
boggle	jingle	straggle
bugle	juggle	strangle
dangle	jungle	struggle
eagle	mangle	tangle
entangle	mingle	tingle
finagle	rectangle	triangle
giggle	shingle	untangle
goggle	single	wiggle
haggle	smuggle	

FINISH IT!

Fill in the blanks with words from the word list.

1. Tim got a free _____ of the ice cream at the store.

2. Adriana was so excited and nervous to be on T.V., she could not stop _____.

3. "Please _____ those loose pages together," Judy said.

4. The clown _____ five peaches.

5. Jessie hit a _____ into right field.

6. The _____ is a tropical fruit.

7. An _____ a day keeps the doctor away.

8. "I like to hear those bells _____," Pete said.

9. Jacob drew a _____ to represent a tent.

10. Jean had a _____ supper of soup and bread.

WORD LIST

juggled	giggling
jingle	apple
simple	pineapple
staple	triangle
single	sample

Name _____ **Date** _____

A GAME OF CATEGORIES

Choose words from your word list that belong in each category.

RELATING TO NUMBERS

_____

_____

_____

_____

_____

TO HARM

_____

_____

_____

_____

_____

TYPES OF TREES OR PLANTS

_____

_____

_____

_____

SHAPES OR RELATING TO SHAPES

_____

_____

_____

_____

WORD LIST

crumple	multiple
angle	rumple
quadruple	quadrangle
apple	crabapple
maple	triple
quintuple	rectangle
mangle	trample
triangle	pineapple
cripple	single

Name _____ **Date** _____

LOOK IT UP!

Look up the listed words in your dictionary. Then match each word with its correct definition.

1. wimple
2. toggle
3. grapple
4. boondoggle
5. wangle
6. supple

7. quadrangle
8. duple

9. joggle
10. dapple

a. to hold tight
b. flexible and limber
c. to have spots, such as on an animal's skin
d. consisting of two
e. to move or shake
f. a cloth that winds around and covers a woman's head and neck

g. a figure with four sides
h. a device such as a bolt that keeps a rope or chain from slipping

i. to gain by trickery or persuasion
j. to do work that is not considered important

Now choose five words from the above list and use each one in a sentence.

1. _____

_____

2. _____

_____

3. _____

_____

4. _____

_____

5. _____

_____

Name _____   **Date** _____

LIST IT!

Animals are fascinating creatures with their own unique characteristics. Choose whether you would like to learn about the eagle or the beagle. Consult books like:

1. *Where the Bald Eagles Gather* by Dorothy Hinshaw Patent, photographs by William Muñoz (Clarion Books, Ticknor and Fields, a Houghton Mifflin Co., 1984)

2. *The Reader's Digest Illustrated Book of Dogs,* Second Revised Edition (The Reader's Digest Association, Inc., 1993)

Also see if there are people you could talk with who know about these animals. Then list interesting facts about the eagle or the beagle.

_____

_____

_____

_____

_____

_____

_____

_____

_____

_____

_____

_____

Name _____   **Date** _____

WRITE ON!

"Multiple" means that something has more than one part. Write a story that has multiple points of view.

To begin, think of a situation involving at least two people where a crisis is occurring. For example:

Joel watched in horror as the paint he had just spilled oozed slowly over his teacher's new notebook.

Then, write the story first from the point of view of Joel and then from the point of view of his teacher.

Joel could begin:

I'm in trouble now. She's never liked me. This will be it. She'll call my parents and I'll be grounded for the rest of my life. What should I do? Okay, I'll say that . . .

The teacher could begin:

All right, I'm going to stay calm. He's just a kid. It was just an accident, clearly an accident. That clumsy oaf! But he looks so terrified. All right, I'll . . .

Select this situation or invent one of your own, and write a multiple story.

_____

_____

_____

_____

_____

_____

_____

Name _____ **Date** _____

CONSONANT-LE SYLLABLES
"tle, fle, cle, kle"

GETTING STARTED

Ask your students to give examples of words that contain the four types of consonant-le syllables presented in the last two lessons: "ble," "dle," "ple," and "gle." Then give your students time to make a page for their notebooks for "ple" and "gle."

INTRODUCING NEW INFORMATION

"Today, we are going to continue to work with consonant-le syllables."
Present the following lists of words:

circle	ankle	baffle	beetle
obstacle	freckle	rifle	cattle
spectacle	pickle	shuffle	gentle
uncle	sprinkle	trifle	little
vehicle	twinkle	waffle	title

Read these words to your students, and then ask them to read them silently to themselves.

"What sound do you hear at the end of these words?"

"Yes, an /ull,/ as in 'bull' or 'pull.' What generalization can you make about the sound of consonant-le syllables?"

"That's right. They take the sound of their consonant and then add the /ull/ sound. Now look at the lists of words and name four other consonants that are often seen in consonant-le syllables."

"Yes, there are several words that end in 'cle,' 'kle,' 'fle,' and 'tle.'"

❖ PRACTICING WITH INDIVIDUAL WORDS

Select a manageable number of words from the word list provided on page 329 for your students to spell.

⑤ PRACTICING SPELLING IN CONTEXT

Select a manageable number of sentences from the following list for your students to write.

The title of the book is *The Wind in the Willows.*

Janet ate a dill pickle and a bag of chips at snack time.

"When will we tackle that job?" Fran asked.

David stifled his sniffles.

Betty got a little tired running the five-mile race.

"Look at the hundreds of ruffles," Kate said as she picked up the dress in the shop.

"That dog is so gentle with those kittens," Jane said.

Andy asked his uncle to let him drive the speedboat to the end of the lake.

The little kid had lots of freckles.

"My lack of study time is a big obstacle to my passing the math test," Joseph said.

◼ REINFORCING ACTIVITIES

Allow your students to choose from the following list of activities:

1. Write sentences, each of which contains more than two words with consonant-le syllables. You can choose words with any consonant-le syllable you like. An example is, "'I'd rather learn about Aristotle than Constantinople,' my uncle said." If you wish, illustrate one or more of your sentences.

2. Play a "Little" word game. You can play this game alone or with friends. Start with a little word such as "a." Then add one or more letters to this word to create a new word. Then add to that word; for example, you might write: "a," "as," "asp," "hasp." Can you go further? The challenge is to make the string of words as long as you can.

   Good little words to begin with are: "on," "am," "to," "no," and "it." If you start a string and it ends quickly, you can always begin again, as with "a," "an," "and," "sand," "sands," "sandstone," "sandstones." Dictionaries are very helpful to use to help you think of good words to add.

3. We have all heard stories of desperate people who, when marooned on a desert island, send a message in a bottle to summon help. Why wait to be marooned to send a message?

   Find a bottle, such as a clean fruit juice bottle. Then write one or more messages to put in the bottle. These messages can be favorite riddles or jokes, or they can be interesting facts you have learned; for example, you could write, "Did you know that tarantulas molt?"

   To find interesting facts, you can look in books or you can talk with people who are knowledgeable in a certain subject. You, also, right now, have a wide range of knowledge that could make interesting messages. For example, do you know a lot about skateboarding? If so, write messages about that.

   Talk with your teacher about when would be a good time to share your messages. Also, invite other people to contribute messages to the bottle.

4. LITERATURE CONNECTION: *A Wrinkle in Time* by Madeleine L'Engle (Farrar, Straus, 1962) is about a girl, Meg, and her friend and little brother who journey to another place and time to rescue Meg's father. If you enjoy this classic tale of fantasy, read the next two books in the trilogy: *A Wind in the Door* and *A Swiftly Tilting Planet*.

⧉ EXTRA INTERESTING FACTS

The word "uncle" comes originally from the Latin "avunculus," which means one's mother's brother. "Uncle" was modified by the English and the French people, until it now means "a brother of one's parents." Its meaning has also extended to indicate the spouse of one's aunt.

It is most interesting, however, to examine the many ways "uncle" is used in modern American English. Three main uses are:

1. Uncle Sam ("born" during the War of 1812) refers to the United States. Do you think the name might have been inspired by the initials U.S.?

2. In African-American communities, an uncle is a person who is servile to white people. This comes from the character Uncle Tom in Harriet Beecher Stowe's *Uncle Tom's Cabin.*

3. When someone cries "uncle," it means that he has recognized and admitted his lack of power.

One curiosity of consonant-le syllables is that when a "tle" syllable is preceded by an "s," the "t" becomes silent. Examples of words where this occurs are: "castle," "hustle," "thistle," "wrestle," "whistle."

WORD LIST

CONSONANT-LE SYLLABLE: TLE

battle	gentle	resettle	teakettle
beetle	kettle	scuttle	throttle
belittle	little	Seattle	title
bottle	mantle	settle	unsettle
brittle	mistitle	shuttle	whittle
cattle	prattle	subtitle	
entitle	rattle	tattle	

CONSONANT-LE SYLLABLE: FLE

baffle	reshuffle	shuffle	trifle
muffle	rifle	sniffle	truffle
raffle	ruffle	stifle	waffle

CONSONANT-LE SYLLABLE: KLE

ankle	fickle	ramshackle	tickle
buckle	freckle	shackle	trickle
cackle	heckle	sickle	twinkle
chuckle	pickle	sprinkle	
crackle	prickle	tackle	

CONSONANT-LE SYLLABLE: CLE

clavicle	follicle	receptacle	uncle
cubicle	obstacle	spectacle	vehicle
cuticle	pinnacle		

FINISH IT!

Fill in the blanks with words from the word list.

1. The _____ of the Bulge is an historic event of World War II.

2. Jamal brought the _____ back to the store to be recycled.

3. Kara fell down and sprained her _____.

4. "Stop that jumping! You're making a _____ of yourself," Bruce said.

5. Jean was interested in studying insects, especially _____.

6. "I certainly need a new _____," Keisha said as she looked despairingly at her old car.

7. With a _____ in her eye, Jill began to count the money she had earned.

8. The _____ grazed peacefully in the meadow.

9. The crime _____ the detective, and she did not know how to proceed.

10. Pete made _____ with maple syrup and bananas for breakfast.

WORD LIST

beetles   cattle

baffled   Battle

vehicle   waffles

bottles   twinkle

spectacle   ankle

Name _____   **Date** _____

A GAME OF CATEGORIES

Choose words from your word list that belong in each category.

PARTS OF THE BODY

_____

_____

_____

_____

_____

WAYS TO HARM SOMEONE

_____

_____

_____

_____

_____

SOUNDS

_____

_____

_____

_____

CONTAINERS

_____

_____

_____

_____

WORD LIST

cuticle	crackle
cackle	freckle
tackle	kettle
bottle	belittle
clavicle	rattle
battle	tattle
chuckle	teakettle
receptacle	throttle
ventricle	ankle

Name _____   Date _____

LOOK IT UP!

Look up the listed words in your dictionary. Then match each word with its correct definition.

1. pinnacle   a. unimportant, silly talk
2. truffle   b. the pointed top of a mountain
3. hackle   c. to put irregular spots or streaks of color on a surface
4. disentitle   d. a type of blackbird
5. mottle   e. a type of edible fungi that grows in the earth
6. baffle   f. a remedy
7. piffle   g. the long neck feathers of a bird such as a rooster
8. treacle   h. to make unhappy
9. disgruntle   i. to take away a claim or right
10. grackle   j. to confuse

Now choose five words from the above list and use each one in a sentence.

1. _____

_____

2. _____

_____

3. _____

_____

4. _____

_____

5. _____

_____

Name _____   **Date** _____

LIST IT!

When something baffles a person, it confuses or puzzles. There are many things in our world that baffle us. Three of these are:

1. the Abominable Snowman

2. the Bermuda Triangle

3. the Loch Ness Monster

Choose one of these baffling mysteries and read about it. Then write a list of facts about the legend.

_____

_____

_____

_____

_____

_____

_____

_____

_____

_____

_____

_____

Name _____ **Date** _____

△ △ △ △ △ △ △ △ △ △ △ △ △ △ △ △

WRITE ON!

It is usually considered bad to tattle or "tell on" other people. For this activity, however, you are going to pretend to be a champion tattler.

First, choose an historic event such as Paul Revere's ride during the Revolutionary War. Next, do research so that you become familiar with the important facts. Then pretend you are a person who was there and who knows that what has been reported in the history books is definitely *not* the truth. Write your own account of the famous event. And don't forget to tell your readers why the story has been wrong all these years!

_____

_____

_____

_____

_____

_____

_____

_____

_____

_____

_____

_____

_____

_____

Name _____ **Date** _____

SPELLING GENERALIZATION "ch, tch"

▣ GETTING STARTED

Discuss the consonant-le syllable type. Ask your students to look around the room and to check in books to find some examples of common consonant-le words. Then provide time for your students to make a page for their notebooks for "tle," "fle," "cle," and "kle."

◖ INTRODUCING NEW INFORMATION

"Today, we are going to work with a spelling generalization."
Say the following words: coach, goldfinch, inch, mulch, peach, speech.
"What sound do you hear at the end of these words?"
"Yes, you hear a /ch/ sound, as in 'chin.'"
Record the following words: coach, goldfinch, inch, mulch, peach, speech.
"What do you see at the end of these words?"
"I agree that you see the letters 'ch.' This is the usual way that we spell the /ch/ sound."
Say the following words: catch, ditch, hutch, itch, sketch, topnotch.
"What do you hear at the end of these words?"

335

"That's right. You hear the same /ch/ sound as in 'chin.'"
Record the following words: catch, ditch, hutch, itch, sketch, topnotch.
"What three letters do you notice at the end of these words?"
"Yes, each of these words ends with 'tch.'"
Place both lists of words side by side. *"Can you figure out when the /ch/ sound is spelled with a 'tch' at the end of a word, rather than with a 'ch'?"*
"That is right. When a /ch/ sound is heard at the end of a word and it is preceded by a single short vowel, the sound is usually spelled with a 'tch.' In all other cases, the /ch/ is spelled with the regular 'ch.'"
Record the following words: approached, catching, clenched, matching, teaching, stretching.
"What happens when you add suffixes to root words that end in 'ch' or 'tch'?"
"That's right, no change occurs. You simply add the suffix to the root word."

❖ PRACTICING WITH INDIVIDUAL WORDS

Select a manageable number of words from the word list provided on page 338 for your students to spell.

◐ PRACTICING SPELLING IN CONTEXT

Select a manageable number of sentences from the following list for your students to write.

The little kids played hopscotch in the driveway.

"Catch that ball now!" yelled Janet.

Andy and Betty went to the beach to go fishing.

"Steve will teach me how to cook," Jan said.

Jeff stitched a patch on his jeans.

At lunch, Fred had a bag of peanuts and a peach.

"Joan's sketch of Kathy's hands is good," Dave said.

Ben fell off his bike into the ditch.

The biggest branch of the tree fell down on the road.

"If each of us can take away a bag of trash, that will help a lot to clean up this mess," Emily said.

◼ REINFORCING ACTIVITIES

Allow your students to choose from the following list of activities:

1. Select pairs of words, one which ends with a "ch," and the other which ends with a "tch"; for example, "hunch" and "fetch," and "reach" and "watch." Write sen-

tences with these words. A sentence for the last pair could be, "Henry watched as his sister reached the finish line." If you wish, illustrate one or more of your sentences.

2. The Dutch people live in the Netherlands, also known as Holland. This small European country lies northwest of Germany. Find an encyclopedia in your library and read about the people and culture of the Netherlands. Then find a globe or map and locate the country where the Dutch people live.

3. All of us have unique skills and talents we can teach to each other. Do you, for example, jump rope very well? Do you know how to knit, bake an apple pie, draw comic strip characters, run a slide projector, change a tire on a car? Think carefully about the skills you possess. Then select one you would like to teach to someone else. Find a willing student and go ahead and TEACH.

4. LITERATURE CONNECTION: There is a lot of debate over whether or not witches exist. Some people say they do and that witches are evil. Others argue that witches exist to do good in the world. Still others say that witches are just imaginary characters made up by people.

   Much literature has been written about witches and the works are extremely diverse. They range from humorous books like *The Witches* by Roald Dahl (Farrar, Straus and Giroux, Inc., 1983) to serious works like the play *The Crucible* by Arthur Miller, which can be found in the book *Arthur Miller's Collected Plays* (Viking Press, 1957). *The Crucible* is based on the Salem witch trials that occurred in Salem, Massachusetts in the 1600s.

   There are also many books that simply tell stories about witches. One of these is *Yankee Witches*, edited by Charles G. Waugh, Martin H. Greenburg and Frank D. McSherry, Jr., illustrated by Peter Farrow (Lance Tapley, Publisher, 1988). Another is *Strega Nona,* written and illustrated by Tomie de Paola (Simon and Schuster Books for Young Readers, 1975). This humorous old tale tells of a "Grandma Witch" who helps people with headaches, warts, and love. Trouble only comes when her helper tries to perform some magic by himself.

⧉ EXTRA INTERESTING FACTS

Have you ever heard the expression, "She made a last ditch effort?" This means that the person tried her best, even if she was not successful.

This expression originated in war and was based on soldiers digging trenches or "ditches" to ward off oncoming invaders. The last ditch was the final stand. This expression is recorded in writing as early as the 1700s.

There are a few words in which the /ch/ sound is preceded by a single short vowel, but the word does not end in "tch." These major exceptions are: "such," "rich," "much," "which," "sandwich."

WORD LIST

WORDS ENDING IN "CH"

beach	finch	pooch
beech	flinch	punch
bench	French	ranch
bleach	goldfinch	reach
branch	hunch	roach
brunch	inch	screech
bunch	leech	scrunch
clench	lunch	speech
clinch	mulch	stagecoach
coach	munch	stench
crunch	peach	teach
drench	pinch	trench
each	poach	

WORDS ENDING IN "TCH"

backstitch	homestretch	snatch
backstretch	hopscotch	snitch
batch	hutch	stitch
bewitch	itch	stretch
catch	latch	switch
clutch	match	thatch
crutch	mismatch	topnotch
dispatch	notch	topstitch
ditch	nuthatch	twitch
Dutch	patch	unlatch
etch	pitch	unstitch
fetch	rematch	witch
hatch	scratch	
hitch	sketch	

FINISH IT!

Fill in the blanks with words from the word list.

1. José taught his dog how to _____.

2. As Kate sat on the _____, she ate her ice cream cone and watched the world go by.

3. "It's important to _____ your muscles every day to stay healthy and fit," Ms. Palaski said.

4. In the movie, the horse was _____ to a lamppost.

5. There are twelve _____ in one foot.

6. It took Natasha and Luke six hours to _____ the top of the mountain.

7. "That poison ivy will make you _____," Mabel said.

8. Sally had a _____ that Mike wanted to be in the play.

9. In the past, many women were accused of being _____.

10. The _____ talked to the team at halftime.

WORD LIST

reach	coach
hunch	hitched
fetch	witches
itch	inches
stretch	bench

Name _____ **Date** _____

A GAME OF CATEGORIES

Choose words from your word list that belong in each category.

RELATING TO SEWING

_____

_____

_____

_____

_____

BIRDS

_____

_____

_____

_____

_____

RELATING TO FOOD OR DRINK

_____

_____

_____

_____

LIVING THINGS (BUT NOT BIRDS)

_____

_____

_____

_____

WORD LIST

nuthatch	backstitch
cockroach	goldfinch
patch	roach
lunch	hemstitch
bullfinch	chaffinch
stitch	quench
leech	topstitch
peach	punch
finch	pooch

Name _____   **Date** _____

LOOK IT UP!

Look up the listed words in your dictionary. Then match each word with its correct definition.

1. broach   a. to take away the color

2. splotch   b. to blame someone for doing something wrong

3. filch   c. a spot or mark

4. dispatch   d. a winter ceremony of Northern Pacific people dur-
                      ing which gifts are exchanged

5. blanch   e. to establish and protect

6. potlatch   f. a skewer for cooking meat, or to introduce a topic

7. botch   g. a pen for little animals

8. reproach   h. to steal with caution

9. hutch   i. to do a job poorly

10. entrench   j. to send a message

Now choose five words from the above list and use each one in a sentence.

1. _____

   _____

2. _____

   _____

3. _____

   _____

4. _____

   _____

5. _____

   _____

Name _____   **Date** _____

LIST IT!

The word "sandwich" represents an exception to the "tch" spelling generalization. Even though the /ch/ sound follows a single short vowel, this word does not end with "tch."

Perhaps this is because "sandwich" originates in a name: the fourth Earl of Sandwich. Lord Sandwich liked to gamble, but he did not like to stop for meals. He, instead, insisted that meat be brought to him between two slices of bread. Thus, the sandwich was born.

Even though the Earl invented the sandwich, he probably did not use much imagination in thinking up different types. This is what *you* are going to do.

Make a list of fillings for a sandwich. You can either invent humorous sandwiches (chocolate-covered ants with mayo anyone?), or you can seriously try to invent good tasting "new" sandwiches (how about cheese, roasted red peppers, black olives, and honey mustard?).

_____

_____

_____

_____

_____

_____

_____

_____

_____

_____

_____

Name _____   Date _____

WRITE ON!

AN ACCEPTANCE SPEECH

Pretend you are someone else. You can choose to be a famous sports figure, a politician, a character in a book you have read, or a person from history. "You" are being given an award, and you must make a speech of acceptance.

First, figure out what "your" award is going to be.

Will the award be for outstanding achievement, for facing great burdens with courage, for never giving up? Next, plan an outline of things to say as "you" accept this award. Then practice your speech. Last, find an audience and give your speech.

_____

_____

_____

_____

_____

_____

_____

_____

_____

_____

_____

_____

_____

Name _____ **Date** _____

SPELLING GENERALIZATION "ge, dge"

▣ GETTING STARTED

Ask your students to tell you about the spelling generalization with "ch" and "tch." List some common words that illustrate this generalization. Then give your students time to make a page for their notebooks for "ch" and "tch."

◖ INTRODUCING NEW INFORMATION

"Today, we are going to work with another spelling generalization."
Say the following words: age, challenge, exchange, hinge, plunge, refuge.
"What sound do you hear at the end of these words?"
"I agree that you hear a /j/ sound, as in 'jam.'"
Record the following words: age, challenge, exchange, hinge, plunge, refuge.
"What two letters do you see at the end of these words?"
"Good. You see the letters 'ge.' When you hear the /j/ sound at the end of a word, the most common way to spell it is with 'ge.' Now, let's work further with the /j/ sound at the end of words."
Say the following words: bridge, dislodge, fudge, ledge, misjudge, ridge.
"What sound do you hear at the end of these words?"

344

"Yes, you hear the same /j/ sound, as in 'jam.'"
Record the following words: bridge, dislodge, fudge, ledge, misjudge, ridge.
"What three letters do you notice at the end of these words?"
"That's correct. All of these words end with 'dge.'"
Place both lists of words next to each other. *"Can you figure out when the /j/ sound is spelled with a 'dge' at the end of a word, rather than with just 'ge'?"*

"Yes, when a /j/ sound is heard at the end of a word and it is preceded by a single short vowel, the sound is usually spelled with a 'dge.' In all other cases, the /j/ is spelled with 'ge.'

"But let's talk just a little more about the words presented in this lesson. Look at the two lists. What are the syllable types of these words?"

"That's good. 'Age' is a consonant-vowel-e syllable. 'Refuge' has a closed syllable and a consonant-vowel-e syllable. The first syllable of 'challenge' is a closed syllable. But what about the second syllable in 'challenge' and the words 'bridge' and 'hinge' and the others?"

"You're right. This is a syllable type we have not seen before. This demonstrates the irregularities of the English language. Most words have recognizable syllable types, but some do not. In the case of 'ge' and 'dge,' this may be caused by the fact that English words do not end with the letter 'j.' Instead, 'ge' and 'dge' substitute for this letter, and this makes the syllable type an unusual one."

❖ PRACTICING WITH INDIVIDUAL WORDS

Select a manageable number of words from the word list provided on page 347 for your students to spell.

⑤ PRACTICING SPELLING IN CONTEXT

Select a manageable number of sentences from the following list for your students to write.

The kids played dodge ball.

"That footbridge feels a little shaky," Fran said.

The huge strange bug landed on the tomato plant.

"Look in the fridge and see if the milk is still good," Sam said.

"The challenge is not to win the race, but just to finish it," Midge said.

Pam ate a lot of fudge and then felt a little sick.

Nat made a pledge to help Dan with his problem.

The silly hat had a yellow fringe on its rim.

The edge of the table was clean and smooth.

David went backstage to meet his uncle at the end of the show.

◘ REINFORCING ACTIVITIES

Allow your students to choose from the following list of activities:

1. Select pairs of words, one that ends with "ge" and the other that ends with "dge"; for example, "cage" and "budge," and "stage" and "edge." Write sentences with these words. A sentence for the last pair could be, "The actress stood at the edge of the stage and spoke softly." If you wish, illustrate one or more of your sentences.

2. Calvin Coolidge was president of the United States from 1923 to 1929, the year of the Wall Street crash. Mr. Coolidge was known to be a silent man, but one with great wit. Once, when a woman told him that she had made a bet that she could get him to say more than two words to her, Coolidge responded with, "You lose."

   Many other anecdotes are attributed to him. Find an encyclopedia in your library and read about Calvin Coolidge.

3. Fudge is a candy most of us enjoy. Go to your library or to a person you know who cooks, and find some fudge recipes. One book that contains good fudge recipes is *Lots and Lots of Candy* by Carolyn Meyer (Harcourt Brace Jovanovich, 1976). Once you have selected your recipe, find an adult who is knowledgeable about cooking and willing to help you, and make some fudge.

4. LITERATURE CONNECTION: *The Bridge to Terabithia* by Katherine Paterson (Crowell, 1977) is a story of an unlikely friendship between Jess, a lonely boy, and Leslie, a girl who moves into a nearby home. Because of their friendship, Jess's life is greatly enriched. When Leslie accidentally dies, however, Jess has to deal with this horrifying loss.

   The Bridge to Terabithia is a story that touches all ages. It is a powerful and ultimately hopeful book.

⊟ EXTRA INTERESTING FACTS

It's time consuming to use long words in everyday speech and, therefore, words are often shortened when used regularly by people. One example of such a shortening is the word "fridge" from "refrigerator." It's interesting that when people began to write the shortened form, they followed the spelling generalization with "dge." Thus, they added the "d" to the word.

There is one main exception to the spelling generalization with "ge" and "dge." When words end with the /ij/ sound, this sound is spelled "age." Examples of these words are: "cottage," "mileage," "package."

WORD LIST

WORDS ENDING IN "GE"

age	huge	sage
avenge	impinge	scavenge
backstage	indulge	singe
bulge	infringe	strange
cage	lunge	substage
challenge	oblige	teenage
cringe	offstage	tinge
divulge	page	twinge
downstage	plunge	unchange
engage	privilege	unhinge
enrage	rage	upstage
exchange	range	wage
fringe	refuge	
hinge	revenge	

WORDS ENDING IN "DGE"

abridge	edge	Midge
badge	footbridge	misjudge
begrudge	fridge	nudge
bridge	fudge	pledge
budge	grudge	prejudge
Coolidge	hedge	ridge
dislodge	judge	trudge
dodge	ledge	wedge
dredge	lodge	

FINISH IT!

Fill in the blanks with words from the word list.

1. The little girl got a shiny new _____ for her sheriff's costume.

2. "It's amazing that he still hikes up mountains at his _____ of eighty-seven," Jack said.

3. The mountain goat stood on the rock _____.

4. Leroy was so overtired, he felt _____ in his muscles.

5. Pat got paid a good _____ for her work.

6. The _____ heard the court case.

7. Tim was so angry that, for a moment, he wanted _____.

8. A new _____ was built over the river.

9. "This coat doesn't fit, so I'm going to _____ it," Bay Ly said.

10. Don had a job mowing lawns and clipping _____.

WORD LIST

wage	age
ridge	revenge
exchange	judge
bridge	hedges
twinges	badge

Name _____   **Date** _____

A GAME OF CATEGORIES

Choose words from your word list that belong in each category.

RELATING TO MOVEMENT

_____

_____

_____

_____

_____

RELATING TO THE THEATER

_____

_____

_____

_____

_____

RELATING TO MAKING DECISIONS

_____

_____

_____

_____

PLACES

_____

_____

_____

_____

WORD LIST

adjudge

dislodge

ledge

backstage

downstage

judge

dodge

ridge

lunge

offstage

misjudge

plunge

edge

prejudge

stage

trudge

bulge

upstage

Name _____   **Date** _____

LOOK IT UP!

Look up the listed words in your dictionary. Then match each word with its correct definition.

1. abridge   a. a machine that scrapes the bottoms of bodies of water, such as bays

2. sage   b. to complain, especially about someone else's good luck

3. divulge   c. a type of anchor

4. flange   d. to make shorter and more concise

5. sedge   e. a raised edge that holds and guides a wheel

6. begrudge   f. a type of grass

7. impinge   g. to be very wise

8. dredge   h. to burn a little on the surface

9. singe   i. to reveal information

10. kedge   j. to fight against, to try to take away something that belongs to another

Now choose five words from the above list and use each one in a sentence.

1. _____

_____

2. _____

_____

3. _____

_____

4. _____

_____

5. _____

_____

Name _____ **Date** _____

LIST IT!

STRANGE FACTS

Do you know that polar bears can run up to twenty-five miles an hour, faster than reindeer? Or that it hadn't rained in Calama, a town in the Chilean desert, for four hundred years until one day in 1971? On that day, the town got so much rain, it was flooded and washed away.

Our world is full of wondrous, strange facts. Check books in your library. The two facts recorded above were learned from *Weird and Wonderful Science Facts* by Dr. Magnus Pyke, illustrated by Terry Burton (Sterling Publishing Co., 1984). Ask friends if they know of any truly weird facts. Then make a list of strange facts.

_____

_____

_____

_____

_____

_____

_____

_____

_____

_____

_____

_____

Name _____   **Date** _____

WRITE ON!

Challenges force us to consider our actions and our goals. In many ways, even though they are not always welcome, they can enrich our lives.

Write a statement about a challenge. This can be a challenge you are currently facing, a challenge for your city or town, for your country, or for the world. In your statement, discuss what is causing the challenge, and what you feel needs to be done to meet it successfully.

_____

_____

_____

_____

_____

_____

_____

_____

_____

_____

_____

_____

_____

_____

Name _____   **Date** _____

R-CONTROLLED
SYLLABLE
"ar"

▣ GETTING STARTED

Discuss the spelling generalization with "ge" and "dge." Ask your students to list some common words that illustrate this generalization. Then provide time for your students to make a page for their notebooks for "ge" and "dge."

◖ INTRODUCING NEW INFORMATION

"Today, we are going to work with a new syllable type. This will be the last major syllable type that we will study."
Say the following words: arm, card, dark, march, sharp, star.
"What vowel sound do you hear in these words?"
"Yes, you hear /ar/ as if you are naming the letter 'r.'"
Record the following words: arm, card, dark, march, sharp, star.
"What letter pattern do you see in these words?"
"I agree that you see an 'a' followed by an 'r.' This type of syllable is called an r-controlled syllable.
"It is similar to a closed syllable in that a vowel is followed by one consonant, but it is considered a special type because the letter 'r' changes the vowel sound of whichever

vowel it follows. 'R' is a powerful letter in this way. Now let's see if r-controlled syllables occur in multisyllabic words."

Record the following words: artist, depart, garden, marble, popular, sparkle.

"Do you see r-controlled syllables in these words?"

"That's right, you do. There are also closed syllables, open syllables, and consonant-le syllables."

❖ PRACTICING WITH INDIVIDUAL WORDS

Select a manageable number of words from the word list provided on page 356 for your students to spell.

§ PRACTICING SPELLING IN CONTEXT

Select a manageable number of sentences from the following list for your students to write.

The stars sparkled in the sky.

The artist cleaned his paint brush.

Martha and Amy had a good time playing cards.

Mark went to the barn and started milking the cows.

"Don is smart and charming," June said.

The huge white shark stayed in the deepest part of the sea.

In the park, the little kids played a baseball game.

Bart put the load of paint and varnish in the cart.

It was hard not to see Marta with the scarlet cape.

Tom had six tomato plants and lots of green beans growing in his garden.

▣ REINFORCING ACTIVITIES

Allow your students to choose from the following list of activities:

1. Write a paragraph that contains words with r-controlled syllables with "ar." Challenge yourself to use as many of these words as you can. If you wish, illustrate your paragraph. An example of such a paragraph is:

   It was a sunny day on the farm, and Martha was working in the herb garden. But then the skies started getting dark. Martha hurried to harvest her basil so that she could get it to market before the rains came.

2. The expression "This car is a lemon" means that the car is constantly breaking down and is, generally, a great disappointment to its owner. The literal meaning

of this cliché is very different, however. Illustrate the literal meaning of "This car is a lemon."

3. The planet Mars has fascinated people for many years. It is relatively close to us. From what we now know, it is the planet that would be the easiest for people to explore, since it has the least hostile environment to us. After all, on a hot sunny day, it might reach 0 degrees Centigrade (32 degrees Fahrenheit).

   Go to your library and find information on Mars. You can check the encyclopedia or look for books such as *Rand McNally Discovery Atlas of Planets and Stars* (Rand McNally for Kids, 1993).

4. LITERATURE CONNECTION: Art books contain pictures of some of the world's most beautiful art. These books also give information about artists. Go to your library and see if you can find the section where art books are kept. Also, ask your librarian to show you the section where the oversized books are stored, because many art books are large and are, therefore, kept in this special place.

   A Young Painter, The Life and Paintings of Wang Yani—China's Extraordinary Young Artist by Zheng Zhensun and Alice Low (a Byron Press/New China Pictures Book, Scholastic Inc., 1991) tells of a young girl's amazing ability with art. Born in 1975, Yani began painting at an early age. Her father recognized her great talent when she was just three years old. Read *A Young Painter* to learn about Yani and to see pictures of some of her brush paintings.

⧉ EXTRA INTERESTING FACTS

Many people are familiar with Scotland Yard because of the famous detectives who have connections there. But where did Scotland Yard get its name?

Many years ago, Scottish kings used to visit London. When in town, they lived in a palace that was on the site where the current Scotland Yard now exists. The building, therefore, got its name from where it was built.

The most common sound of the r-controlled syllable with "ar" is the one we have studied in this lesson, where the "ar" sounds like the name of the letter "r." In some words, however, the "ar" sounds like /er/, as in "her." Some of these words are "collar," "dollar," and "blizzard."

WORD LIST

R-CONTROLLED SYLLABLE: AR, ONE-SYLLABLE WORDS

arm	farm	part
art	hard	scar
bar	harm	scarf
bark	harp	shark
barn	harsh	sharp
car	jar	smart
card	lard	snarl
cart	lark	spar
carp	march	spark
charm	mark	star
chart	Mars	start
dark	marsh	tar
dart	mart	yard
far	park	yarn

R-CONTROLLED SYLLABLE: AR, MULTISYLLABIC WORDS

artist	garlic	remark
cargo	garment	scarlet
carpet	harden	sharpen
cartoon	harvest	sparkle
charcoal	marble	startle
darling	market	target
depart	marlin	tarnish
discard	marvel	varnish
garden	party	
gargle	popular	

FINISH IT!

Fill in the blanks with words from the word list.

1. Rob enjoyed all forms of _____, but he especially liked sculpture.

2. Rather than doing her homework, Pamela often drew funny

_____.

3. The month of _____ comes before April.

4. Omar bought some _____ so that he could cook his supper outside on the grill.

5. "It's too _____ to walk, so let's take our bikes," Shanika said.

6. The class sat on the _____ and listened to the story.

7. The night was _____, since clouds hid the moon.

8. The country music band played many places because it was so

_____.

9. "That knife is _____ , so be careful when you cut the carrots," Nick said.

10. The mason built the fireplace mantle out of _____.

WORD LIST

charcoal	March
dark	popular
art	far
marble	cartoons
carpet	sharp

Name _____ **Date** _____

A GAME OF CATEGORIES

Choose words from your word list that belong in each category.

BIRDS AND FISHES

_____

_____

_____

_____

_____

PLACES

_____

_____

_____

_____

_____

RELATING TO COMMUNICATION

_____

_____

_____

_____

NAMES OF PEOPLE

_____

_____

_____

_____

WORD LIST

farm	partridge
Bart	Marta
remark	yard
marlin	snarl
carp	starling
Mark	impart
shark	Martha
barnyard	Mars
marsh	bark

Name _____ Date _____

LOOK IT UP!

Look up the listed words in your dictionary. Then match each word with its correct definition.

1. garb   a. a type of fish
2. parlay   b. someone who is often in trouble
3. ardent   c. clothes, a style of dressing
4. shard   d. a woolen plaid cloth, often worn in Scotland
5. impart   e. a type of soil
6. tartan   f. to bet the winnings from another wager
7. mar   g. to hurt or spoil
8. varmint   h. a little piece that is broken off, often of pottery
9. gar   i. very enthusiastic
10. marl   j. to tell or give, as with information

Now choose five words from the above list and use each one in a sentence.

1. _____

_____

2. _____

_____

3. _____

_____

4. _____

_____

5. _____

_____

Name _____   **Date** _____

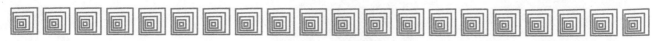

LIST IT!

THE SCAR

You are sitting on a park bench. An elderly man approaches and sits next to you. He seems normal . . . ordinary, until he turns to you and you notice a two-inch scar above his right eyebrow.

Make a list of ways you imagine this man could have gotten this scar. Be as imaginative as you can. Two examples are:

1. He was hiking in the mountains and a piece of meteorite hit him.

2. He is a veterinarian who once performed surgery on a lion. During surgery, the lion woke up and . . . .

_____

_____

_____

_____

_____

_____

_____

_____

_____

_____

_____

_____

Name _____   Date _____

△ △ △ △ △ △ △ △ △ △ △ △ △ △ △ △

WRITE ON!

Make your own post cards. First, find some sturdy paper and cut out rectangles 4-1/4 inches wide by 6 inches long. Larger post cards are more expensive to send than this standard size.

Next, decide how you are going to illustrate your card. You can paint an abstract design, draw a picture of a place you have recently visited, even draw a cartoon.

Then decide to whom you are going to send your card and write a message. You don't have to send your card to someone who lives far away. You could surprise a nearby friend by mailing him or her a message.

_____

_____

_____

_____

_____

_____

_____

_____

_____

_____

_____

_____

_____

Name _____ **Date** _____

R-CONTROLLED SYLLABLE "or"

▣ GETTING STARTED

Ask your students to talk about the six types of syllables they have discovered. List them and record examples of each.

Select a paragraph from a book or magazine. Together, look at the individual words and discuss their syllable types. Notice any that are irregular. Talk about how most English words are made up of the six major syllables, but that there are some that are irregular.

Give your students time to make a page in their notebooks for the r-controlled syllable with "ar."

◖ INTRODUCING NEW INFORMATION

"Today, we are going to continue to work with r-controlled syllables."
Say the following words: cord, fork, horn, porch, storm, thorn.
"What vowel sound do you hear in these words?"
"Yes, you hear /or/ as in the word 'or.'"
Record the following words: cord, fork, horn, porch, storm, thorn.
"What letter pattern do you see in these words?"

"That's right. You see an 'o' followed by an 'r.' This is a second kind of r-controlled syllable. Let's see if 'or' is found in multisyllabic words."

Record the following words: acorn, category, export, forty, platform, shortwave.

"Do you see r-controlled syllables in these words?"

"I agree. There are also open, closed, and vowel-consonant-e syllables."

"We need to work more with the r-controlled syllable with 'or.' This is because, in some instances, the 'or' represents the /er/ sound as in 'her.'"

Record the following words: word, work, world, worm, worry, worth.

"Can you figure out when 'or' represents the /er/ sound?"

"That's good. If 'or' occurs after a 'w,' the sound represented is /er/. There is one other case where 'or' represents /er/."

Record the following words: actor, alligator, doctor, harbor, labor, tractor.

"Can you figure out the other time that 'or' represents the /er/ sound?"

"I agree. When 'or' occurs at the end of a multisyllabic word, it usually represents the /er/ sound. Will you please summarize what you have discovered today."

"Yes, the r-controlled syllable with 'or' usually represents the /or/ sound. When 'or' follows a 'w,' however, or when it occurs at the end of a multisyllabic word, it represents the /er/ sound."

❖ PRACTICING WITH INDIVIDUAL WORDS

Select a manageable number of words from the word list provided on page 365 for your students to spell.

☯ PRACTICING SPELLING IN CONTEXT

Select a manageable number of sentences from the following list for your students to write.

Bob had corn on the cob at the picnic.

Beth went to Florida to study alligators.

The tornado came in the middle of the day.

"That class is so boring," Kim said.

Ron took the bus up north to visit his uncle.

"I like all sports. I like baseball, basketball, track, swimming, and even javelin throwing," Janet said.

Alex picked up his fork and started to eat.

Yoko stood on the platform and waited for the train.

The porcupine rested in the hollow of the tree.

"It will be a lot of hard work, but it will be worth it," Pam said, as she started painting the cabin.

◼ REINFORCING ACTIVITIES

Allow your students to choose from the following list of activities:

1. Write a paragraph that contains words with r-controlled syllables with "or." Challenge yourself to use as many of these words as you can. An example of such a paragraph is:

   Rick had a memory of sitting on a porch and seeing a short man walk by. The man was wearing some sort of uniform. Suddenly, the man stopped and began to juggle some small objects. Rick realized that they were acorns! After a few minutes, the man placed the acorns back in his pocket and walked away toward the horizon.

   If you wish, illustrate your paragraph.

2. Record a literature tape for a friend. Ask a teacher or librarian to help you locate a tape recorder and a blank tape. Then select either pieces you have written, or look in favorite books for selections of poems, stories or nonfiction pieces to read. Plan your reading choices carefully and then record them. Be sure to say where each selection comes from. Then find a friend who wants to listen to your tape.

3. Many fascinating animals inhabit our world. Two common ones are porcupines and alligators. But have you ever heard of worm lizards? Go to your library and look for information on these animals. One good book, often found in the reference section, is *Macmillan Illustrated Animal Encyclopedia, a visual who's who of all the world's creatures,* edited by Dr. Philip Whitfield, foreword by Gerald Durrell (Macmillan Publishing Co., 1984).

4. LITERATURE CONNECTION: Short stories are a unique form of literature. A writer who has mastered this form is Langston Hughes. His story "Thank You, M'am" tells of a young boy who attempts to steal a woman's purse. The boy is not successful, but the story does not end with the foiled theft. It twists and turns until we really care for the woman and the boy.

   Read "Thank You, M'am" in *Something in Common and Other Stories* by Langston Hughes (American Century Series, Hill and Wang, a division of Farrar, Straus and Giroux, 1963).

⧉ EXTRA INTERESTING FACTS

Would you find it odd to sit down at the dinner table and not find a fork by your plate? If you lived before the 1600s in England, you would think it was normal because forks were not used before that time.

It's said that Thomas Coryate brought forks to England in the early 1600s after he had seen people use them in Italy. Do you think the English people applauded Mr. Coryate's efforts to make their dining habits more efficient? What they did, in fact, was laugh at his idea.

In spite of people's initial reluctance, forks did eventually become popular. The word "fork" itself is derived from the Old English word "forca." This was the word for "pitchfork."

WORD LIST

R-CONTROLLED SYLLABLE: "OR," ONE-SYLLABLE WORDS

born	form	or	sort
cord	fort	porch	sport
cork	forth	pork	stork
corn	horn	port	storm
for	lord	scorch	thorn
ford	nor	scorn	torch
fork	north	short	torn

R-CONTROLLED SYLLABLE: "OR," MULTISYLLABIC WORDS

absorb	escort	horizon	platform
acorn	export	hornet	porcupine
boring	forest	inform	portray
borrow	forgave	memorize	record
category	forget	memory	reform
corncob	formula	morning	shortstop
cornmeal	forty	northwest	shortwave
deformity	glory	organic	transport
distort	history	orbit	uniform

R-CONTROLLED SYLLABLE: "OR" AFTER A "W"

word	world	worry	worth
work	worm	worship	worthy

R-CONTROLLED SYLLABLE: "OR" AT THE END OF MULTISYLLABIC WORDS

actor	editor	labor	terror
alligator	error	mentor	tractor
captor	harbor	splendor	victor
doctor	horror	sponsor	visitor

✠ ✠ ✠ ✠ ✠ ✠ ✠ ✠ ✠ ✠ ✠ ✠ ✠ ✠ ✠ ✠ ✠ ✠

FINISH IT!

Fill in the blanks with words from the word list.

1. The old coat was dirty and _____.

2. The squirrel dug a hole and stored his _____ in the ground.

3. Oceans cover a large percentage of our _____.

4. Linda worked hard and was finally able to _____ her whole speech.

5. "I've grown so tall this summer, that all my pants are too _____ for me," Bernard said.

6. The _____ played three different roles in the play.

7. Peter did not want to get stung, so he avoided walking near the _____ nest.

8. "Mike was _____ in Alaska, so he is a U.S. citizen," Helga said.

9. Many fascinating animals and plants live in the rain _____.

10. The people sat on the _____ and talked about old times.

WORD LIST

short	torn
actor	porch
acorn	forest
born	world
memorize	hornet's

Name _____   Date _____

A GAME OF CATEGORIES

Choose words from your word list that belong in each category.

THINGS THAT PEOPLE CAN BE

_____

_____

_____

_____

_____

FROM THE ANIMAL KINGDOM

_____

_____

_____

_____

_____

PARTS OF THE BODY

_____

_____

_____

_____

RELATING TO COMMUNICATION

_____

_____

_____

_____

WORD LIST

bachelor	stork
torso	thorax
visitor	doctor
corn meal	corn bread
alligator	hornet
aorta	corncrib
porcupine	lord
corncob	cortex
actor	horned toad

Name _____   **Date** _____

LOOK IT UP!

Look up the listed words in your dictionary. Then match each word with its correct definition.

1. orb		a.	lack of agreement or harmony
2. hortatory		b.	to be very unhappy
3. tort		c.	a legal term that stands for damages against which a civil suit can be filed
4. ornate		d.	a circular body, especially as relates to the planets, sun, and moon
5. discord		e.	an uproar, a sustained noise
6. forlorn		f.	to fight back with words
7. amoral		g.	giving encouragement
8. candor		h.	not based on standards of morality
9. clamor		i.	very fancy, with much ornament
10. retort		j.	to express oneself with openness and honesty

Now choose five words from the above list and use each one in a sentence.

1. _____

_____

2. _____

_____

3. _____

_____

4. _____

_____

5. _____

_____

Name _____   **Date** _____

LIST IT!

THE MAN IN ARMOR

You walk into your classroom. You think the room is empty until you notice a suit of armor in the corner. But wait. It's moving! There's a man in that armor. And he is coming toward you.

Make a list of possible explanations for why there is a person in a full suit of armor in your classroom. Two possibilities are:

1. **He is a time traveler from an earlier era.**

2. **He is an actor who has lost his way to the stage.**

Be imaginative. For this activity, the rules of reality do not have to stifle your creativity.

_____

_____

_____

_____

_____

_____

_____

_____

_____

_____

_____

Name _____ **Date** _____

WRITE ON!

Select an historical event you would like to learn about. You can choose one with which you are familiar or you can look through books to discover an interesting occurrence.

A good series to refer to is *Great Events, the Twentieth Century,* a Magill Book from the Editors of Salem Press (Salem Press, Inc., 1992). One interesting story you will find recorded in Book One is the formation of the NAACP.

Read about your selected event and think about how you feel about what occurred. Then write a report.

For this report, you are going to pretend you are living in the place where and when the event happened. Record the facts, but also discuss your feelings and opinions. Remember, you are *there*.

_____

_____

_____

_____

_____

_____

_____

_____

_____

_____

_____

_____

Name _____   **Date** _____

R-CONTROLLED
SYLLABLE
"er, ir, ur"

▣ GETTING STARTED

Ask your students to look through their notebooks and to select some information about the spelling of English they wish to tell you about. Discuss this information, and record words that illustrate the syllable type, generalization, rule, or exception they present. Then provide time for your students to make a page in their notebooks for the r-controlled syllable with "or."

◖ INTRODUCING NEW INFORMATION

"Today, we are going to continue to work with r-controlled syllables."
Say the following words: perch, verb, bird, girl, hurt, turn.
"What vowel sound do you hear in these words?"
"Yes, you hear /er/ as in the word 'her.'"
Record the following lists of words:

fern	bird	church
germ	first	fur
her	girl	hurt
perch	third	turn

371

"Do you see the same vowel combination in all these words?"

"I agree that you don't. What do you see instead?"

"Yes, you see an 'e' combined with an 'r,' an 'i' combined with an 'r,' and a 'u' combined with an 'r.' All of these r-controlled syllables make the same sound: /er/ as in the word 'her.' Let's see if these syllables occur in multisyllabic words."

Record the following lists:

carpenter	circle	absurd
entertain	dirty	disturb
sister	thirteen	purple
termite	whirlpool	Thursday

"Do you see r-controlled syllables with 'er,' 'ir,' and 'ur' in these words?"

"Yes, you do. There are also closed syllables, consonant-le syllables, vowel combination syllables, a vowel-consonant-e syllable, and an r-controlled syllable with 'ar.'"

"Because the /er/ sound can be spelled with three different r-controlled syllables, this can feel confusing. When you are confronted with spelling this sound, take a good guess and then either check it with a dictionary or with a computer spell check."

❖ PRACTICING WITH INDIVIDUAL WORDS

Select a manageable number of words from the word list provided on page 374 for your students to spell.

❂ PRACTICING SPELLING IN CONTEXT

Select a manageable number of sentences from the following list for your students to write. If your students have not mastered the use of apostrophes to indicate possession, provide a model for this where appropriate.

"It is Tommy's third birthday on Thursday," Abe said.

While surfing, Jane hurt her foot.

Joan invited thirteen girls to her party.

"Turn left at the white church," Henry said.

The stern man did not smile at the baby.

At first, the girl liked the black skirt, but then she got sick of it.

The huge fern shaded the little plants growing under it.

In the north, the weather starts getting cool in September or October.

"Do not disturb me," Mark said. "I am tired and grumpy."

The kids had burgers, green beans, chips, and milk for lunch.

◩ REINFORCING ACTIVITIES

Allow your students to choose from the following list of activities:

1. Write a paragraph that contains words with r-controlled syllables with "er," "ir," and "ur." Challenge yourself to use as many of these words as you can. An example of such a paragraph is:

   The large turtle was resting near the ferns. Because he was thirsty, he started lumbering toward the brook. Suddenly, the birds stopped their chirping. It was obvious that something had disturbed them. The turtle stopped and listened.

   If you wish, illustrate your paragraph.

2. Limericks are short, funny poems that follow a standard form. They are five lines long. The subject of the limerick is stated in the first line. The action is begun in the second. The third and fourth lines continue the action, with the fifth line usually being the punch line of the joke. The first, second, and fifth lines rhyme, as do the third and fourth. An example of a limerick is:

   > *There was a young fellow named Jake*
   > *Who loved eating slices of cake.*
   > *He liked chocolate the best,*
   > *But would eat all the rest,*
   > *Til Jake got a huge stomach ache.*

   Read more about limericks in an encyclopedia. Then, try writing some limericks of your own.

3. The cliché "Money burns a hole in her pocket" means that the person has a hard time saving money, and that she spends whatever she has very quickly. The literal meaning of this cliché, however, is quite specific and humorous. Illustrate the literal meaning of "Money burns a hole in her pocket."

4. LITERATURE CONNECTION: During World War II, some German prisoners were brought to the U.S. and placed in special prison camps. *Summer of My German Soldier* by Bette Greene (Bantam Books, 1973) tells the story of Patty, a young Jewish girl who befriends and shelters Anton, an escapee from such a camp near her home in Arkansas. Patty and Anton find friendship and understanding, something that is lacking in both of their lives.

   If you enjoy reading *Summer of My German Soldier*, you can also read the sequel *Morning Is a Long Time Coming* by Bette Greene (an Archway Paperback published by Pocket Books, 1978).

⧉ EXTRA INTERESTING FACTS

The hamburger that we know today comes from Hamburg, Germany. It started out as Hamburg steak. When German immigrants brought this food with them to the United States in the mid 1800s, both the food and the word changed. The steak got placed between slices of bread. For the word, the capital was dropped and an "er" was added.

WORD LIST

R-CONTROLLED SYLLABLE: "ER," ONE-SYLLABLE WORDS

berth	serf
fern	stern
germ	term
her	tern
perch	verb

R-CONTROLLED SYLLABLE: "ER," MULTISYLLABIC WORDS

carpenter	remainder
chowder	rooster
December	September
eager	sister
entertain	sooner
imperfect	speaker
interpret	sweater
lantern	termite
leader	thunder
monster	tiger
November	underneath
October	usher
partner	verdict
perfect	whisper
reader	yesterday

R-CONTROLLED SYLLABLE: "IR," ONE-SYLLABLE WORDS

birch	girl
bird	shirt
birth	sir
chirp	skirt
dirt	stir
firm	third
first	thirst
flirt	twirl

R-CONTROLLED SYLLABLE: "IR," MULTISYLLABIC WORDS

birthday	skirmish
birthrate	stirrup
circle	thirteen
circus	thirsty
dirty	thirty
girdle	whirlpool

R-CONTROLLED SYLLABLE: "UR," ONE-SYLLABLE WORDS

blur	hurl
burn	hurt
church	lurk
curl	surf
fur	turn

R-CONTROLLED SYLLABLE: "UR," MULTISYLLABIC WORDS

absurd	purple
burden	return
burlap	Saturday
burrow	sturdy
curly	suburb
disturb	surplus
furnish	surprise
further	survive
hurdle	Thursday
murder	turnip
murmur	turtle

FINISH IT!

Fill in the blanks with words from the word list.

1. Dan and Helen _____ to each other, because they did not want to disturb the other students.

2. "Dear _____" began the letter.

3. The events of Jean's day happened so fast, her memory of them was just a _____.

4. The towels were _____, so Pat washed them.

5. The cat sat in the sun and cleaned his _____.

6. The _____ made an oak table for the kitchen.

7. Maria sewed the button back on her _____.

8. Chin made an arrangement of yellow and _____ flowers.

9. "Wash your hands to get rid of _____," Jake said.

10. "It's true that _____ are not my favorite vegetable," Zoe said.

WORD LIST

blur	sir
turnips	shirt
germs	fur
whispered	purple
carpenter	dirty

Name _____ **Date** _____

A GAME OF CATEGORIES

Choose words from your word list that belong in each category.

DIRECTIONS

_____

_____

_____

_____

_____

FROM THE ANIMAL KINGDOM

_____

_____

_____

_____

_____

MONTHS

_____

_____

_____

_____

RELATING TO THE NUMBER THREE

_____

_____

_____

_____

WORD LIST

turtle	northern
third	thirteen
panther	termite
western	northwestern
September	November
thirty	tiger
eastern	thirty-three
October	northeastern
rooster	December

Name _____   **Date** _____

LOOK IT UP!

Look up the listed words in your dictionary. Then match each word with its correct definition.

1. irk   a. to relate to

2. turbulent   b. not strong or able

3. tern   c. a small amount implying poverty

4. curt   d. to unlawfully take over

5. usurp   e. to anger

6. gird   f. to reject with scorn

7. meager   g. to fasten or enclose, as with a belt

8. spurn   h. being boisterous or disturbing

9. appertain   i. a type of bird

10. infirm   j. short and rude

Now choose five words from the above list and use each one in a sentence.

1. _____

   _____

2. _____

   _____

3. _____

   _____

4. _____

   _____

5. _____

   _____

Name _____   **Date** _____

LIST IT!

THIRTY SILVER DOLLARS

You have been home all afternoon studying in your room. You have been **alone, or so you thought.** You go to the kitchen to get a snack. When you turn **on the light,** you see them: thirty silver dollars placed in a perfect circle on the table.

Make a list of possibilities of how the silver dollars got there. Two examples are:

1. The tooth fairy is finally paying me (with interest) for all those teeth I lost as a kid.

2. An ex-burglar with a guilty conscience is leaving strangers money.

If you prefer, you can also write a list of things you might do with the **thirty silver dollars.**

_____

_____

_____

_____

_____

_____

_____

_____

_____

_____

Name _____ **Date** _____

WRITE ON!

Newspapers provide space where they print letters readers write. These letters to the editor are often written to express opinions and beliefs.

Choose a topic about which you have strong feelings. For example, do you feel the U.S. legal system is fair? Do you believe kids should be allowed to drop out of school before they are sixteen? What do you feel about the problem of people being homeless?

Once you have chosen your topic, write your letter to the editor. Then, if you wish, send your letter to your local newspaper.

_____

_____

_____

_____

_____

_____

_____

_____

_____

_____

_____

_____

_____

Name _____ **Date** _____

FINAL VOWEL COMBINATION SYLLABLES
"tion" and "sion"

▣ GETTING STARTED

Discuss r-controlled syllables with your students. Ask them to illustrate the various types of these syllables and the different sounds they make. Then give your students time to make a page in their notebooks for the r-controlled syllables with "er," "ir," and "ur."

◖● INTRODUCING NEW INFORMATION

"Today, we are going to work with a syllable that always occurs at the ends of words."
Say the following words: addition, celebration, imitation, locomotion, reaction, solution.
"What sound do you hear at the end of these words?"
"Yes, you hear /shun/ as in the word 'action.'"
Record the following words: addition, celebration, imitation, locomotion, reaction, solution.

"What do you see at the end of these words?"

"That's right. You see the vowel combination syllable 'tion.' This is the most common way of spelling the sound /shun/ when it occurs at the end of a word. Let's look now at a less common way of spelling this sound."

Record the following words: admission, comprehension, discussion, impression, pension, session.

"What do you see at the end of these words?"

"Good. You see the vowel combination syllable 'sion,' which is a less common way of spelling /shun/ when it is at the end of a word. There is one other thing we need to study."

Say the following words: decision, explosion, illusion, provision, revision, television.

"What sound do you hear at the end of these words?"

"That is right. You hear the /zhun/ sound as in the word 'vision.'"

Record the following words: decision, explosion, illusion, provision, revision, television.

"What do you see at the end of these words?"

"Yes, you see the vowel combination syllable 'sion.' This vowel combination syllable always represents the sound /zhun/ when it's at the end of a word. Please summarize what you have discovered today."

"Good. The most common way of spelling the sound /shun/ in the final position in a word is with the vowel combination syllable 'tion.' A less common way of spelling this sound is with the vowel combination syllable 'sion.' The sound /zhun/ at the end of a word is always spelled with the vowel combination syllable 'sion.'"

❖ PRACTICING WITH INDIVIDUAL WORDS

Select a manageable number of words from the word list provided on page 383 for your students to spell.

❙ PRACTICING SPELLING IN CONTEXT

Select a manageable number of sentences from the following list for your students to write.

The celebration went on for three days.

Luke studied the addition of fractions in math class.

"The admission price to the movies is five dollars," Emily said.

Judy sent a wedding invitation to Sam and Lee.

"The translation of the book is hard to understand," Pete said to Kim.

Steve got the information he needed at the garden shop.

Betty felt a lot of satisfaction when she finished the race.

The discussion went on until the afternoon.

"I got the impression that Sally is going to quit her job soon," Bruce said.

The trick illusion worked well for the clown at the party.

◼ REINFORCING ACTIVITIES

Allow your students to choose from the following list of activities:

1. Write a paragraph that contains words with "tion" and "sion." Challenge yourself to use as many of these words as you can. An example of such a paragraph is:

   Tom's exploration of the valley was going well. He had gathered much new information. His identifications of the plants and animals in the valley were done with precision, and they already filled three notebooks. It had always been Tom's ambition to study a place that had spent many years in isolation, so he felt that a celebration was now well deserved.

   If you wish, illustrate your paragraph.

2. People have to fill out many applications in their lives: for jobs, bank accounts, library cards, colleges, and other purposes. Ask your teacher to get you one or more applications that you will practice filling out. You can also go to local businesses and ask them for samples of their applications. The more you practice filling these forms out, the easier this task becomes.

3. Have you ever stopped and wondered who invented some of the things that we now take for granted? Who, for example, thought of making pencils? Who put erasers on the end of pencils?

   For this activity, you will investigate an invention. First, select the invention you wish to explore, and then go to your library to research its history. Refer to books such as *100 Inventions That Shaped World History* by Bill Yenne, Dr. Morton Grosser, Consulting Editor (A Bluewood Book, 1993) and *They All Laughed, From Light Bulbs to Lasers: The Fascinating Stories Behind the Great Inventions That Have Changed Our Lives* by Ira Flatow (Harper Collins, 1992).

   Sometimes, encyclopedias will have information on the invention being explored. And, if you get stuck, you can always fall back on an old research tool: ask your librarian, or other person who might know how to proceed, for help.

4. LITERATURE CONNECTION: *The Education of Little Tree* by Forrest Carter (Delacorte Press, 1976 and the University of New Mexico Press, 1990) tells the true story of the author's childhood. Forrest Carter went to live with his full Cherokee grandmother and half Cherokee grandfather at the age of five after both his parents died. Living with his grandparents in the hills of Tennessee, he received much love and a valuable education. At the age of ten, when both grandparents were dead, Forrest set off to take care of himself.

   Read *The Education of Little Tree* for a rich and moving reading experience.

⧉ EXTRA INTERESTING FACTS

How would you feel if someone accused you of being guilty of "pumpkinification"? You would probably be surprised and confused because in our modern times most people have never heard of the word.

"Pumpkinification" is a word that has not survived in the English language. It used to mean "acting in a pompous way"; in other words, not being humble, or puffing oneself up like a pumpkin.

WORD LIST

FINAL VOWEL COMBINATION SYLLABLE: "TION"

action	description	invention	**reaction**
addition	education	investigation	**relation**
admiration	election	invitation	**satisfaction**
affection	emotion	isolation	selection
ambition	exhibition	location	sensation
application	expectation	locomotion	situation
attention	explanation	mention	solution
celebration	exploration	motion	station
circulation	fraction	nomination	suggestion
combination	friction	occupation	tradition
composition	identification	opposition	translation
concentration	illustration	population	transportation
conversation	imagination	position	vacation
cooperation	imitation	presentation	
creation	instruction	probation	

FINAL VOWEL COMBINATION SYLLABLE: "SION"

admission	expansion	mission	revision
comprehension	explosion	obsession	session
decision	expression	pension	suspension
depression	illusion	precision	television
dimension	impression	profession	tension
discussion	intermission	provision	version
division	invasion	repercussion	vision

✠ ✠ ✠ ✠ ✠ ✠ ✠ ✠ ✠ ✠ ✠ ✠ ✠ ✠ ✠ ✠

FINISH IT!

Fill in the blanks with words from the word list.

1. The child had a sad _____ on his face.

2. "Please pay _____ to this because it's important," the teacher said.

3. Amy wrote her _____ on paper and then left it on the boss's desk.

4. Fred's father gave him _____ to drive the family car.

5. Carlos got his _____ about elephants from the encyclopedia.

6. Malik waited at the railroad _____.

7. The _____ between the two acts of the play lasted for fifteen minutes.

8. Jennifer drew a beautiful _____ for Martha's story.

9. "My _____ is perfect with glasses," Alia said.

10. "The train is my favorite mode of _____," Jeff said.

WORD LIST

permission   expression

intermission   vision

attention   station

illustration   transportation

information   suggestion

Name _____   **Date** _____

A GAME OF CATEGORIES

Choose words from your word list that belong in each category.

POSITIVE FEELINGS

_____

_____

_____

_____

_____

NEGATIVE FEELINGS

_____

_____

_____

_____

_____

RELATING TO BOOKS

_____

_____

_____

_____

RELATING TO THE SEEKING OF KNOWLEDGE

_____

_____

_____

_____

WORD LIST

elation

translation

satisfaction

frustration

experimentation

dissatisfaction

revision

appreciation

investigation

revulsion

admiration

publication

exploration

apprehension

affection

edition

observation

confusion

Name _____   **Date** _____

LOOK IT UP!

Look up the listed words in your dictionary. Then match each word with its correct definition.

1. premonition   a. a way of speaking
2. digression   b. a separation or division
3. ration   c. a specified amount, often of food
4. elocution   d. a feeling that something is about to happen
5. junction   e. a greeting, a welcoming
6. partition   f. a connecting place
7. admonition   g. giving a great amount, often implying being wasteful
8. dissension   h. a warning or gentle scolding
9. salutation   i. a turning away from the main topic
10. profusion   j. a disagreement or quarrel

Now choose five words from the above list and use each one in a sentence.

1. _____

_____

2. _____

_____

3. _____

_____

4. _____

_____

5. _____

_____

Name _____   **Date** _____

LIST IT!

THE INVITATION

An invitation addressed to you has just arrived by special messenger. "Your presence is requested this afternoon at 4 o'clock on the front steps of the Art Museum," the invitation reads. "Please dress formally, but bring an umbrella and an old pair of shoes." The invitation is signed, "Edna Maria Barbanzian."

You have never heard of Ms. Barbanzian.

Make a list of possibilities of why you have been sent this invitation. Include information, if you wish, on why you've been asked to bring the umbrella and shoes. Two examples follow:

1. Your friends are giving you a surprise party at your home, and this is just a trick to get you out of the house.

2. Ms. Barbanzian has randomly selected people to visit the museum. During your tour, the sprinkler system will be tested.

_____

_____

_____

_____

_____

_____

_____

_____

_____

_____

Name _____   Date _____

WRITE ON!

Write an ad for television. You can create your ad for a service or product you actually can offer, such as a lawn mowing service or a line of hand-painted note cards. If you prefer, you can invent something imaginary to sell.

It is helpful to watch some television ads so that you can study how they are written. Then write either a serious or a humorous ad. Once your ad is written, "perform" it for your class if you wish.

_____

_____

_____

_____

_____

_____

_____

_____

_____

_____

_____

_____

_____

_____

_____

Name _____   **Date** _____

THE DOUBLING RULE WITH MULTISYLLABIC WORDS

▣ GETTING STARTED

Ask your students to look through their notebooks and to choose a piece of information that interests them about the spelling of English. Discuss the syllable type, rule, generalization, or exception they present. Then provide time for your students to make a page in their notebooks for the final vowel combination syllables with "tion" and "sion."

◖● INTRODUCING NEW INFORMATION

"Today, we are going to learn more about the Doubling rule. What do you remember about this spelling rule? If you need to, you can refresh your memory by referring to your notebook."

"In our past work, we discovered that the last consonant is doubled in a one-syllable word when a suffix is being added if three conditions are present: if the root word has one vowel, if it ends in one consonant, and if the suffix being added begins with a vowel."

In the past, we only worked with one-syllable words. What do you think happens with multisyllabic words? Let's check."

Record the following list:

admit + ed = admitted

forget + ing = forgetting

refer + ed = referring

"Look at the last syllable in these words. Is the last consonant doubled?"
"Yes, and these last syllables have one vowel, end in one consonant, and a suffix beginning with a vowel is added. But we have to look further."
Record the following list:

enter + ed = entered

garden + ing = gardening

open + ed = opening

"The last syllables in these words also have one vowel and end in one consonant. The suffixes being added all begin with vowels. Can you figure out why the last consonants in these root words are not doubled?"

Place both lists side by side in front of your students. *"Say both sets of root words out loud to help you."*

"Congratulations, you have figured it out. For the last consonant to be doubled in a multisyllabic word, the last syllable also has to be emphasized or accented. Therefore, the 't' in 'permit' + 'ed' = 'permitted' is doubled, but the 't' in 'visit' + 'ed' = 'visited' is not. Please state the final rule."

"Good. If the last syllable in a multisyllabic word is accented, has one vowel, ends in one consonant, and a suffix beginning with a vowel is added, the consonant is doubled."

❖ PRACTICING WITH INDIVIDUAL WORDS

Select a manageable number of words from the word list provided on pages 393 and 394 for your students to spell.

⑤ PRACTICING SPELLING IN CONTEXT

Select a manageable number of sentences from the following list for your students to write.

Stephen kept forgetting to do his homework.

Patty permitted her cat to sleep on the sofa.

Jessie admitted that she had played the trick on Dan.

"That movie is upsetting," Mike said.

Kate lifted the shade and opened the window.

Ned regretted his decision to not go to the party.

Martha omitted telling Andy that she already had plans for Friday afternoon.

"Go back to the beginning of the story and look for good descriptions," the teacher said.

Max gathered sticks to start the fire.

Fran visited Jane in San Francisco for the weekend.

◼ REINFORCING ACTIVITIES

Allow your students to choose from the following list of activities:

1. Write a paragraph that contains words that illustrate the Doubling rule with multisyllabic words. Challenge yourself to use as many of these words as you can. An example of such a paragraph is:

   Anthony regretted that he had permitted himself to sleep late. He admitted to himself that he should have gotten up earlier. He would have preferred to have had more time to get ready for the camping trip. But Anthony gathered his sleeping bag and clothes and finally left on his adventure.

   If you wish, illustrate your paragraph.

2. Write story beginnings. To do this, you can either make up story ideas from your imagination, or you can look at pictures in magazines for inspiration.

   This activity is fun to do with a group of people. You each write one story beginning. Then exchange papers so that a second person continues with the story. If you wish, you can continue to exchange papers, so that, in the end, several people have worked on one story.

   You may also prefer to do this activity yourself. In that case, write several story beginnings and file them until a later time when you may want to continue working on one or more of them.

3. Play the "Quick Sort" game with multisyllabic words. Gather small pieces of paper such as 3 × 5 index cards and a stopwatch. Refer to your notebook, and select some multisyllabic words that end with closed syllables, r-controlled syllables, vowel-consonant-e syllables, and open syllables with "y."

   Write these words on your cards, one per card. It's good to have at least thirty cards.

   Then play "Quick Sort." The purpose of the game is for one person to divide the pack into three groups: (a) words where the Doubling rule is used when a suffix is added to the root word; (b) words where the "E" rule is used when a suffix is added to the root word; and (c) words where the "Y" rule is used when a suffix is added to the root word. The challenge is to sort your words as quickly as you can. Ask a friend to time you with the stopwatch, or compete with a friend to see who is faster. As you repeat this activity, you will become faster at it.

4. LITERATURE CONNECTION: *Call It Courage* by Armstrong Sperry (Macmillan Publishing Co., 1940) is a tale of suffering. It is a legend that takes place in the

South Seas before the Europeans arrived. It tells of the suffering of Mafatu, a boy who is afraid of the sea. Mafatu was with his mother on the water when a hurricane struck; Mafatu was spared, but his mother was not.

Driven by desperation to overcome his terror of the sea, Mafatu finally gets his canoe and sets out into the ocean with his dog and albatross to face his fear. He finds much adventure but, mostly, he finds his own courage.

⊟ EXTRA INTERESTING FACTS

When we are "equipped" to handle something, we have what we need. The word "equip" was originally a nautical term. It came via the French "equiper," which meant to provide what was necessary for a ship.

Apparently, the French word had evolved from the Old Norse term "skipa" which also meant to prepare a ship for a journey with provisions and crew. It is not known how "equip" left its original origins of only referring to ships and how it became a more general term in English.

WORD LIST

MULTISYLLABIC WORDS WHERE THE LAST SYLLABLE IS ACCENTED AND THE LAST SINGLE CONSONANT IS DOUBLED WHEN A VOWEL SUFFIX IS ADDED

acquit + ed = acquitted

annul + ed = annulled

admit + ing = admitting

begin + ing = beginning

defer + ed = deferred

deter + ed = deterred

dispel + ed = dispelled

embed + ed = embedded

entrap + ed = entrapped

equip + ed = equipped

excel + ing = excelling

forbid + ing = forbidding

forget + ing + forgetting

infer + ed = inferred

occur + ed = occurred

omit + ed = omitted

patrol + ed = patrolled

permit + ed = permitted

prefer + ed = preferred

propel + ing = propelling

recur + ing = recurring

refer + ed = referred

regret + ing = regretting

remit + ing = remitting

submit + ing = submitting

transfer + ing = transferring

transmit + ed = transmitted

upset + ing = upsetting

MULTISYLLABIC WORDS WHERE THE LAST SYLLABLE IS ACCENTED BUT THE LAST CONSONANT IS NOT DOUBLED WHEN A VOWEL SUFFIX IS ADDED

adjust + ed = adjusted

attempt + ed = attempted

attend + ed = attended

disgust + ing = disgusting

disrupt + ed = disrupted

disturb + ing = disturbing

enlist + ed = enlisted

insist + ing = insisting

instruct + ed = instructed

insult + ed = insulted

invent + ed = invented

mistrust + ed = mistrusted

neglect + ed = neglected

perform + ing = performing

prevent + ing = preventing

resent + ed = resented

respect + ed = respected

subtract + ing = subtracting

support + ed = supported

suspect + ed = suspected

WORD LIST

(continued)

MULTISYLLABIC WORDS WHERE THE LAST SYLLABLE IS NOT ACCENTED AND THE LAST CONSONANT IS NOT DOUBLED WHEN A VOWEL SUFFIX IS ADDED

benefit + ing = benefiting

blunder + ed = blundered

cancel + ed = canceled

differ + ed = differed

enter + ing = entering

garden + ing = gardening

gather + ed = gathered

happen + ing = happening

limit + ed = limited

number + ed = numbered

offer + ing = offering

open + ed = opened

pilot + ed = piloted

profit + ing = profiting

recover + ed = recovered

remember + ing = remembering

scatter + ed = scattered

shiver + ing = shivering

suffer + ed = suffering

tunnel + ed = tunneled

thunder + ing = thundering

visit + ing = visiting

FINISH IT!

Fill in the blanks with words from the word list.

1. The ball game was _____ because of the rain.

2. It _____ to Yani that she should call her mom to tell her she was going to be late.

3. Dave _____ bread crumbs on the pavement for the pigeons.

4. After yawning five times, Lorenzo finally _____ to himself that he was tired.

5. "Beth _____ me," Sam said, "and I'm mad at her."

6. Ted _____ the message over the telegraph wire.

7. Ann _____ her story to the contest.

8. Beth _____ the kitchen to get a snack.

9. The soldiers _____ outside the gate to prevent a surprise attack.

10. Jane _____ from the cold.

WORD LIST

scattered	submitted
patrolled	admitted
canceled	entered
shivered	occurred
transmitted	insulted

Name _____   **Date** _____

A GAME OF CATEGORIES

Choose words from your word list that belong in each category.

NEGATIVE FEELINGS

_____

_____

_____

_____

_____

TO HAVE MOVED

_____

_____

_____

_____

_____

**TO HAVE NOT ALLOWED
SOMETHING TO OCCUR**

_____

_____

_____

_____

**TO HAVE DONE SOMETHING
POSITIVE**

_____

_____

_____

_____

WORD LIST

transported	scattered
disgusted	prevented
permitted	resentful
insulted	benefited
disrupted	transferred
instructed	supported
mistrustful	deterred
disturbed	regretful
propelled	entered

Name _____ **Date** _____

LOOK IT UP!

Look up the listed words in your dictionary. Then match each word with its correct definition.

1. annulled
2. deferred

3. remitted
4. slandered
5. allotted
6. befitting
7. recurring
8. bombarded
9. relentless
10. dispelled

a. repeating, happening again
b. to have lied about another person and, thus, to have hurt his or her reputation
c. to have scattered
d. to be suitable or correct
e. to have canceled and made not valid
f. to have forgiven or excused
g. to be without pity
h. to have delayed an action or a decision
i. to have attacked
j. to have set aside a certain portion

Now choose five words from the above list and use each one in a sentence.

1. _____

_____

2. _____

_____

3. _____

_____

4. _____

_____

5. _____

_____

Name _____ **Date** _____

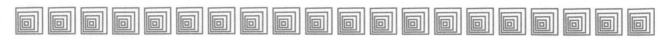

LIST IT!

THE RECURRING DREAM OF THE FORGETFUL FRIEND

You are having a recurring dream. In it, your best friend rushes up to you with something important to tell you. Suddenly, he stops and shouts, "I forgot! I forgot!" He holds out his hands. He is holding a seashell and a broken watch. Somehow, you know these objects hold the secret to the message.

Write a list of possibilities of what this message might be. Two examples are:

1. You lost your watch at the beach.

2. Time is running out! Go surfing now!

_____

_____

_____

_____

_____

_____

_____

_____

_____

_____

_____

Name _____ **Date** _____

WRITE ON!

REMEMBERING

Older people have important memories about how life was lived in the past. Find an older person who is willing to be interviewed. Then decide with that person about the time of his or her life he or she wishes to discuss: early childhood, adolescence, or a part of his or her adult life. Then prepare questions like:

1. What were your clothes like?

2. What did you eat?

3. Did you go to the movies?

4. How much money did an ice cream cone cost?

Once you have prepared your questions, conduct your interview. You can then either write a summary of the information you obtain or do an oral report for your class.

To help you with this project, you may wish to refer to the *Foxfire* books published by Anchor Books, Anchor Press/Doubleday. This series of books records information about earlier times in the Appalachian mountains, as reported by older people who lived there.

_____

_____

_____

_____

_____

_____

_____

_____

Name _____   **Date** _____

ANSWER KEYS

Lesson One

FINISH IT!

1. raft	2. glad	3. lamp	4. van	5. jam
6. map	7. cab	8. ran	9. stamp	10. sand

A GAME OF CATEGORIES

PEOPLE: man, lad, tramp, Sam, Gram
THINGS PEOPLE DO: ask, brag, gasp, grasp, clap
THINGS PEOPLE FEEL: mad, sad, glad, bad
ANIMALS: ant, clam, rat, cat

LOOK IT UP!

1. f	2. d	3. i	4. b	5. j
6. a	7. h	8. e	9. c	10. g

Lesson Two

FINISH IT!

1. bandit	2. trip	3. crib	4. catnip	5. print
6. picnic	7. hip	8. napkin	9. sip	10. fish

A GAME OF CATEGORIES

THINGS PEOPLE DO: grin, skip, swim, admit, insist
PARTS OF THE BODY: rib, lip, chin, skin, hip
FOOD: fig, shrimp, fish, mint
MATERIALS: plastic, tin, fabric, silk

LOOK IT UP!

1. d	2. f	3. i	4. b	5. h
6. e	7. a	8. j	9. g	10. c

Lesson Three

FINISH IT!

1. frog	2. drop	3. Scotland	4. blond	5. hop
6. contract	7. cop	8. gossip	9. hotrod	10. pond

A GAME OF CATEGORIES

ANIMALS: hog, bobcat, frog, tomcat, cod
PEOPLE: cop, frogman, convict, Don, Tom
PLACES: Wisconsin, Scotland, pond, bog
WAYS OF MOVING: jog, trot, plod, hop

LOOK IT UP!

1. c	2. h	3. j	4. g	5. a
6. f	7. e	8. i	9. b	10. d

Lesson Four

FINISH IT!

1. club	2. drum	3. cactus	4. dump	5. album
6. Gulf	7. campus	8. sum	9. insult	10. pump

A GAME OF CATEGORIES

FOOD (NOT FROM THE ANIMAL KINGDOM): pumpkin, plum, gumdrop, muffin, nut
ANIMALS: cub, possum, mollusk, pup, thrush
SOUNDS WE MAKE: hum, grunt, hiccup, gulp
THINGS THAT CAN HOLD WATER: tub, mug, cup, jug

LOOK IT UP!

1. d	2. f	3. j	4. i	5. b
6. e	7. h	8. g	9. a	10. c

Lesson Five

FINISH IT!

1. desk	2. dentist	3. slept	4. hen	5. problem
6. cobweb	7. men	8. trumpet	9. net	10. rent

A GAME OF CATEGORIES

HAVING TO DO WITH NUMBERS: hundred, octet, triplet, ten, seven
FROM THE ANIMAL KINGDOM: hen, kitten, ferret, insect, mussel
CONTAINERS: basket, keg, goblet, vessel
THINGS TO WEAR: bonnet, belt, helmet, mitten

LOOK IT UP!

1. b	2. g	3. f	4. c	5. j
6. a	7. e	8. i	9. h	10. d

Lesson Six

FINISH IT!

1. dress	2. hill	3. grass	4. chess	5. miss
6. fell	7. shell	8. toss	9. ill	10. yell

A GAME OF CATEGORIES

PEOPLE: Jill, Jeff, Russ, Bill, Bess
RELATING TO SOUND: shrill, yell, trill, bell, hiss
RELATING TO OUR NOSES: whiff, smell, sniff, snuff
LAND FORMATIONS: cliff, hill, bluff, dell

LOOK IT UP!

1. c	2. f	3. h	4. d	5. b
6. a	7. i	8. e	9. g	10. j

Lesson Seven

FINISH IT!

1. chicken	2. back	3. luck	4. shock	5. flashback
6. rock	7. check	8. pocket	9. snack	10. speck

A GAME OF CATEGORIES

BEHAVIORS THAT ARE NOT POSITIVE: to henpeck, to mock, to trick, to ransack, to attack
THINGS PEOPLE WEAR: backpack, lipstick, locket, jacket, sock
RELATING TO MONEY: rollback, buck, check, kickback
RELATING TO THE OCEAN: haddock, pollack, shipwreck, dock

LOOK IT UP!

1. e	2. g	3. b	4. i	5. f
6. c	7. j	8. h	9. a	10. d

Lesson Eight

FINISH IT!

1. face	2. shade	3. escape	4. bake	5. grade
6. pavement	7. take	8. lake	9. whale	10. translate

A GAME OF CATEGORIES

RELATING TO AN ERROR: mistake, misplace, misname, misstate, mistranslate
FOOD: pancake, hotcake, cupcake, kale, grape
RELATING TO FIRE: inflame, blaze, flame, bake
ANIMALS: ape, drake, crane, whale

LOOK IT UP!

1. c	2. h	3. f	4. a	5. d
6. i	7. b	8. g	9. j	10. e

Lesson Nine

FINISH IT!

1. kite	2. slice	3. bonfire	4. time	5. bride
6. write	7. price	8. vampire	9. mile	10. inside

A GAME OF CATEGORIES

RELATING TO NUMBERS: five, nine, prime, twice, thrice
COMPARED TO SOMETHING ELSE: catlike, lifelike. rocklike, apelike, gemlike
TYPES OF FIRE: grassfire, brushfire, campfire, gunfire
SOMETHING TO EAT OR DRINK: Sprite®, wine, lime, rice

LOOK IT UP!

1. d	2. g	3. j	4. b	5. e
6. a	7. c	8. h	9. i	10. f

Lesson Ten

FINISH IT!

1. wrote	2. disclose	3. spoke	4. froze	5. close
6. handwrote	7. hose	8. postpone	9. doze	10. cone

A GAME OF CATEGORIES

BONES: backbone, hipbone, chinbone, ringbone, wishbone
STONES: limestone, gemstone, millstone, sandstone, gallstone
TO DISTURB SOMETHING: explode, poke, expose, bulldoze
FOOD: sole, cone, scone, compote

LOOK IT UP!

1. c	2. a	3. e	4. i	5. g
6. b	7. h	8. d	9. j	10. f

Lesson Eleven

FINISH IT!

1. flute	2. theme	3. rude	4. fuse	5. excuse
6. Crete	7. athlete	8. assume	9. concrete	10. truce

A GAME OF CATEGORIES

PEOPLE: Steve, Luke, Pete, Bruce, Gene
THINGS PEOPLE DO: intrude, dispute, accuse, exclude, include
CHARACTERISTICS OF PEOPLE: rude, crude, cute, huge
RELATING TO MUSIC: flute, lute, postlude, tune

LOOK IT UP!

1. f	2. i	3. b	4. j	5. a
6. e	7. c	8. h	9. d	10. g

Lesson Twelve

FINISH IT!

1. shells	2. swiftest	3. spotless	4. likeness	5. asking
6. bashful	7. statement	8. lunches	9. richest	10. rudeness

A GAME OF CATEGORIES

ANIMALS: cats, pups, kittens, rabbits, chickens
FOUND IN THE KITCHEN: glasses, dishes, napkins, cups, plates
POSITIVE CHARACTERISTICS OR FEELINGS: skillful, hopeful, helpful, grateful
ACTIONS: rocking, rushing, packing, picking

LOOK IT UP!

1. d	2. a	3. f	4. i	5. b
6. j	7. e	8. h	9. c	10. g

Lesson Thirteen

FINISH IT!

1. smelled	2. hunted	3. fished	4. wilted	5. camped
6. spilled	7. yelled	8. lifted	9. missed	10. spelled

A GAME OF CATEGORIES

RELATING TO COMMUNICATION: yelled, ranted, called, asked, hinted
JOBS PERFORMED BY HANDS AND ARMS: dusted, mended, sanded, packed, picked
ACTIONS PERFORMED BY FEET: jumped, kicked, limped, stamped
RELATING TO FEELINGS: trusted, wished, thrilled, shocked

LOOK IT UP!

1. e	2. c	3. g	4. a	5. i
6. b	7. d	8. f	9. j	10. h

Lesson Fourteen

FINISH IT!

1. chased	2. admired	3. hopeful	4. voted	5. misplaced
6. safest	7. riding	8. vampires	9. baked	10. dining

A GAME OF CATEGORIES

RELATING TO FIRE AND HEAT: fires, flames, blazing, baking, smoking
RELATING TO MOVEMENT: driving, biked, hiked, riding, sliding
RELATING TO HAPPY FEELINGS: admired, excited, smiled, hoping
WORDS THAT DESCRIBE FOOD: stalest, ripest, boneless, glazed

LOOK IT UP!

1. h	2. d	3. j	4. b	5. g
6. a	7. f	8. i	9. c	10. e

Lesson Fifteen

FINISH IT!

1. rabid	2. Canada	3. adopted	4. Kenya	5. agent
6. abolished	7. amazing	8. nature	9. awoke	10. label

A GAME OF CATEGORIES

COUNTRIES: Libya, Japan, Kenya, Canada, Gabon

CITIES AND STATES: Tampa, Atlanta, Alabama, Alaska, Montana

ASPECTS OF LANDSCAPE: delta, vista, tundra, savanna

OUT OF THE ORDINARY: sacred, amazing, gala, ultra

LOOK IT UP!

1. f	2. c	3. a	4. e	5. i
6. b	7. j	8. h	9. d	10. g

Lesson Sixteen

FINISH IT!

1. quiet	2. divide	3. Africa	4. hifi	5. minus
6. sensitive	7. substitute	8. digest	9. optimistic	10. Chinese

A GAME OF CATEGORIES

RELATING TO NUMBERS: biped, tripod, trisect, trident, bisect

CHEMICAL ELEMENTS: nitric, nitrate, silicon, silicone, platinum

PLACES: Africa, China, Iran, Ireland

RELATING TO FEELINGS: optimistic, sentiment, tirade, disquiet

LOOK IT UP!

1. i	2. h	3. d	4. f	5. a
6. c	7. j	8. b	9. g	10. e

Lesson Seventeen

FINISH IT!

1. potato	2. broken	3. hoping	4. rodents	5. coconut
6. violin	7. San Francisco	8. open	9. ago	10. Ohio

A GAME OF CATEGORIES

STATES IN THE U.S.: Ohio, Idaho, Iowa, Arizona, Oklahoma

CITIES: Toronto, Sacramento, Copenhagen, Oslo, San Francisco

COUNTRIES IN AFRICA: Angola, Morocco, Congo, Togo

COUNTRIES OR ISLANDS NOT IN AFRICA: Oman, Poland, Mexico, Samoa

LOOK IT UP!

1. e	2. j	3. g	4. b	5. d
6. f	7. i	8. a	9. c	10. h

Lesson Eighteen

FINISH IT!

1. secret	2. tuba	3. zero	4. aluminum	5. erupt
6. decided	7. future	8. deposited	9. result	10. duels

A GAME OF CATEGORIES

PLACES: Cuba, Korea, Sweden, Munich, Pasadena
RELATING TO FEELINGS: regret, respect, detest, repent, elated
RELATING TO MATHEMATICS: tabulate, calculate, zero, cubic
PEOPLE: we, she, he, me

LOOK IT UP!

1. c	2. g	3. e	4. i	5. b
6. j	7. h	8. a	9. d	10. f

Lesson Nineteen

FINISH IT!

1. hobby	2. fifty	3. pony	4. fly	5. windy
6. navy	7. fry	8. shiny	9. spy	10. silly

A GAME OF CATEGORIES

NUMBERS: twenty, fifty, sixty, seventy, ninety
HOW OR WHAT YOU CAN FEEL: angry, happy, silly, grumpy, envy
WORDS THAT DESCRIBE THE WEATHER: sultry, sunny, chilly, windy
RELATING TO APPEARANCE: shabby, filthy, dusty, shiny

LOOK IT UP!

1. d	2. i	3. c	4. f	5. a
6. g	7. j	8. e	9. b	10. h

Lesson Twenty

FINISH IT!

1. biggest	2. clapped	3. selling	4. bragged	5. tossed
6. stopped	7. wagging	8. camped	9. sitting	10. melted

A GAME OF CATEGORIES

RELATING TO COMMUNICATION: telling, calling, begging, bragging, chatting
TO HAVE HIT: bashed, smashed, thrashed, jabbed, clubbed
RELATING TO THE PREPARATION OF FOOD: chopping, cutting, melting, mashing
RELATING TO MOVEMENT: stepping, spinning, jumping, hopping

LOOK IT UP!

1. h	2. a	3. e	4. i	5. j
6. b	7. f	8. c	9. g	10. d

Lesson Twenty-One

FINISH IT!

1. transatlantic	2. reruns	3. inhale	4. receded	5. unspoken
6. misquoted	7. invented	8. mistrusts	9. unsafe	10. subject

A GAME OF CATEGORIES

HAVING NEGATIVE CHARACTERISTICS: unfit, unjust, unsafe, unwise, misfit

THINGS YOU DO WITH WORDS: translate, transcribe, rewrite, reprint, inscribe

RELATING TO MOVEMENT: recede, invade, repel, transit

RELATING TO GEOGRAPHY: subcontinent, transatlantic, subtropics, inland

LOOK IT UP!

1. d	2. f	3. i	4. b	5. h
6. g	7. a	8. j	9. e	10. c

Lesson Twenty-Two

FINISH IT!

1. nail	2. exclaimed	3. sprained	4. pail	5. painful
6. mail	7. remain	8. trail	9. quail	10. train

A GAME OF CATEGORIES

RELATING TO THE MAIL: mailbag, mailbox, mailing, mailman, postpaid

THINGS DEFINED AS "NOT SOMETHING": unafraid, unchained, unexplained, unpaid, unpainted

TO DO SOMETHING AGAIN: reclaim, repaint, retrain, regain

WAYS TO RESPOND TO FEELINGS: bewail, wail, exclaim, explain

LOOK IT UP!

1. c	2. g	3. a	4. f	5. j
6. i	7. b	8. d	9. h	10. e

Lesson Twenty-Three

FINISH IT!

1. Sunday	2. painful	3. play	4. rain	5. paint
6. stray	7. explain	8. essay	9. train	10. stay

A GAME OF CATEGORIES

RELATING TO TRANSPORTATION: runway, pathway, subway, railway, train

PEOPLE: maid, Ray, Fay, saint, maiden

RELATING TO INJURY OR ILLNESS: ailment, faint, sprain, strain

PARTS OF THE BODY: braid, brain, pigtail, waist

LOOK IT UP!

1. d	2. b	3. g	4. j	5. f
6. h	7. i	8. e	9. a	10. c

Lesson Twenty-Four

FINISH IT!

1. speech	2. asleep	3. feed	4. beehive	5. screech
6. meeting	7. sweet	8. referee	9. feel	10. weekend

A GAME OF CATEGORIES

THINGS THAT PEOPLE CAN BE: nominee, trainee, refugee, trustee, escapee

TYPES OF WEEDS: chickweed, milkweed, ragweed, pigweed, duckweed

NUMBERS: fifteen, sixteen, seventeen, nineteen

FROM THE ANIMAL KINGDOM: chickadee, chimpanzee, bee, sheepdog

LOOK IT UP!

1. e	2. h	3. j	4. c	5. i
6. a	7. g	8. d	9. b	10. f

Lesson Twenty-Five

FINISH IT!

1. throat	2. goals	3. loaded	4. roasted	5. tugboat
6. toast	7. coat	8. road	9. soapbox	10. loan

A GAME OF CATEGORIES

TYPES OF BOATS: gunboat, lifeboat, sailboat, speedboat, tugboat

TYPES OF COATS: raincoat, redcoat, tailcoat, topcoat, waistcoat

RELATING TO ROADS: roadblock, roadbed, roadside, roadway

RELATING TO SOAP: soapbox, soapflakes, soapsuds, soapy

LOOK IT UP!

1. d	2. i	3. a	4. g	5. f
6. j	7. b	8. e	9. h	10. c

Lesson Twenty-Six

FINISH IT!

1. ready	2. eaglet	3. beach	4. threaded	5. seals
6. defeated	7. dream	8. health	9. east	10. team

A GAME OF CATEGORIES

FROM THE ANIMAL KINGDOM: flea, peacock, weasel, seal, eaglet

FOOD: oatmeal, bread, bean, peach, peanut

SOUNDS: squeal, squeak, scream, creak

TO USE WORDS TO COMMUNICATE: plead, appeal, preach, speak

LOOK IT UP!

1. e	2. g	3. j	4. i	5. b
6. h	7. c	8. f	9. d	10. a

Lesson Twenty-Seven

FINISH IT!

1. field	2. pie	3. weird	4. brief	5. friends
6. goalie	7. tie	8. shield	9. deceit	10. relief

A GAME OF CATEGORIES

THINGS PEOPLE CAN BE: caddie, goalie, chief, thief, bailie

RELATING TO A FIELD: field day, field hand, field gun, field music, field glass

FEMALE NAMES: Annie, Christie, Connie, Bonnie

RELATING TO THE SUPERNATURAL: zombie, genie, fiend, weird

LOOK IT UP!

1. d	2. h	3. f	4. c	5. j
6. a	7. g	8. b	9. i	10. e

Lesson Twenty-Eight

FINISH IT!

1. spoonfuls	2. shook	3. moon	4. brook	5. footprints
6. broom	7. good	8. balloons	9. proof	10. notebook

A GAME OF CATEGORIES

TYPES OF ROOMS: bedroom, bathroom, clubroom, lunchroom, playroom

TYPES OF BOOKS: chapbook, checkbook, cookbook, copybook, daybook

TYPES OF WOODS: boxwood, deadwood, dogwood, driftwood

RELATING TO THE FOOT: clubfoot, splayfoot, flatfoot, footprint

LOOK IT UP!

1. g	2. e	3. a	4. j	5. i
6. b	7. f	8. c	9. h	10. d

Lesson Twenty-Nine

FINISH IT!

1. clown	2. snow	3. growling	4. crow	5. downtown
6. dishtowel	7. down	8. window	9. throw	10. fishbowl

A GAME OF CATEGORIES

FROM THE ANIMAL KINGDOM: cow, crow, owl, minnow, blowfish

RELATING TO SNOW: snowflake, snowdrift, snowman, snowball, snowcap

CITIES: Allentown, Cape Town, Glasgow, Moscow

RELATING TO GOING DOWN: downhill, downshift, downfall, downgrade

LOOK IT UP!

1. d	2. i	3. f	4. h	5. a
6. j	7. c	8. g	9. b	10. e

Lesson Thirty

FINISH IT!

1. cried	2. flying	3. skinniest	4. fries	5. candies
6. studied	7. tiniest	8. played	9. bunnies	10. dismayed

A GAME OF CATEGORIES

NEGATIVE DESCRIPTIVE WORDS: sloppiest, messiest, shabbiest, flimsiest, grubbiest
POSITIVE DESCRIPTIVE WORDS: coziest, classiest, tidiest, dandiest, spiffiest
FOOD: jellies, candies, fries, taffies
RELATING TO NUMBERS: twenties, fifties, sixties, seventies

LOOK IT UP!

1. c	2. g	3. a	4. j	5. b
6. e	7. f	8. i	9. h	10. d

Lesson Thirty-One

FINISH IT!

1. poodle	2. fumble	3. saddle	4. puddle	5. possible
6. candle	7. table	8. needle	9. resembles	10. flexible

A GAME OF CATEGORIES

THINGS FOUND IN THE KITCHEN: griddle, ladle, noodles, soap bubbles, table
POSITIVE CHARACTERISTICS: agreeable, capable, credible, dependable, humble
RELATING TO MOVEMENT: amble, waddle, ramble, skedaddle
RELATING TO HORSES: packsaddle, saddle, bridle, sidesaddle

LOOK IT UP!

1. d	2. e	3. i	4. c	5. g
6. a	7. h	8. j	9. f	10. b

Lesson Thirty-Two

FINISH IT!

1. sample	2. giggling	3. staple	4. juggled	5. single
6. pineapple	7. apple	8. jingle	9. triangle	10. simple

A GAME OF CATEGORIES

RELATING TO NUMBERS: quadruple, quintuple, multiple, triple, single
TO HARM: crumple, trample, cripple, rumple, mangle
TYPES OF TREES OR PLANTS: apple, crabapple, pineapple, maple
SHAPES OR RELATING TO SHAPES: angle, triangle, quadrangle, rectangle

LOOK IT UP!

1. f	2. h	3. a	4. j	5. i
6. b	7. g	8. d	9. e	10. c

Lesson Thirty-Three

FINISH IT!

| 1. Battle | 2. bottles | 3. ankle | 4. spectacle | 5. beetles |
| 6. vehicle | 7. twinkle | 8. cattle | 9. baffled | 10. waffles |

A GAME OF CATEGORIES

PARTS OF THE BODY: freckle, cuticle, ventricle, clavicle, ankle
WAYS TO HARM SOMEONE: tackle, battle, belittle, tattle, throttle
SOUNDS: cackle, chuckle, crackle, rattle
CONTAINERS: bottle, receptacle, kettle, teakettle

LOOK IT UP!

| 1. b | 2. e | 3. g | 4. i | 5. c |
| 6. j | 7. a | 8. f | 9. h | 10. d |

Lesson Thirty-Four

FINISH IT!

| 1. fetch | 2. bench | 3. stretch | 4. hitched | 5. inches |
| 6. reach | 7. itch | 8. hunch | 9. witches | 10. coach |

A GAME OF CATEGORIES

RELATING TO SEWING: patch, stitch, backstitch, hemstitch, topstitch
BIRDS: nuthatch, bullfinch, finch, goldfinch, chaffinch
RELATING TO FOOD OR DRINK: lunch, peach, punch, quench
LIVING THINGS (BUT NOT BIRDS): cockroach, leech, roach, pooch

LOOK IT UP!

| 1. f | 2. c | 3. h | 4. j | 5. a |
| 6. d | 7. i | 8. b | 9. g | 10. e |

Lesson Thirty-Five

FINISH IT!

| 1. badge | 2. age | 3. ridge | 4. twinges | 5. wage |
| 6. judge | 7. revenge | 8. bridge | 9. exchange | 10. hedges |

A GAME OF CATEGORIES

RELATING TO MOVEMENT: dislodge, dodge, lunge, plunge, trudge
RELATING TO THE THEATER: backstage, downstage, offstage, stage, upstage
RELATING TO MAKING DECISIONS: adjudge, judge, misjudge, prejudge
PLACES: ledge, ridge, edge, bulge

LOOK IT UP!

| 1. d | 2. g | 3. i | 4. e | 5. f |
| 6. b | 7. j | 8. a | 9. h | 10. c |

Lesson Thirty-Six

FINISH IT!

1. art	2. cartoons	3. March	4. charcoal	5. far
6. carpet	7. dark	8. popular	9. sharp	10. marble

A GAME OF CATEGORIES

BIRDS AND FISHES: marlin, carp, shark, partridge, starling
PLACES: farm, barnyard, yard, marsh, Mars
RELATING TO COMMUNICATION: remark, snarl, impart, bark
NAMES OF PEOPLE: Bart, Mark, Martha, Marta

LOOK IT UP!

1. c	2. f	3. i	4. h	5. j
6. d	7. g	8. b	9. a	10. e

Lesson Thirty-Seven

FINISH IT!

1. torn	2. acorn	3. world	4. memorize	5. short
6. actor	7. hornet's	8. born	9. forest	10. porch

A GAME OF CATEGORIES

THINGS THAT PEOPLE CAN BE: bachelor, visitor, lord, doctor, actor
FROM THE ANIMAL KINGDOM: alligator, porcupine, stork, hornet, horned toad
PARTS OF THE BODY: torso, aorta, thorax, cortex
RELATING TO CORN: corn meal, corncob, corn bread, corncrib

LOOK IT UP!

1. d	2. g	3. c	4. i	5. a
6. b	7. h	8. j	9. e	10. f

Lesson Thirty-Eight

FINISH IT!

1. whispered	2. sir	3. blur	4. dirty	5. fur
6. carpenter	7. shirt	8. purple	9. germs	10. turnips

A GAME OF CATEGORIES

DIRECTIONS: western, eastern, northern, northwestern, northeastern
FROM THE ANIMAL KINGDOM: turtle, panther, rooster, termite, tiger
MONTHS: September, October, November, December
RELATING TO THE NUMBER THREE: third, thirty, thirteen, thirty-three

LOOK IT UP!

1. e	2. h	3. i	4. j	5. d
6. g	7. c	8. f	9. a	10. b

Lesson Thirty-Nine

FINISH IT!

1. expression	2.attention	3. suggestion	4. permission
5. information	6. station	7. intermission	8. illustration
9. vision	10. transportation		

A GAME OF CATEGORIES

POSITIVE FEELINGS: elation, satisfaction, appreciation, admiration, affection

NEGATIVE FEELINGS: frustration, dissatisfaction, revulsion, apprehension, confusion

RELATING TO BOOKS: translation, revision, publication, edition

RELATING TO THE SEEKING OF KNOWLEDGE: experimentation, investigation, exploration, observation

LOOK IT UP!

1. d	2. i	3. c	4. a	5. f
6. b	7. h	8. j	9. e	10. g

Lesson Forty

FINISH IT!

1. canceled	2. occurred	3. scattered	4. admitted	5. insulted
6. transmitted	7. submitted	8. entered	9. patrolled	10. shivered

A GAME OF CATEGORIES

NEGATIVE FEELINGS: disgusted, insulted, mistrustful, resentful, regretful

TO HAVE MOVED: transported, propelled, scattered, transferred, entered

TO HAVE NOT ALLOWED SOMETHING TO OCCUR: disrupted, disturbed, prevented, deterred

TO HAVE DONE SOMETHING POSITIVE: permitted, instructed, benefited, supported

LOOK IT UP!

1. e	2. h	3. f	4. b	5. j
6. d	7. a	8. i	9. g	10. c

BIBLIOGRAPHY

Much valuable information was gained from the following books regarding the history of English, the etymology of individual words, and the continuing evolution of the language. The author wishes to express gratitude to the authors of these books, and to recommend the books for use in further study.

Ayto, John. *Dictionary of Word Origins.* Boston: Arcade Publishing, Little, Brown & Co., 1990.

Barnhart, Robert K., Sol Steinmetz, and Clarence L. Barnhart. *Third Barnhart Dictionary of New English, Three Decades of Changes and Additions to the English Language.* Bronx, NY: The H.W. Wilson Company, 1990.

Ciardi, John. *A Browser's Dictionary, A Compendium of Curious Expressions and Intriguing Facts.* New York: Harper & Row, 1980.

_____. *A Second Browser's Dictionary and Native's Guide to the Unknown American Language.* New York: Harper & Row, 1983.

_____. *Good Words to You: An All-New Browser's Dictionary and Native's Guide to the Unknown American Language.* New York: Harper & Row, 1987.

Feldman, David. Illustrated by Schwan, Kassie. *Who Put the Butter in Butterfly? ...And Other Fearless Investigations Into Our Illogical Language.* New York: Harper & Row, 1989.

Funk, Wilfred. *Word Origins and Their Romantic Stories.* New York: Wilfred Funk, Inc., 1950.

McCrum, Robert, William Cran, and Robert MacNeil. *The Story of English,* New York: Elisabeth Sifton Books, Viking, 1986.

Morris, William and Mary. *Dictionary of Word and Phrase Origins.* New York: Harper & Row, 1962.

_____. *Dictionary of Word and Phrase Origins, Vol. III,* New York: Harper & Row, 1971.

Onions, C. T., Editor. *The Oxford Dictionary of English Etymology.* London: Oxford at the Clarendon Press, 1982.

Rosenthal, Peggy and George Dardess. Illustrations by The Crag and Peter LaVigna. *Every Cliche in the Book.* New York: William Morrow and Company, Inc., 1987.

Shipley, Joseph T., Ph.D. *Dictionary of Word Origins.* Totowa, New Jersey: Littlefield, Adams and Co., 1979.

Sperling, Susan Kelz. Illustrated by George Moran. *Poplollies and Bellibones, A Celebration of Lost Words.* New York: Clarkson N. Potter Publishing, Distributed by Crown Publishers, Inc., 1977.

The Compact Edition of the Oxford English Dictionary, Vols. 1 and 2. New York: Oxford University Press, 1971.